From Mounds to Megachurches

From Mounds to Megachurches

Georgia's Religious Heritage

DAVID S. WILLIAMS

The University of Georgia Press

Athens & London

Title page image: The oldest public building in
Georgia is Jerusalem Lutheran Church (Effingham
County), built in 1767–1769.

© 2008 by the University of Georgia Press
Athens, Georgia 30602
www.ugapress.org
All rights reserved
Set in Adobe Garamond by
Graphic Composition, Inc., Bogart, Georgia
Printed and bound by Thomson-Shore
The paper in this book meets the guidelines for
permanence and durability of the Committee on
Production Guidelines for Book Longevity of the
Council on Library Resources.

Printed in the United States of America
08 09 10 11 12 C 5 4 3 2 1

Library of Congress Cataloging-in-Publication Data
Williams, David S. (David Salter)
From mounds to megachurches : Georgia's
religious heritage / David S. Williams.
p. cm.
Includes bibliographical references and index.
ISBN-13: 978-0-8203-3175-1 (hardcover : alk. paper)
ISBN-10: 0-8203-3175-9 (hardcover : alk. paper)
1. Georgia—Religion. 2. Religion and state—
Georgia—History. 3. Georgia—History. I. Title
BL2527.G46W55 2008
200.9758—dc22   2008010957

British Library Cataloging-in-Publication Data available

For RaRa

Contents

Acknowledgments

I appreciate the help and guidance provided by Nancy Grayson, associate director and editor-in-chief of the University of Georgia Press, as well as the assistance of the Press staff. Countless staff members in churches, libraries, museums, and parks across the state also assisted me, and I am especially thankful to those in the University of Georgia Libraries.

It would not have been possible for me to complete the project without the understanding and support of Provost Arnett Mace, Vice President for Instruction Jere Morehead, and my valued colleagues in the Department of Religion and the Honors Program at the University of Georgia. I am particularly grateful to my administrative assistants during the writing of the book, Kristen Ruhland and Heather Carlson.

A number of scholarly colleagues gave me helpful answers and advice. Del Dunn, Robert Gardner, Charles Hudson, Sandy Martin, and Jace Weaver deserve to be singled out, but above all John Inscoe was generous with his time and offered acute observations. The good suggestions provided by the anonymous readers for the Press also strengthened the book considerably. Any mistakes that remain are, of course, mine.

I have had the opportunity to teach the material in this book as an Honors seminar on several occasions at the University of Georgia. The students in these courses have given me wonderful and spirited responses. One of them, Hariqbal Basi, continued to assist me after the course was completed, and his astute readings of various chapter drafts supplied valuable feedback.

My friends have contributed in many ways, from providing encouragement or a missing nugget of information to reading parts or all of the manuscript. My thanks go especially to Bob Boehmer, Sheffield Hale, Hamilton Jordan, Mike McNulty, Penny Overcash, and Jane Willson.

My family has been a mainstay. My father, C. V. Williams, and mother-in-law, Hera Reines, provided important lay perspectives. I owe my career, ultimately, to my mother, Jean Hayes, who convinced me when I was young that I should be a teacher. Only my wife, Jen, truly knows the depth of both my debt and my gratitude to her. She has been with me every step of the way and had to make many sacrifices for this book to come to be. I wrote the book for our daughter, RaRa, and lovingly dedicate it to her—from one Georgian to another.

Athens, Georgia
May 28, 2007

Prologue

Given the vital role that religion has played in Georgia, it seems appropriate that the oldest public building in the state is Jerusalem Lutheran Church, located in Effingham County.[1] Close inspection shows that some of the church's bricks still bear the imprints of the hands that made them more than two hundred years ago. The persons who shaped those bricks spoke the German language, yet their community was an integral part of the British colony of Georgia, a vivid illustration of the diversity that has marked the state since its beginnings.[2] Indeed, one historian of colonial Georgia has observed that "Georgians were not a homogeneous people. By 1736, to function well in all parts of the colony, a person ideally needed what probably no one in Georgia had—fluency in English, French, German, and Gaelic. A knowledge of Spanish would also have been helpful. English was the language of record, but many Georgians did not speak it at all."[3]

Nearly twenty miles southeast of Jerusalem Lutheran Church is Georgia's first town, Savannah, where two other churches sit a third of a mile apart in the historic district, one facing in the direction of the other. Christ Episcopal Church, facing west, and First African Baptist Church, facing east, stare mutely toward one another, but the polarities embodied in these churches convey some core themes of religion in Georgia.

James Oglethorpe, who led the effort to found colonial Georgia, planned Savannah as a grid of city squares. Oglethorpe laid out the first four squares in 1733, and eighteen others were added throughout the eighteenth and nineteenth centuries. Johnson Square was the first established by Oglethorpe, and its design called for a church on the eastern side of the square, on the lot where Christ Church now stands. Although the present building was constructed in the nineteenth century, the congregation that it houses dates to the very beginnings of the colony. The Christ Church congregation was founded by the first settlers who arrived with Oglethorpe on a high bluff above the Savannah River in February 1733.

I

Christ Church is one of more than ten religious congregations that face Savannah's squares today. They include Mickve Israel, the synagogue of one of the oldest Jewish congregations in the United States; the Independent Presbyterian Church, which served as the site of the wedding of Woodrow Wilson; the Cathedral of St. John the Baptist, one of the largest Roman Catholic churches in the Southeast; and the Lutheran Church of the Ascension, which stems from the Austrian Salzburgers who came to Savannah the year following its founding and who eventually built Jerusalem Lutheran Church.

In addition to the Salzburg Lutherans, a wide range of religious groups lived in colonial Georgia, such as English Anglicans, German- and Spanish-speaking Jews, and Scottish Presbyterians. It is important to note as well that Spanish Catholic missionaries had worked along the coast proselytizing Indians close to 150 years before Oglethorpe stepped ashore, and, as we will see, that Indians had been practicing their own native religious traditions long before that. Taken together, these groups reflect Georgia's variegated religious heritage.

When one exits Christ Church and steps into Johnson Square, the top of the steeple of First African Baptist can be seen in the distance above buildings and trees. First African Baptist sits facing in the direction of Christ Church on the far, western side of Franklin Square, which was laid out in 1790, five years after Oglethorpe died. It is fitting that a Baptist church has a reverse orientation from an Episcopal church, for, as a recent encyclopedia of religion in the South suggests: "The history of religion in Georgia since the Revolution is largely the story of the growth of Evangelical Protestant denominations, especially the Baptist and the Methodist."[4] As a one-sentence summary, this cuts to the heart of the demographic realities. The first congregation to appear in colonial Georgia was Anglican, and the Church of England would become the official religion of the colony in 1758. But today Baptists and Methodists are the two largest denominations in Georgia, with Baptists being by far the more numerous. Baptists are now the religious majority in virtually every county in the state.[5]

It may be accidental that Christ Church and First African Baptist face toward one another. Yet we may draw significant meaning from their placement, since it suggests more than just the numerical triumph of evangelicalism over the mainline colonial congregations. For First African Baptist is not only an evangelical Protestant church, it is also one of the oldest African American congregations in North America and was established by slaves. Thus, beyond the transition from the mainline colonial denominations to evangelicalism, the juxtaposition of Christ Church and First African Baptist draws our attention to the intertwining of religion and race in Georgia. To paraphrase former Governor Roy E. Barnes, while the state is known for its red clay, its history has been written in black and white.[6] Therefore, in order to fully grasp the religious heritage of Georgia, we must return again and again to racial matters.

The polarities that Christ Church and First African Baptist reflect—established colonial religion and upstart evangelicalism, white and black—together form the essence of the religious history of Georgia. Consequently, they also suggest some major themes of this book: the triumph of the evangelicals, and the profound role of race. The religious heritage of Georgia, however, is far more complex than just the rise of evangelicalism, both white and black. It is important to alert the reader from the outset that while we will trace the growth of the major denominations in the state, we will also take an expansive view of the term *religion*. We will explore religious expressions that have existed alongside the recognized denominations, reflecting how disparate people have sought to explain their existence as distinct communities. These matters have continued relevance today as Georgians grapple with new issues of tolerance and intolerance in the face of increasing ethnic and religious pluralism.

Finally, it is important to note as well what this book is and is not, and what is and is not intended. This is not primarily a history of denominational institutions and movements. The scope of the book is meant to be representative and balanced, rather than comprehensive and encyclopedic. In addition, at times matters of social and political history that extend beyond religious concerns must be discussed in order to set the stage for religious developments. Above all, the chief aim in these pages is to explore the role that religion has played in determining and explaining what it has meant, and means, to be a Georgian.

CHAPTER ONE

Before Georgia

In 1818, having returned from "a tour of considerable extent in the United States," New York minister Elias Cornelius wrote to the editor of the *American Journal of Science* regarding various geological and other natural features he had examined. Near the end of his report Cornelius discussed a few curiosities he had also encountered. The last items he mentioned were three earthen mounds beside the Etowah River in northwest Georgia, near modern Cartersville. Cornelius had seen such mounds before but never of such dimensions as the largest of the three, which he described as a "stupendous pile." Accompanying him at the time of the discovery were "eight Indian chiefs," who, he reported, gazed on the mounds "with as much curiosity as any white man." Cornelius asked the Indians what the origin of the mounds was. None could say. All ended up agreeing that "they were never put up by our people." Cornelius concluded: "It seems probable they were erected by another race, who once inhabited the country. . . . Who they were, and what were the causes of their degeneracy, or of their extermination, no circumstances have yet explained."[1]

It may seem surprising that the Indians (presumably Cherokees) who accompanied Cornelius had no knowledge of mound building.[2] The popular perception is that Cherokees and Creeks inhabited Georgia for several centuries, extending back before Europeans arrived in the New World, and that they were responsible for virtually all of the pieces of pottery, projectile points ("arrowheads"), and mounds that can be found and seen across the state.[3] Yet such "tribes" actually formed during the colonial period out of the survivors of earlier chiefdoms with names like Coosa and Ocute. It was the members of these chiefdoms who built nearly all the mounds in Georgia, an activity that appears to have ceased, for various reasons, by the close of the sixteenth century.[4] The tribal (or, better, coalescent) groups that succeeded the chiefdoms represent a social transformation so great that little memory remained of the chiefdoms and what had befallen them.[5]

Archaeologists have determined that the earliest human inhabitants of what is today Georgia arrived approximately thirteen thousand years ago. Those first people, referred to today as Paleoindians, were hunter-gatherers who roamed the land in small groups.[6] During the succeeding Archaic period, beginning roughly ten thousand years ago, the inhabitants established short-term settlements.[7] The Woodland period, which began some three thousand years ago and lasted until approximately the year 1000, produced even more dramatic changes, as settlements increased in size, complexity, and year-round permanence.[8] Two significant innovations were the introduction of maize (corn), which did not yet constitute a large part of the diet, and the beginning of extensive mound-building activity.[9]

One of the most impressive of all Woodland sites is the Kolomoki mound complex in southwest Georgia, near Blakely, which is maintained as Kolomoki Mounds State Historic Park. There are several preserved mounds at Kolomoki, and archaeological exploration of them has uncovered numerous artifacts, including a variety of ceramic vessels, with some in the shapes of various animals.[10] A number of these vessels have precut decorative holes in them, suggesting they were intended for ceremonial usage.[11]

The ritual vessels at Kolomoki reflect another important development during the Woodland period: the appearance of certain designs on stone and ceramic artifacts. These designs include circles and four-fold figures, as well as various birds. Rock Eagle, a large bird effigy mound near Eatonton, in Putnam County, probably belongs to the Woodland period. The bird, which may represent a buzzard, is constructed of quartz stones and extends more than one hundred feet from wingtip to wingtip. A smaller and less well-known effigy rock pile, which seems to depict a hawk, is also located in Putnam County.[12] The symbolic importance of birds to Southeastern Indians will be discussed later in this chapter.

Chiefdoms emerged with the Mississippian period (ca. 1000 to 1540).[13] Scholars have suggested several ways of defining or describing Mississippian culture. Commonly singled out is an emphasis on centralized political authority with ranked hereditary rulers, including a chieftain.[14] Mississippians were farmers, and corn became the staple of their diet, eventually joined by beans and squash. Mississippians grew enough corn to provide surpluses, which accrued to the chief, who controlled their distribution. This was an important element of the broad social system of a chiefdom, which generally bound together various towns, villages, and farms.[15] In addition, Mississippian society featured a broadly dispersed ceremonial pattern that included temple mounds and shared artistic motifs.[16]

Two of the most important of the Mississippian sites in the Southeast are located in Georgia: Ocmulgee National Monument in Macon, and Etowah Indian Mounds State Park in Cartersville. Ocmulgee reached its height at approximately 950, and Etowah flourished a bit later, around 1250.[17] At Ocmulgee, a visitor can view a restored earth lodge. The lodge has a bird-shaped seating platform with graduated heights and spacing, probably representing the relative social positions of nobles and leaders from towns and villages within the chiefdom.[18] The museum at Etowah features marble statues of a man and a woman, each in a sitting or kneeling posture, who may represent important ancestral figures.[19] James Adair, who lived among Southeastern Indians in the mid-eighteenth century, mentioned that he had seen a similar carved wooden statue in a Creek town, which he thought represented a hero from the past, and contemporary scholars agree that such statues were likely part of an ancestor cult.[20]

When Europeans arrived during the sixteenth century, perhaps close to fifteen chiefdoms existed in the territory that is now Georgia. The chiefdoms appeared throughout the physiographic regions, such as Coosa in the Ridge and Valley, Ocute in the Piedmont, and Ocmulgee on the upper edge of the Coastal Plain. Most (though not all) of the chiefdoms belonged to a subcategory of Mississippian culture known as Lamar. These Lamar chiefdoms had a common material culture, seen most clearly in pottery, and many of them also shared a language family, Muskogean.[21] When the chiefdoms came to an end, for reasons to be discussed, some of the survivors banded together to form the Creek Confederacy, which maintained the use of Muskogean languages. Other languages that were spoken in late prehistoric Georgia include Cherokee, Timucuan, and Yuchi.[22]

The food surplus of the Mississippian chiefdoms not only reinforced rulers' authority but also allowed them to support a class of at least part-time artisans. Hence, the Mississippian period is marked by an abundance of artifacts and relics, such as engraved shells and pendants, hair ornaments, intricately designed pottery, and embossed copper sheets and plates.[23] In the 1930s and 1940s, scholars identified a widespread system of symbols appearing on objects found at Etowah as well as at Moundville in Alabama and at an additional mound site near Spiro, Oklahoma. The symbolic system behind these shared motifs became known as the Southeastern Ceremonial Complex, which consists of a series of geometric patterns, representations of either deities or people impersonating them, and weaponry.[24] The geometric designs include an assortment of circles and squares (similar in style to those of the Woodland period), as well as depictions of arrows and eyes, while the spirits (or human impersonators) include a bird-man figure and assorted anomalous beings, such as snakes with horns and sometimes wings.[25] War clubs of various kinds dominate representations of weapons.

The items in this shared set of motifs are not random. Rather, they represent important aspects of the worldview of the Southeastern Indians. To take but one example, four-fold designs, including assorted crosses and squares, appear not only in Woodland period artifacts but also extend through the Mississippian period and are integral even to later coalescent groups such as the Creeks. Indeed, the typical Creek housing arrangement featured four-fold patterns. William Bartram, an eighteenth-century visitor to a Creek town on the Tallapoosa River in modern Alabama, observed that "every habitation consists of four oblong square houses . . . so situated as to form an exact square." And modern historian Joel W. Martin notes that Creek "civic and ceremonial life centered on the square ground, and almost every village was affiliated with a square ground town."[26]

Presumably, the four-fold patterns in Southeastern Indian life reflect the four cardinal directions, but interpretation of many other Mississippian motifs is hampered by the fact that, while we have quite a bit of information on symbolism from archaeology, there is next to nothing from before the era of the coalescent societies to tell us how the natives themselves viewed the designs. The continuation of motifs such as the four-fold patterns across major time periods and Indian societies, however, suggests that it is reasonable to use later Cherokee and Creek myths and practices to flesh out earlier shared iconography in an effort to reconstruct the belief system of Mississippian chiefdoms.[27]

One of the most important later stories that we may assume reflects Mississippian beliefs is the earth-diver myth, which is set against the backdrop of a watery chaos. One Cherokee account relates: "The earth is a great island floating in a sea of water, and suspended at each of the four cardinal points by a cord hanging down from the sky vault, which is of solid rock."[28] In different versions of the earth-diver myth, a small creature such as a beetle dives deep into the waters and retrieves mud from the bottom. Then, a bird, such as a buzzard, flaps its wings over the mud, drying it, and the new land is illuminated in stages by the Star, the Moon, and the Sun, which leads to the emergence of life, including the first people.[29]

Such stories reveal an understanding of a tripartite cosmos with an Upper World (populated by celestial beings), This World (populated by animals, people, and spiritual beings), and an Under World (populated by fish and water creatures, as well as other beings). Charles Hudson observes that the Southeastern Indians "believed that they existed—literally—in the center of the world. And all around them, in the four cardinal directions as well as above and below, were spiritual beings who were attentive to what went on among the people—the principal people—who lived in the center of the world. One sought to keep these spiritual beings balanced off against each other, so that none got the upper hand."[30]

In the Creek understanding, holding everything together was a creator being, the Master of Breath. In daily life Southeastern Indians acknowledged numerous other deities and spirits, and items of jewelry or decoration featured such beings. In opposition to the gigantic inhabitants of the Upper World—such as the sun, the moon, stars, and thunder—in the Under World there lived a second major class of beings, some of which were considered dangerous. Reflecting the regular patterns of the celestial bodies, the Upper World was thought to represent order, while the Under World was characterized by disorder. Because of the strength of the opposing powers of the Upper and Under Worlds, it was most important to preserve a proper balance among the three levels of being and to respect boundaries between them. Accordingly, Creeks did not extinguish fire (representing the Upper World) with water (representing the Under World) but rather with sand (a substance belonging to This World).[31]

The dangers of crossing boundaries, not only between Worlds but also with respect to food and other taboos, are related in several myths. James Mooney, who collected myths and stories among late nineteenth-century Cherokees, related one such tale:

> Two hunters, both for some reason under a tabu [taboo] against the meat of a squirrel or turkey, had gone into the woods together. When evening came they found a good camping place and lighted a fire to prepare their supper.

One of them had killed several squirrels during the day, and now got ready to broil them over the fire. His companion warned him that if he broke the tabu and ate squirrel meat he would become a snake, but the other laughed and said that was only a conjurer's story. He went on with his preparation, and when the squirrels were roasted made his supper of them and then lay down beside the fire to sleep. Late that night his companion was aroused by groaning, and on looking around he found the other lying on the ground rolling and twisting in agony, and with the lower part of his body already changed to the body and tail of a large water snake. The man was still able to speak and called loudly for help, but his companion could do nothing, but only sit by and try to comfort him while he watched the arms sink into the body and the skin take on a scaly change that mounted gradually toward the neck, until at last even the head was a serpent's head and the great snake crawled away from the fire and down the bank into the river.[32]

It may be observed that, since he broke the taboo, the errant hunter was forced to relocate from This World to the Under World.

Birds held a special place in the Southeastern Indian worldview, for, unlike other animals, some birds, such as the kingfisher, readily navigate all three Worlds because they are able to fly, walk the ground, and dive into water to spear fish. Even those birds that do not fish can easily traverse land and sky (This World and the Upper World), making them not only worthy of emulation by wearing bird feathers or bird symbols on jewelry, but also important beings thought to possess the ability to carry messages from the Upper World to This World.[33]

Along with myths and symbols, Southeastern Indians had important rituals and festivals that reinforced their worldview. While the yearly cycle probably included several festivals, perhaps the most important was what some Muskogean speakers called the *posketa*, an elaborate annual multiday festival of renewal in late summer or early fall, associated with the time when corn was ripe enough to be eaten green.[34] Charles Hudson has described the essential elements of the festival. First, people from various towns within a chiefdom would gather at their ceremonial center and eat large amounts of food in anticipation of fasting. Then they renovated buildings as well as the hearth at the center of the town's square ground. The square ground itself was swept clean, and a new layer of sand or dirt was spread out, with no one allowed to walk on it.[35] Following the initial preparations, men fasted, save for sipping an emetic drink, which induced vomiting.[36] They took counsel while fasting and reviewed crimes committed during the preceding year in order to resolve them before moving forward into a new year. Eventually, the men broke their fast and a new fire was created. Since the Master of Breath was associated with the sun, his earthly image was the sacred fire that was kept burning in the square ground throughout the year. This fire was put out at the *posketa* ceremony, together with all other fires in the town. A priest created a new fire using friction, and earlier fires were rekindled from this central fire.[37] There was then feasting, dancing, and games to celebrate an important ritual transition.[38]

The Mississippian chiefdoms thrived for nearly five hundred years, but they did not survive more than three generations following initial contact with Europeans. From 1539 to 1543 Spanish explorer Hernando de Soto led an extensive expedition, with close to six hundred soldiers, through parts of several contemporary Southeastern states, including Georgia.[39] For reasons to be explained, platform mound building ceased less than sixty years later. Throughout the second half of the sixteenth century chiefdoms were disintegrating. Those Indians who survived formed new groups such as the Creeks, who became entangled with Europeans in a complicated web of interrelationships.[40] The ancient ways of life, including religious traditions, either disappeared or were transformed.

To appreciate the scale of the developments that occurred after European contact, it is helpful to consider the rapid collapse of the chiefdom of Coosa in northwest Georgia, which De Soto visited in the late summer of 1540 before he headed into what is now Alabama, never to return to Georgia.[41] Later Spanish expeditions and explorers did travel into Georgia, including a detachment of Tristán de Luna's expeditionary force that came to Coosa in 1560.[42] Available accounts make it clear that the Coosa chiefdom the Luna group encountered had suffered severe decline since De Soto's expedition. In 1540, when De Soto observed Coosa, it was a paramount chiefdom—that is, one that had achieved either dominance over, or alliances with, neighboring chiefdoms. One member of De Soto's expedition described Coosa as being "thickly settled in numerous and large towns, with fields between, extending from one to another." Indeed, archaeological evidence suggests that the population of the entire paramount chiefdom (which stretched from modern eastern Tennessee to central Alabama and held at least seven chiefdoms in all) was then perhaps between thirty and fifty thousand. Therefore, when Luna's men, including some who were veterans of the De Soto expedition, arrived at

Coosa only twenty years later and found it "unimproved and full of thistles and weeds," they were shocked. Those men who had seen Coosa with De Soto declared that "they must have been bewitched when this country seemed to them so rich and populated."[43]

Why had Coosa deteriorated so much, so soon? In addressing this question, it is important to note that Coosa was not alone. There are widespread indications of chiefdom degeneration throughout the Southeast during the second half of the sixteenth century.[44] In fact, scholars estimate that the indigenous population of the Southeast fell by as much as 90 to 95 percent in the two hundred years following European contact.[45] While a number of factors likely contributed to this decline, it appears that the primary reason was the effect of European diseases on Indian groups. Simply put, while Spanish expeditionary soldiers killed many Indians in their path, the Old World diseases they carried, such as smallpox, measles, and bubonic plague, did far more damage than their swords.[46] Such diseases, which spread quickly, devastated native New World populations that lacked any resistance to them.[47] Archaeologists have established that over a period of several decades the residents of three main population clusters in Coosa near modern Rome and Cartersville, which collectively tallied nearly twenty villages, moved in a southwestern direction and ended up merging into one village, near Childersburg, Alabama.[48] In all, Coosa's fate illustrates that by the close of the seventeenth century the chiefdoms that De Soto and his men had encountered were largely gone, and the refugees were forging new societies.[49]

In 1565, around the time that Coosa Indians were migrating out of northwest Georgia into northeast Alabama, Spain founded St. Augustine in Florida; soon thereafter Spanish missionaries began to work in coastal Georgia. Initial efforts to convert Georgia's Indians were led by Jesuits in the late 1560s, but they were unsuccessful. Beginning in the mid-1580s, however, a number of Franciscan missionaries were able to launch several missions, including San Pedro de Mocama on present-day Cumberland Island. Additional missions were located farther north, in what was known as the Guale region of the Georgia coast, including Santa Catalina de Guale, which gave St. Catherines Island its name. There were also missions on the mainland. In 1597 Guale Indians revolted, in large measure because the Franciscans had tried to modify some of their existing social practices. Five friars were killed and several missions were destroyed. Eventually, priests were able to reestablish a coastal mission system. Those missions north of Cumberland Island became known collectively as Guale, while the region from Cumberland southward was Mocama.[50]

Following the Guale rebellion and less violent forms of negotiation, the Franciscans and Indians eventually established a mixed culture, which offered benefits to both sides. The Spanish priests came to have responsibility for religious matters, but they learned to work within existing social structures and under the authority of remaining Indian nobles. By respecting the authority of Indian leaders, the friars developed relationships with them, and when such leaders converted to Christianity, most of the population loyal to them followed suit. Consequently, for a time the priests were able to turn Indians into converts, while the Indians gained access to European goods and materials.[51]

The Santa Catalina mission on St. Catherines Island has been extensively studied by archaeologists. The site is of great historical interest since it was the northernmost Spanish outpost along the coastline for many years. In addition, it appears to be the location of the earliest church in Georgia. Finding the mission proved difficult since it was built using wooden stakes and woven cane, which were plastered with a mixture of sand, marsh mud, and plant fibers, and topped with a thatch roof. Such buildings are biodegradable, making their presence almost impossible to discover except by accident. As it happens, however, the Santa Catalina chapel is known to have burned, and thus the walls were fired. Archaeologists determined that the marsh mud used for plastering contained microscopic iron participles that, when subjected to great heat, point north. A device was used to locate anomalous magnetic readings in selected locations on St. Catherines Island, which allowed archaeologists to find and examine the mission site. Together with other material and documentary evidence, the excavations, which uncovered hundreds of graves of Christianized Indians, reveal the extensive commingling of Spanish and Indian cultures that occurred at and near the missions.[52]

Dennis Blanton of the Fernbank Museum of Natural History in Atlanta has drawn attention to the abundance of items buried with Indians at the St. Catherines site, a ritual once thought to have been banned by the friars. According to Blanton, "the Catholics believed that you can't take it with you, but the Indians believed otherwise. . . . These artifacts talk to us about a compromise." David Hurst Thomas, who was the lead archaeologist at the St. Catherines excavations, explains the necessity of compromise on the part of the friars: "At one point there were about 1,000 Guale Indians living around the mission, and it was a system that became mutually beneficial. . . . Consider that you have, at the most, two barefoot friars dropped off at a site where there were about 300 armed Indian warriors. There is going to be give-and-take."[53]

The priests who were resident in the missions served Indians in satellite villages, which might be as much as ten or so miles away.[54] Comments made by Baltasar Lopez of the San Pedro mission on Cumberland Island reflect both the dedication of the missionaries as well as the nature of the Spanish-Indian culture. In a letter dated September 15, 1602, Father Lopez wrote: "Of the 17 years that I have been in this land I have spent all of them among the Indians. And, thus, because I know from such experience and from knowing the language of this Province . . . and from having made expeditions into the hinterland, I am aware of their capacity and customs. . . . They come to Mass very willingly and take part in the chanted divine services and some already know how to read and write."[55]

Despite the success that the Franciscan priests had in getting Indians to participate in Catholic rituals, it is clear that the Indian belief system was not fully replaced by Christianity. Instead, the available evidence suggests that traditional beliefs went underground, with some elements still surfacing from time to time. For instance, Jerald T. Milanich relates an account of a traditional game played with a deer-skin ball that was enjoyed by Indians in Apalachee, located in northern Florida and southern Georgia. For some time, the Spanish missionaries in the area did not realize it, but the game had traditional religious features, and it was associated with supernatural beings linked to a successful harvest. The game was forbidden after some of the Indians admitted that it featured non-Christian symbolism.[56]

Overall, the mission system increased the level of interaction between Indians and Spaniards. As a result, epidemic diseases continued to negatively impact converted Indian societies, as did the effects of a draft labor system that the Spanish introduced. The combination led to continued population decline, such that the Spanish missions in Georgia began to weaken.[57] The expansionism of the English colonies of Virginia and Carolina represented the final straw for Georgia's Spanish missions. Indeed, from the 1660s into the initial decades of the 1700s, what can be characterized as an undeclared war between English and Spanish entities was waged, and eastern Georgia was the primary battleground.[58] As part of this conflict, from about 1660 to 1680, Indians known as Westos, who had migrated from the Northeast, terrorized

Indians of the Georgia interior as well as mission Indians along the coast, resulting from a complex trading system with English colonists. In a nutshell, Virginians, and later Carolinians, armed the Westos in exchange for Indian slaves captured by the Westos in the Southeast.[59]

Robbie Ethridge has written about this overall process and its impact. She explains that English traders would provide guns to an Indian group and require that slaves be exchanged to pay for them. These Indians would then attack an unarmed Indian group in order to obtain the slaves. In turn, the unarmed Indians would themselves seek guns for defensive purposes, and they would have to obtain them by the same procedure. Ethridge summarizes: "The Native Americans depended on the European trade for flintlock guns as well as for shot and powder. Therefore, anyone needing guns had to become a slave raider. In this way a cycle of dependency emerged." The violence that this cycle spawned had a far-reaching impact, with vulnerable Indians migrating to avoid enslavement and formerly disparate factions joining forces to try to survive. Along the way, many Indian groups were wiped out or lost their identity due to the combined effects of disease and slaving.[60] Thus Ethridge aptly refers to areas where this slave trade was practiced as "shatter zones."[61]

Matters intensified after Carolina became the primary sponsor of the Westo slave-raiders, as well as various pirates. Georgia's mission Indians were increasingly threatened and attacked, and several interior villages and towns were destroyed. Refugees fled to the south and west. Ultimately, the Westos themselves fell victim to the spiraling violence. When the Westos came to be viewed as a hindrance by Carolinians, other Carolina-sponsored Indians eliminated them in 1680.[62] A pirate raid in late 1684 "left Georgia's remaining missions in ruins."[63]

The considerable social disruption among Indians following European contact left Georgia sparsely populated by the late seventeenth century.[64] At this time Cherokees were moving into unoccupied northern Georgia, while a number of Muskogean speakers were congregating in southwest Georgia along the Chattahoochee River and in central Georgia on the Ocmulgee River, where an English trading post stood. That area was then known as Ochese Creek (from the former name of the chiefdom of Ichisi), and consequently the society that was developing there became known as the Creek Indians. The chiefdoms had collapsed and the survivors were having to reconstruct themselves. Out of the remains of former chiefdoms, the Creeks forged a multiethnic confederacy held together by a common language and shared needs. Given the appearance of the Cherokees and Creeks, and the increasing tension between English Carolina and Spanish Florida, "the stage was set for Oglethorpe's Georgia."[65]

The story of the European settlement of Georgia during the eighteenth century, as well as the further missionization of Indians, will be related in upcoming chapters. To complete the picture of Southeastern Indian spiritual traditions, we must now skip over the colonial period to an episode of the early nineteenth century, the Redstick revolt of 1813–1814. Events leading up to the conflict demonstrated that many of the major elements of the ancient Southeastern Indian worldview were still present in a residual yet powerful way.[66]

By the early nineteenth century the Creeks had suffered the loss of millions of acres of land. In 1805, for instance, Creeks were forced to cede to the state more than two million acres between two central Georgia rivers, the Oconee and the Ocmulgee. One Creek leader, Hopoithle Miko, tried to plead his case directly to President Thomas Jefferson: "The [Creek] land is become very small. . . . When a thing began to grow scarce it is natural to love it. . . . What we have left we cannot spare." Yet white settlers were already beginning to press beyond the Ocmulgee toward the Flint River in southwest Georgia. Not surprisingly, Creeks developed a special name for Anglo-Americans, *Ecunnaunuxulgee*, or "people greedily grasping after all lands."[67]

In 1812 Creek prophets related messages they claimed to have received from the Master of Breath, who, they said, could no longer tolerate things as they were. The land had to be returned to its former state, which would bring back the balance of the entire cosmos. Such restoration, however, necessitated revolt against Anglo-American invaders. Throughout 1813 the rebellion grew and warriors took up the ancient war club. Those war clubs, which were painted red, gave the Redstick revolt its name.[68]

The revolt did not end the way that the Creek prophets and rebels had desired. At the Battle of Tohopeka (Horseshoe Bend) in March 1814, one thousand Creek warriors carrying war clubs were confronted by fifteen hundred white soldiers armed with rifles and cannon, who were supported by five hundred Cherokees. Approximately eight hundred Creeks died, and the revolt was crushed. The Creeks were forced by the Treaty of Fort Jackson, signed soon after the battle, to cede several million more acres to the United States, enlarging Georgia in the process. Whites and their black slaves quickly settled this land, contributing to the development of the "Cotton Kingdom."[69] By then, Southeastern Indian religious traditions had become what one scholar refers to as "the beliefs of a marginalized underclass."[70]

In 1835, some two decades after the end of the Redstick revolt, John Howard Payne, writing from Macon, Georgia, sent a letter to a relative in New York describing a Green Corn ceremony, or *busk* (deriving from a Muskogean word meaning "a fast"), that he had recently attended among Creeks in Alabama:

> The chosen spot [for the ceremony] is remote from any habitations, and consists of an ample square, with four large log houses, each one forming a side of the square, at every angle of which there is a broad opening into the area. . . . Behind the angle of one of the four broad entrances to the square, rises a high, cone-roofed building, circular and dark; . . . some one said it was a councilhouse. It occupied one corner of an outer square. . . . In the center of this outer square was a very high circular mound. This, it seems, was formed from the earth accumulated yearly by removing the surface of the sacred square thither. At every Green-Corn Festival, the sacred square is strewn with soil yet untrodden; the soil of the year preceeding being taken away, but preserved as above explained. No stranger's foot is allowed to press the new earth of the sacred square until its consecration is complete.[71]

The similarity of this ceremony to the Mississippian *posketa* described earlier in this chapter is clear.[72] Indeed, owing to the work of archaeologists and historians, it is obvious to us today that many symbolic forms of ancient usage among Southeastern Indians can be seen in Payne's account of this renewal ceremony, from the square surrounded by four buildings to the circular mound.[73] As we saw at the outset of this chapter, the Indians who were with Elias Cornelius at Etowah in 1818 believed that the mounds they encountered "were never put up by our people." Just so, it is quite possible that neither Payne nor the Creeks he observed knew that the ceremony he was watching was reenacting religious practices of lost mound-building Mississippian chiefdoms, dating to a time long before Europeans trod the ground that would become Georgia.

CHAPTER TWO

Seeds Are Sown

During the initial decades of the eighteenth century, European powers
bordered what would become Georgia, involved in an intricate political
dance. Above the Savannah River sat the British colony of Carolina, and
below the St. Mary's River was Spanish Florida. Each claimed at least par-
tial possession of the land between, leading some historians to dub the coast
of Georgia at that time "the debatable land."[1] In the 1720s a lone military
outpost sat between them, Fort King George, which was built in 1721 at the
mouth of the Altamaha River.[2] The English troops who garrisoned the fort
were unable to tame their environs, and eventually they fell prey to unsanitary
water and malaria. The fort was abandoned by 1732, and the debatable land
lay unoccupied by European forces. A few years before the soldiers left Fort
King George, a Creek Indian named Tomochichi created a splinter group,
the Yamacraw, that settled near an English trading post close to the Savannah
River.[3] A spot of land that became known as Yamacraw Bluff, above the river,
is the site of Savannah, Georgia's first town.

The dispute between England and Spain over the debatable land forms
one element of the background of the colonization of Georgia. Another key
development took place in England as Tomochichi organized his new Indian
group in America. In 1729 James Oglethorpe, a member of the British Parliament, was part of an effort to reform prisons in England, which eventually
led to the creation of a group that became interested in creating a colony in
America as a refuge for deserving poor. The location they selected was the
land between the Savannah and the Altamaha rivers. The group became trustees of the new colony and received a royal charter in 1732 from King George
II, which gave them jurisdiction for twenty-one years. In honor of the king,
the colony would be named Georgia.[4] Though the concept of the colony had

grown out of philanthropic motives, by the time it was established political and economic motives had taken center stage. The colony was meant not only to provide new opportunities for deserving settlers, but also to serve as a buffer between Carolina and Florida, as well as a location for what the trustees hoped would be lucrative agricultural experimentation. Oglethorpe, a politician as well as a man with military experience, was the perfect person to spearhead the colony and look after the various aspects of its mission.[5]

On February 12, 1733, following an ocean voyage from England, Oglethorpe led approximately one hundred colonists ashore and up to the top of Yamacraw Bluff. There he met with Tomochichi, assisted by a woman named Mary Musgrove, who served as interpreter for the two men.[6] Musgrove, also known as Coosaponakeesa, was one of the most interesting and important people in early Georgia. The daughter of an English trader and a Creek woman, she was reared in the Carolina colony as well as in the Creek village of Coweta. Thus she was thoroughly conversant with both the English and Muskogean languages, as well as British and Indian cultures. Andrew K. Frank nicely summarizes her importance: "As Pocahontas was to the Jamestown colony and Sacagawea was to the Lewis and Clark expedition, so was Musgrove to the burgeoning Georgia colony."[7]

The year before the colony was founded, the trustees gained the assistance of the Society for the Propagation of the Gospel in Foreign Parts, which effectively meant that the Church of England would be promoted in Georgia. Yet, while Anglicanism was favored, the colony's charter explicitly offered freedom of religion, save to Catholics (in part out of fear that an influx of Catholics into the colony might provide assistance to the Spanish in Florida).[8] The charter stated: "We do . . . Ordain . . . for ever hereafter there shall be a liberty of conscience allowed in the Worship of God to all persons Inhabiting . . . our said Province And that all such persons Except Papists shall have a Free Exercise of their Religion."[9] This principle of religious freedom was tested very early in the life of Georgia when, only a few months after the colony was established, approximately forty Jews joined it.[10]

A group of Lutherans also came to the young colony. In 1731 Roman Catholic Archbishop Leopold von Firmian expelled Protestants from Salzburg (in present-day Austria), leading tens of thousands of Lutherans to seek safe haven. Two ministers, John Martin Bolzius and his assistant Israel Christian Gronau, brought a group of around fifty of the Salzburg Lutherans to Savannah in 1734.[11] Most of the Jews in Savannah were Spanish speakers, but some who spoke German befriended the Salzburg immigrants. Bolzius, whose copious writings are of great assistance for understanding early life in Georgia, recorded that when they arrived a "Jew, who had also received some land here, took the Salzburgers in and treated them to breakfast with a good rice-soup."[12]

The Jew who met the Salzburgers was Benjamin Sheftall.[13] Sheftall was the patriarch of what would become the leading Jewish family in the colony, and he and his sons were instrumental in founding Mickve Israel, the third-oldest Jewish congregation in the United States (after congregations in New York and Rhode Island).[14] Sheftall had been a member of the first group of Jews to arrive in Georgia. The Torah scroll they brought with them is still in the possession of the congregation in Savannah today. In 1748 Sheftall also had *tefillin* (phylacteries) brought over from England for his son Mordecai's bar mitzvah, "the first recorded observance of this rite in America."[15]

The Salzburgers received approval from Oglethorpe to establish their own town, Ebenezer, north of Savannah. After two years, having experienced flooding and other problems associated with their original site, they moved about five miles west and established New Ebenezer, near modern Rincon, some twenty miles northwest of Savannah.[16] The brick edifice of their church building, Jerusalem Lutheran Church, which still survives, was begun in 1767 and completed in 1769. Throughout the colonial period these Lutherans modeled the trustees' ideal of yeomanry.[17] Bolzius and his congregation worked hard on their land, and they lived and worshipped together as a community. Bolzius wrote that the group led "a calm and quiet life of blessedness and honesty."[18] One element that he cited as a key to his flock's success was the trustees' rule, made equivalent to law in 1735, that there would be no slavery in the colony.[19] This policy became a strain on relations within the colony at large, however, and was ultimately overturned.

In 1735 and 1736 two additional religious groups came to Georgia; they would have very different experiences in the colony. First, beginning in April 1735 a small number of Moravians (less than fifty in all at any given time) appeared in Savannah as part of their worldwide missionary efforts.[20] Moravians, a Protestant group with origins in the fifteenth century, take their name from Moravia, a region in the former Czechoslovakia, where many of the faith lived. Moravians are pacifists. Therefore, when the threat of hostilities with Spanish forces increased in the late 1730s and Georgians prepared for war, it created a difficult situation for the Moravians. Scholars generally hold that when the Moravians were pressured to serve in defense of the colony, they left in stages, culminating in 1740.[21] Some Moravians would again appear in Georgia by 1800, though, to conduct missionary activities among Indians.

In contrast to the pacifist Moravians, Scottish Highlanders were recruited to come to Georgia because of their renowned skill in warfare.[22] A group of more than fifty Highlanders arrived in January 1736 and settled near the spot of the old Fort King George, at a site that became known as Darien.[23] There they helped to protect the southern flank of Georgia. These Highlanders worshipped as Presbyterians and were led by their minister, John McLeod. As we will see, the Highlanders were vocal in protesting the introduction of slavery into Georgia and argued that owning slaves was immoral. As Thomas A. Scott has observed: "Such arguments were rare anywhere in the early eighteenth century. For them to come from military outposts in the empire's backwaters was remarkable."[24]

Hostilities in the New World between Spain and England finally broke out in late 1739 in the War of Jenkins' Ear.[25] In 1740, as part of the conflict, Oglethorpe tried to seize St. Augustine.[26] The campaign ended as a failure. Oglethorpe withdrew his remaining forces to Fort Frederica on the island of St. Simons and waited for a retaliatory Spanish strike, which came nearly two years later. In the summer of 1742 Spanish ships appeared off the Georgia coast. Though scores of soldiers were prepared to do battle, large-scale conflict did not occur. Rather, in two skirmishes on St. Simons, Oglethorpe's forces routed the Spanish, who retreated and fled. Warfare between England and Spain over conflicting claims in the New World ceased with a later treaty and a tacit agreement that the St. Johns River would serve as a boundary between Georgia and Florida. The dispute over the debatable land had ended.[27]

In 1743 Oglethorpe went to England to settle some financial and political matters, and he never returned to America. His absence left an opening for the supporters of slavery in Georgia. A proslavery group, eventually referred to as the malcontents, had emerged in the colony as early as 1735.[28] When Thomas Stephens became a supporter of the malcontents, it represented a significant moment in the debate about slavery in Georgia.[29] Stephens was a lobbyist in Parliament, and in 1742 he published a pamphlet on behalf of the malcontents titled *The Hard Case of the Distressed People of Georgia*.[30] Betty Wood notes that before this time the debate over slavery was largely a matter for discussion between the trustees and the settlers. Thereafter, primarily because of Stephens, Parliament began to take much more interest in the

situation in Georgia. As a result, the trustees found themselves fighting a losing battle.[31]

In Georgia itself the ban on slavery was a matter of intense debate. In a
petition signed in January 1739, the Presbyterian Highlanders at Darien urged
Oglethorpe to maintain the ban, stating: "It's shocking to human Nature,
that any Race of Mankind, and their Posterity, should be sentenced to perpetual Slavery. . . . Freedom to them must be as dear as to us."[32] According to
some historians, this was the first written protest of the use of African slaves
in America.[33] A few months later, in March 1739, the Lutheran Salzburgers at
Ebenezer led by Bolzius lent their support to the Presbyterian Highlanders'
petition.[34]

Not all religious figures in Georgia agreed with the opposition to slavery.
George Whitefield, a priest who served the Anglicans in Savannah from 1738
to 1740, supported slavery as both an opportunity to convert what he considered to be heathens as well as a vital economic need. Whitefield advocated
what is known as the "climatic necessity" argument, which holds that blacks
have a greater capacity than whites for working in hot climates such as that
of the American South. Such a view contends that Europeans are naturally
challenged when they work in semitropical settings, whether at hard labor or
mental tasks.[35] Accordingly, one visitor to Savannah commented about some
lawyers he encountered there that "in this warm climate these gentlemen can
only spend about three hours a day on brain work and must have the rest of
the time for recreation."[36] At Ebenezer, Bolzius and his fellow hardworking
Salzburgers scoffed at such notions: "We [were] told by several people after
our arrival that it proves quite impossible and dangerous for white people to
plant and manufacture any rice, being a work only for Negroes, not for European people. . . . We laughed at such a tale."[37]

Following the conclusion of the War of Jenkins' Ear, arguments for ban-
ning slavery based on the concern that runaway slaves would flee to Florida and aid the Spaniards lost their effect. Given the removal of the Spanish
threat, as well as the lobbying of Thomas Stephens, the trustees' opposition
to slavery was increasingly futile. After 1742, even if it was not yet lawful,
slavery was being practiced in Georgia.[38] In the mid-1740s a growing number
of Georgia colonists, particularly those who lived close to the South Carolina
border, flaunted the antislavery proscription and made illicit use of slaves.
By 1748 there were open slave sales in Savannah and, as Michael Thurmond
observes, "'Negro Fever' had even taken hold in Darien, where a majority

of the Scots now supported repeal of the slavery ban. All but forgotten was their 1739 antislavery petition."[39] In 1750 Bolzius too reluctantly accepted slavery in a letter to the trustees.[40] The trustees themselves were left with little choice but to legalize slavery in Georgia, which took effect on January 1, 1751. Shortly after the ban on slavery was lifted, South Carolina planters and their slaves began to stream into Georgia, and additional immigrants came from Virginia. In 1741 fewer than fifteen hundred people lived in the colony of Georgia, the vast majority of whom were white. By 1773 Georgia held some thirty-three thousand inhabitants, with eighteen thousand free whites and fifteen thousand black slaves.[41]

One of the groups that migrated from South Carolina was a community of Congregationalists who had organized a church in 1696 at Dorchester, near Charlestown. Following a congregational vote, they moved en masse to Georgia in 1752 with their slaves. The group was led by their longtime pastor John Osgood, who served them from 1735 to 1773. They settled in Midway (named because of its location between Darien and Savannah), as well as at the port of Sunbury (now abandoned), and worshipped primarily at Midway Congregational Church.[42]

The Congregationalists and their slaves worshipped together. A slave gallery can still be seen in Midway Church, the second oldest church in Georgia of those still standing.[43] More typically, however, slaves in colonial Georgia had relatively little to do with Christianity. Since many of the slaves in Georgia at that time had been born in Africa, there were language barriers to be overcome, and some slaves remained devoted to the indigenous religions they had known. Leonard Haynes, for instance, recalled that, "my grandfather . . . came over from the Gold Coast of Africa and was sold to a Mr. Haynes in Georgia. My grandfather was an African priest. This fact made him hostile to Christian preachers and to the religion of the Christians. Hence, he refused to join with the other slaves in their religious gatherings." Even if a slave was not unreceptive to Christianity, the standard approach to conversion by the leading colonial denominations involved catechesis, which demanded extended study. As will be noted below, there were few active clergy in colonial Georgia, hampering such religious education efforts.[44]

At the time of the Congregationalist migration, Georgia itself was moving from being a trusteeship to a royal province.[45] There were three royal governors prior to the Revolution. The third, James Wright, is widely considered to have been the most successful and efficient of the three.[46] Among

Wright's achievements was expanding the land occupied by colonists. He accomplished this by convincing Indians to cede lands to the province. The extent of what Harold E. Davis calls Wright's "remarkable, if morally ambiguous, accomplishments" in regard to Indian cessions can be ascertained by the sheer number of acres he was able to add to the colony. When Wright became governor white Georgians had undisputed use of some 1.5 million acres, but through Indian cessions he obtained an additional 5.5 million acres.[47] In order to encourage white settlers to populate lands gained through cessions, Georgia's royal government created a number of new towns.

One such town was Wrightsborough, named after the governor, which was set aside for Quaker immigrants. Beginning in 1768, numerous families migrated from North Carolina to Wrightsborough, located in today's McDuffie County. It is debatable how many of these families were actually Quakers, but there were a sufficient number to form a Quaker community. The presence of some non-Quakers was actually encouraged by the leader of the Wrightsborough Quakers, James Maddock, who, realizing the need for protection, permitted some arms-bearing settlers to live among the pacifist Quakers.[48]

In addition to Indian cessions and an increase in population, royal control was marked after 1758 by the establishment of the Church of England as the official religion of the colony. The effect on non-Anglican or "dissenting" churches was not overly oppressive, since the establishment statute explicitly expressed as "the true intent and Meaning of this Act" that "no Rector or Minister . . . shall hereby be invested with any Power or Authority to exercise any Eclesiastical Law or Jurisdiction whatsoever."[49] This statement ensured that members of non-Anglican churches were free to worship as they saw fit.

John J. Zubly (born Hans Joachim Züblin in St. Gall, Switzerland), who served as minister of an Independent Presbyterian congregation in Savannah beginning in 1759, was the leading dissenter.[50] Zubly was a gregarious man and made a good fit for the multiculturalism of early Georgia since he was capable of preaching in English, French, and German. In addition to his clerical talents, Zubly ran a ferry and was known throughout the colonies for his learning (he earned two degrees from the College of New Jersey, later Princeton University).[51] Among his friends was Ezra Stiles, who was at one time president of Yale College.[52] Zubly's library in Savannah was one of the very best in America. In 1774 Rev. Henry Muhlenberg, the leading figure among American Lutherans, came to Georgia from Pennsylvania to adjudicate a dispute between ministers at Ebenezer and visited with Zubly. Muhlenberg found Zubly's library to be a "fine collection of old and new books, the like of which I have seldom seen in America." Indeed, Muhlenberg noted that "the external appearance of his library and study is hardly inferior to that of the most famous in Europe."[53]

The year before Muhlenberg visited him, Zubly wrote a letter in which he addressed the issue of how many clergy were present in Georgia at the time. Given his general studiousness and degree of contact with his fellow colonists, Zubly's 1773 list is a precious resource. Zubly began his survey by observing that Georgia was divided into twelve parishes, but that there were clergy in only two of them: Tim Lawton served in Christ Church (Savannah) and James Seymour in St. Paul (Augusta). Zubly thought that there might be churches in two additional parishes operating without benefit of clergy. There were "three English Congregations of protestant dissenters," which were located at Midway (served by John Osgood), Sunbury (also served by Osgood), and Savannah (served by Zubly himself). In addition, Zubly noted that there was a "Society of Presbyterians on Alatamaha, who have had ministers occasionally among them," and some "German Dissenting Congregations . . . of the Lutheran Persuasion," located at Ebenezer (served by John Martin Bolzius and Israel Christian Gronau) and Savannah. Zubly added that there was "a considerable body of people at Wrightsborough, Queensborough, & Bryar Creek, chiefly Presbyterians" who were "very desirous" of having a regular minister, but were without one. Finally, he concluded that "there is no baptist Church in the Province."[54]

In all, Zubly referred to only six ministers: two Anglicans (Lawton and Seymour); two Lutherans (Bolzius and Gronau); one Congregationalist (Osgood); and one Presbyterian (Zubly). Even if we allow for a few Baptist ministers in the backwoods of whom Zubly had no knowledge—as well as the fact that Jews and Quakers, whom Zubly did not mention, conducted their own services—the tally reflects that there were perhaps fewer than ten persons functioning as clergy in Georgia in 1773, which then held more than thirty thousand inhabitants.[55]

What should we make of this situation? Did most Georgians in Zubly's day desire a local clergyperson but there just were not enough to go around, or does the relative lack of clergy reflect low interest in religion? It seems likely that, following the establishment of the Anglican Church in 1758, most Georgians felt that they had some allegiance to it.[56] Nevertheless, we should not underestimate the degree of indifference to religion in early Georgia. In fact, even in those places where ministers were present, certain persons were simply not interested, a condition that lasted throughout the colonial period. In 1735 Samuel Quincy, the first rector of Christ Church in Savannah, wrote to the trustees in England to tell them that they need not be concerned about Catholics coming to Georgia and making converts, since "Religion seems to be the least minded of any thing in the place."[57] In the late 1750s it was reported to the archbishop of Canterbury that there was a party in the Georgia assembly "such as Care for no Churches at all." In 1769 a minister then in Georgia, Samuel Frink, remarked that Georgia settlers seemed to have "but very little more Knowledge of a Saviour than the Aboriginal natives."[58] And at the end of his 1773 letter Zubly himself referred to "the low Estate of vital Religion every where" in Georgia.[59]

A compelling view of the toll this overall situation could take on an earnest minister can be found in the journal entries of Charles Wesley during the roughly five months in 1736 (March 9 to July 26) when he was in Georgia to serve as secretary to James Oglethorpe and as a minister. Charles had come to Georgia with his brother, John, who was to serve as rector of Christ Church. His term of service began well. He recorded on March 9 that he had set foot on the island of St. Simons about three in the afternoon and "immediately [his] spirit revived." He felt that God had given him, "like Saul, another heart," and he was received well by Oglethorpe and the other colonists. In the evening he led a prayer service and felt that the lesson of the day gave him "the fullest direction, and greatest encouragement."[60] Almost immediately, though, he began to experience various difficulties and frustrations.

In his second entry, from March 10, Wesley mentions trying to reconcile one woman with another, referred to as "M. H.," and the following day he had to console M. H.'s maid, whom she had struck. Difficulties with M. H. become a feature of his entries thereafter. In his third entry, on March 11, Wesley mentioned that he had "heard the first harsh word from Mr. Oglethorpe." The entirety of his March 16 entry is as follows: "I was wholly spent in writing letters for Mr. Oglethorpe. I would not spend six days more in the same manner for all Georgia." By March 25 relations between the two men had deteriorated to the point that Oglethorpe charged Wesley with "mutiny and sedition" for supposedly stirring up people to leave the colony. The day before, Wesley had written that he had prayed "earnestly for my enemies, particularly Mr. Oglethorpe, whom I now looked upon as the chief of them."

On April 6 Wesley recorded: "Today Mr. Oglethorpe gave away my bedstead from under me, and refused to spare one of the carpenters to mend me up another." John Wesley was able to intercede between Oglethorpe and his sibling to some degree. Still, when Charles Wesley wrote his final Georgia entry on July 26, he concluded: "When the boat put off I was surprised that I felt no more joy in leaving such a scene of sorrows."[61]

It seems certain that Charles Wesley would have agreed with John J. Zubly's later characterization of "the low Estate of vital Religion" in the colony. In the second entry of his Georgia journal, Wesley recorded that he spoke with a "Mrs. W." and that he "laboured to guard her against the cares of the world, and to give herself to God in the Christian sacrifice; but to no purpose." He felt that his words had made "no impression." On March 21 his Sunday service was interrupted by a doctor practicing shooting outside. On March 26 Oglethorpe chastised Wesley and asserted that there was not "true religion among the people, but instead of that, mere formal prayers." Wesley responded that in reality the people had "no more of the form of godliness than the power" and said that he seldom had "above six at the public service." On April 5 he glumly reported: "My congregation in the evening consisted of two Presbyterians and a Papist."[62] Harvey H. Jackson points out that by this time Oglethorpe had undertaken a campaign to discredit Wesley, which further reduced the size of his congregation. Nevertheless, Jackson also concludes that, with very few exceptions (such as the Salzburgers and the Jews), most Georgians gave a low priority to religion, and thus that Anglican clergy were forced to minister to an apathetic flock.[63]

The trustees tried to foster interest in religion by distributing religious books. The contents of the library in Augusta, which was established in 1751 when the trustees sent 166 volumes, are suggestive. The books consisted of multiple copies of the Book of Common Prayer and the Bible, as well as *Companion for the Sick, Whole Duty of Man, Faith and Practice of a Church of England Man, Help and Guide to Christian Families, Showing How to Walk with God, The Great Importance of a Religious Life Considered, The Young Christian Instructed,* and spelling books. But another shipment, which was sent in 1735 to Frederica, is more representative of the overall climate for religion in Georgia. The collection consisted of 722 total volumes. Three hundred of the volumes were one hundred copies each of hornbooks, primers, and catechisms. Another 222 volumes were multiple copies of the Bible and the New Testament, the Book of Common Prayer, a book on the Eucharist, the

Christian Monitor and Companion to the Altar, and the *Christian Monitor and Answer to Excuses*. The largest set of books, however, was two hundred copies of the *Friendly Admonition to the Drinkers of Brandy*.[64]

In addition to widespread low interest, part of the problem with regard to the promotion of religion in colonial Georgia was the poor quality of most of the clergy who served the colonists. Among the dissenters, in addition to Zubly, both Bolzius and Osgood may be singled out as having achieved success and esteem. But, as Harold E. Davis observes, save one exception, Anglican clergy in Georgia "were either fractious, overzealous, youthful and inexperienced, discouraged, narrow, immoral, made useless by Revolutionary ferment, or were in their posts too brief a time a demonstrate their strengths or weaknesses." The exception was Bartholomew Zouberbuhler, who served in Savannah for twenty years (1746 to 1766). Zouberbuhler was revered by his parishioners and provided strong leadership. In 1750, for instance, a long-awaited building for the Christ Church congregation was completed, which was expanded in 1765 to hold additional pews.[65] Zouberbuhler was so effective, not only in the construction of Christ Church but also in his guidance of the congregation, that the trustees were greatly concerned about losing him. In 1765 they wrote: "He has perform'd his Duty so well hitherto, and so much better than any of his Predecessors that the Loss of him, could not easily be repair'd."[66]

That the trustees were right to be concerned is underscored by an incident near the end of Zouberbuhler's life. When his health began to decline, Zouberbuhler sought to resign from the Christ Church rectorship. Yet he would not abandon his post until a proper successor could be identified. In 1761 the Society for the Propagation of the Gospel in Foreign Parts sent the Reverend William Duncanson as the intended replacement for Zouberbuhler. Upon interviewing Duncanson, however, the leaders of Christ Church declared him unsuitable. After he had been deemed unacceptable for service in Savannah, St. Paul Parish in Augusta called for Duncanson to serve there since their rectorship was vacant at the time. Things did not go well: "Duncanson was not there six weeks before he was disgraced as a drunkard and a vile talker. He was shortly under a peace warrant from a man he challenged to fight, attempted to horsewhip, and menaced with a loaded pistol. A little later he was accused of seeking to debauch his landlord's daughter."[67] One may imagine how relieved the St. Paul parishioners were when he left town.

To be sure, not all Anglican clergy in colonial Georgia were such a disaster. Still, most experienced difficulties of some sort. The case of John Wesley is illustrative. The imposing statue of him that today commands Reynolds Square in Savannah might suggest that the founder of Methodism thrived when he served in the town. Such an impression could be bolstered by the numerous markers and plaques in Savannah that also commemorate his presence, together with others on Cockspur Island and St. Simons Island.[68] A contemporary tourist, seeing all these memorials, might well come to the conclusion that Wesley had a long and successful stay in Georgia. In actuality, he was forced to leave the colony under cover of night.

John Wesley offended many of his Savannah parishioners by his manner, which they found too formal for their frontier setting. He would not administer communion to John Martin Bolzius, for example, because, even though Wesley felt that Bolzius had a "truly Christian piety," he did not approve of the manner of Bolzius's baptism since it had not been performed by a minister "who had been episcopally ordained." Wesley himself observed: "Can any one carry High Church zeal higher than this?"[69] Wesley's downfall in Georgia came when he proposed marriage to one of the colonists, Sophia Hopkey. After she married someone else, Wesley refused to offer her communion as well, which resulted in a warrant against him for defaming her. Eventually, Wesley left Savannah and departed for England from Charlestown.[70] On December 2, 1737, he recorded in his journal: "I shook off the dust of my feet, and left Georgia, after having preached the gospel there . . . not as I ought, but as I was able, one year and nearly nine months."[71]

In another case, a minister was extremely successful in his preaching, but not in a way that directly benefited his Georgia congregants. George Whitefield came to Georgia from England in 1738 and became the fourth rector of Christ Church, succeeding John Wesley.[72] Whitefield spent a significant amount of time outside Savannah, though, preaching throughout the colonies. To be sure, he preached in part to raise money for Bethesda, an orphanage near Savannah.[73] Nevertheless, the bulk of this preaching occurred far away from Georgia, mostly in the Middle and New England colonies, where he became well known. It is telling that in 1740, when Whitefield departed from Boston harbor, he was seen off by a crowd of some thirty thousand, at a time when the total population of Boston was around twenty thousand.[74]

In sum, the growth and spread of religion in colonial Georgia faced numerous challenges, including not only the harsh daily realities involved with hewing a new colony out of the wilderness, but also overall disinterest in religion and a poorly equipped or inattentive clergy. And thus in 1773, just prior to the Revolution, when John J. Zubly took his mental survey of the colony, he could identify only pockets of religious communities, with few clergy, who were present only among the Episcopalians, Congregationalists, Presbyterians, and Lutherans. The first three members of this grouping are not surprising, given that these were the "mainline" denominations throughout the colonies, and at the time of the Revolution the majority of Americans who were active in a religious group belonged to one of them.[75] Yet the situation was about to change dramatically. For while Zubly thought that there was no Baptist church in Georgia in 1773, one had been founded the year before near Kiokee, and in 1773 a second would be formed at Lower Brier Creek. By 1790 there were more than forty Baptist churches in the state.[76] Methodists had also arrived by 1790 and eventually met with great success as well. About a decade before Zubly wrote his survey, his friend Ezra Stiles had used a demographic technique he learned from Benjamin Franklin to calculate that within one hundred years the colonies would hold seven million Congregationalists and less than four hundred thousand Baptists.[77] But the Revolution changed everything. The mainline colonial denominations would not dominate the future of religion in Georgia; rather, the evangelicals would.

CHAPTER THREE

God Is Calling Ev'ry Nation

A lone figure rode on horseback throughout eastern Georgia in March 1791 to observe the status of religion in the region. The rider was Francis Asbury, a bishop in the Methodist Episcopal Church and the "father of American Methodism."[1] Methodism arose following an experience that John Wesley had in May 1738, just a few months after returning to England from Georgia. Wesley, an Anglican minister, had undergone a profound religious experience in which he felt his heart "strangely warmed." This event changed him and made him feel that Anglicanism needed to be reinvigorated in order to awaken emotional as well as intellectual currents in the faith. Wesley began meeting in small groups with like-minded Anglicans, which helped lead to the development of Methodism within, and eventually beyond, Anglicanism. Asbury was ordained a bishop when the Methodist Episcopal Church was founded in 1784, with Wesley's blessing, as an entity that was separate from the Anglican Church and that was intended to develop Methodism in America.[2] The faith reached Georgia in 1786, and Asbury intended to keep a close eye on its development in the new state. Indeed, though he regularly traveled across the eastern seaboard as far north as New York, between 1788 and 1814 Asbury visited Georgia no fewer than nineteen times, with six trips during the 1790s, as he tried to help Methodism gain a foothold. The task was formidable. On March 13, 1791, near the end of his tour through eastern Georgia, Asbury wrote in his journal: "I have ridden about two hundred and fifty miles in Georgia, and find the work, in general, very dead."[3]

What Asbury observed in Georgia extended beyond the problems that fledgling Methodism was having in the new state, for following the Revolution there was what has been called an "ecclesiastical vacuum" in Georgia. The reputation of the Anglican Church had been harmed by its association with England, evangelical denominations were not yet well established, and many non-evangelical congregations were dormant or defunct. As a result of these conditions, some Christians lamented that religion seemed to face a worrisome environment in the state. Such concern was not unfounded.[4]

Roger Finke and Rodney Stark have argued that the nostalgic view of colonial America as an age of widespread piety and faith is out of keeping with the reality that, as they put it, taverns were probably busier than churches. Indeed, there was a low religious adherence rate in the colonial period, with no more than 15 to 20 percent of the American population belonging to a congregation. According to data collected by Finke and Stark, the religious adherence rate for Georgians in 1776 was only 7 percent, the lowest in the colonies. One of the foremost reasons why the rate was so low has to do with the sociology of frontiers, since such areas are typically filled with young, single males. This situation had a direct impact on religious life because the rate of religious adherence suffers when there is a high male-to-female ratio.[5] Given that most of Georgia remained a frontier for several decades after the Revolution, it is not surprising that none of the denominations kept pace with Georgia's overall population growth in the 1790s.[6]

The years following the Revolution utterly transformed Georgia. As already implied, one important change was that church bodies with some prominence in the colony (Episcopalians, Congregationalists, Presbyterians, and Lutherans) were in disorder after the war, with little to hold them together. Another important development was a dramatic redistribution of the Georgia population. The 1790 census disclosed the surprising fact that only 20 percent of Georgians resided in the coastal counties, while a much larger portion of the populace—some 37 percent—lived in Wilkes County, northwest of Augusta.[7] Thus, a great many Georgians were in the backcountry, the extent of which would gradually expand through acquisition of Indian lands. The backcountry offered good soil for the development of cotton, which eventually became the primary cash crop, displacing rice and tobacco. While the fiber in the cotton that could grow along the coast ("Sea Island cotton") allowed for relatively easy removal of seeds, interior areas in the South supported short-staple, upland cotton, and removing the seed from this variety was labor intensive.[8] Such labor was increasingly provided by slaves, and as a result the slave population grew.[9]

The overall post-Revolution conditions afforded an opportunity for evangelicals to flourish, relative to other denominations.[10] Among the evangelicals, however, Baptists and Methodists were able to take greater advantage of this opportunity than Presbyterians. In 1810 Georgia had nearly fifteen thousand Baptists and approximately eight thousand Methodists, but only a couple of hundred Presbyterians.[11] Typically, early Baptist and Methodist ministers were poorly educated, yet they spoke from the heart, which was persuasive in a frontier setting. On the other hand, Presbyterians, who demanded an educated clergy, continually lagged behind the other two evangelical bodies in total numbers because their ministers were not well equipped to rouse common folk.[12] Therefore this chapter will focus (though not exclusively) on Baptists and Methodists, who, as we will see, clearly did know how to stir the backcountry masses in Georgia.

Baptists were present in Georgia in a limited way from the beginning of the colony until the 1770s. The ship that first brought James Oglethorpe to America had on board William Calvert, a Baptist, and his wife, who was also perhaps a Baptist. Additional Baptists arrived from time to time, but in 1750 there were only seven known Baptists in the colony, out of more than two thousand total inhabitants. The first Baptist church established in Georgia came almost a decade later. The Tuckaseeking congregation, in Effingham County, was apparently only in existence from 1759 to 1763 and had about fifteen members. The Baptists who established the church observed the Sabbath on Saturday, the Seventh Day, and worked on Sunday. This led to conflict with other persons in the area, and the group eventually crossed the river into South Carolina and out of Georgia history.[13]

Sustained Baptist growth in Georgia came from other groups, the Particular Baptists and the Separate Baptists, who formed their first churches within a year of one another in the early 1770s.[14] In 1772 Separates established Kiokee Church, in Columbia County, the oldest continuing Baptist church in the state.[15] A year later Particular Baptists formed the Lower Brier Creek congregation in Burke County. Particular Baptists emerged in England during the seventeenth century and emphasized God's sovereignty by stressing the concepts of unconditional election and limited (particular) atonement, principles commonly known as Calvinist, after the Reformer John Calvin. This theology underscores the divine role in salvation and holds that the elect are predestined by God. Accordingly, Particular Baptists tended to be less evangelistic than other Baptist groups. Separates, on the other hand, who began to appear in America and Canada in the 1740s, were only mildly Calvinistic and embraced more emotional approaches to salvation. Separates had their roots in the Great Awakening (to be discussed below) and considered zealousness in saving souls to be appropriate. When Separate churches began to be organized, Particular Baptists also became known as Regular Baptists, with no alteration in meaning implied by the additional name.[16]

The primary leaders of Particular-Regular and Separate Baptists in Georgia were, respectively, Edmund Botsford and Daniel Marshall. The genuine friendship between the two men contributed to a lasting amalgam, which Robert G. Gardner describes as a "Separate evangelistic enthusiasm . . . coupled with a Particular-Regular demand for education and orderliness." For various reasons, by the late eighteenth century nearly all Baptist churches in Georgia were officially Particular-Regular, but, as can be inferred, there continued to be a strong core of Separate influence. In essence, this meant that evangelism would remain a key feature of Baptist life in Georgia, in combination with a strong organizational impetus.[17]

A group of at least fourteen ministers who were associated with Daniel Marshall have come to be known as "Marshall's Mighty Men."[18] These ministers were the catalyst for Baptist growth in Georgia, beginning with the creation of the Georgia Association in 1784.[19] The bulk of the Baptist churches established in Georgia during the eighteenth century trace their origins to these men. While Marshall may be considered the first great leader of Baptists in Georgia, his contemporaries were more impressed by his sincerity than his rhetoric. Even his friend Morgan Edwards described Marshall as "a weak man, a stammerer, and no scholar," as well as "a man of no bright parts, nor eloquence nor learning." Tellingly, though, Edwards considered that "piety, earnestness and honesty are all he can boast of."[20] Such traits were tailor-made to make a positive impression in the rural backcountry of late eighteenth-century Georgia.[21]

Methodists had a later start in Georgia than the Baptists. Although the great founders of Methodism—John Wesley, Charles Wesley, and George Whitefield—had all lived in Georgia, since each spent only a few months or years in the colony the Methodist faith was not homegrown in the state.[22] After John Wesley's religious experience following his return to England, societies of believers emerged who devoted themselves to an experiential form of religiosity, as opposed to the more rationalistic "philosophical Anglicanism" of their day, accompanied by a strict, methodical approach to living a pure life. Although it originally sprang from within Anglicanism, Methodism eventually became a separate Christian denomination. From its inception,

Methodism was meant to have not only a personal appeal, in that it addressed individuals' emotional as well as intellectual needs, but also a strong social conscience. Wesley himself had argued that "Christianity is essentially a social religion and to turn it into a solitary religion is indeed to destroy it."[23]

The initial group of Methodists in Georgia, seventy-eight in all, did not arrive until 1786, settling west of Augusta. The first Methodist chapel in Georgia, Grant's Meeting House, was built near Washington the following year. After some initial success in attracting converts in the 1780s, Methodists found the going tough during the following decade, without a figure comparable to Daniel Marshall to rally behind.[24] During one of his semiannual visits, Francis Asbury succinctly summarized the roadblocks to frontier evangelism as "rum, races, and rioting," as well as the necessary diversions required to build up businesses and towns. Thus, while he was in Georgia in late 1799, Asbury wrote: "The state of religion is low here. . . . I lament the state of religion in these new settlements. New lands, new officers, and new objects occupy the minds of the people." After traveling for several miles beside the Oconee River, going "from one plantation to another," Asbury concluded: "There appears to be more wealth than religion here."[25]

The number of Methodists in Georgia fell from 2,250 in 1790 to 1,663 in 1800, although the number of Baptists in Georgia grew from 3,340 to roughly 5,315 during the same time period and in the same general setting.[26] In addition to Methodists lacking a counterpart to the activities of "Marshall's Mighty Men," a major reason for the different evangelistic fortunes of the two groups in the 1790s was how each regarded slavery. Simply put, the developing cotton culture was making slavery vital to the welfare of Georgia, and the Methodist leadership opposed the practice. Indeed, John Wesley famously regarded slavery as "the sum of all villainies."[27] Internal tensions concerning slavery had the effect of impeding Methodist growth in Georgia. The situation with regard to Baptists was much more straightforward because they operated free from any central episcopal authority. Thus, while in the early 1780s the Methodist Episcopal Church took steps to require Methodists to emancipate their slaves, already prior to 1772 no fewer than ten Georgia Baptists owned one hundred or more slaves.[28]

The Methodist reputation of opposing slavery actually impaired the ability of Methodists to attract black converts, since some slaveholders restricted contact between Methodist ministers and slaves out of concern that the slaves would be encouraged to run away or rebel. Baptists, on the other hand, had direct access to slaves and gained a strong foothold among them, as evidenced by the fact that there were three independent black Baptist churches in Georgia by 1800. In this regard, Baptists were again aided by their denominational structure. For Methodists ultimate authority resided in the hands of denominational authorities. However, Baptists, who cherished local congregational autonomy, could form white, black, or biracial churches without approval from others.[29]

The first black Baptist church in Georgia had its origins around 1773 among slaves in Aiken County, South Carolina, where the black preacher David George was baptizing new converts. Early members included Jesse Galphin and George Liele, who would become important black preachers themselves. For a time there were members on both sides of the Savannah River, but after 1793 a Silver Bluff group in South Carolina diminished and the Springfield Baptist Church of Augusta came to the fore, with Galphin as its minister. Another black Baptist church was established in Savannah in 1777, under Liele's leadership. Liele, who was pro-British, fled to Jamaica during the Revolution, but before he left he baptized Andrew Bryan, who then served as pastor. Bryan was very successful in building the congregation, which would eventually become known as First African Baptist, from sixty-nine members in 1788 to about seven hundred by 1800. A third black Baptist church is less well recorded. Called Beaverdams, it was apparently formed by 1796 in what is now Screven County (but was then part of Burke County). The church appears to have broken up sometime in the early nineteenth century. All told, around 1800 the three black Baptist churches probably had a little more than one thousand members. In addition to the independent black Baptists, a number of blacks also participated in biracial Baptist churches, indicating that the overall number of black Baptists then in Georgia exceeded one thousand by a good measure.[30] By comparison, in 1800 there were only about 250 black Methodists in the state.[31]

Following their overall decline in the 1790s, Methodists regained momentum after the turn of the century through the use of open-air camp meetings for the purpose of evangelism. In the latter months of 1801, Bishop Asbury preached in eastern Georgia and wrote in his journal that while the congregations were "respectable, and very attentive," there had been no conversions. Yet he held out hope that "Georgia promises something great."[32] He seemed to sense, correctly, that he would not have to wait much longer. Earlier in the year, Asbury had sent a letter to Stith Mead, the presiding elder of the

Georgia District Methodists, in which he shared news of some very produc-
tive revivals he had heard about in various parts of the country; it seemed
at the end of the year that Georgia was poised to have a similar experience.
Indeed, by April 1803 Mead was able to write a long letter (presumably to
Asbury) that recorded a number of camp meeting revivals in Georgia, which
had begun in late 1802 and had continued into 1803. Conversions at these
camp meetings were plentiful.[33]

Camp meeting revivalism has its roots in the Great Awakening, which
emerged around 1740. This movement favored informal church organizations
over formal ones because they gave more authority to lay people and carried
more personal appeal.[34] Arguably, the leading figure of the Great Awakening
was George Whitefield.[35] As was noted in the preceding chapter, Whitefield
preached widely throughout the colonies, not only to gain converts but also
to raise money for the Bethesda orphanage near Savannah. In all, Whitefield
delivered more than eighteen thousand sermons over some thirty years. His
style was dramatic and powerful. He tended not to use prepared sermons
but rather spoke extemporaneously, from the heart, appealing to his listeners' emotional and cerebral sides. Whitefield's power to inspire, persuade,
and transform is reflected in an anecdote related by Benjamin Franklin, who
attended one of Whitefield's sermons: "I perceived he intended to finish with
a Collection, and I silently resolved he should get nothing from me. I had in
my Pocket a Handful of Copper Money, three or four silver Dollars, and five
Pistoles in Gold. As he proceeded I began to soften, and concluded to give
the Coppers. Another Stroke of his Oratory made me asham'd of that, and
determin'd me to give the Silver; and he finish'd so admirably, that I empty'd
my Pocket wholly into the Collector's Dish, Gold and all."[36] Whitefield did
not depend solely on his rhetorical prowess, but also used advertising, including pamphlets and newspaper announcements, often long in advance, to
draw attention to his upcoming sermons.[37] His overall approach informed
the nineteenth-century camp meeting preachers.[38]

The rapid outbreak and spread of camp meetings came during what is now
known as the Great Revival of 1801–1805. The Great Revival followed a period
of spiritual doldrums in the South after the Revolution. Many Christians
then feared that they lived in an age of skepticism and religious decline. We
can perceive their concern in journals, letters, and sermons of the 1780s and
1790s. After spending one Sunday in March 1791 at Georgetown at Ogeechee
Shoals (a now abandoned town site in Glascock County), for instance, Bishop

Asbury wrote in his journal: "The peace with the Creek Indians, the settlement of new lands, good trade, buying slaves, etc. . . . take up the attention of the people." Asbury had preached that day on the parable of the sower (Luke 8:4–15), where it is acknowledged that seed sown on rocky ground will not sprout, and he recorded that he was content to "let the Lord look to his own house."[39] Like Asbury, other devout Christians along the frontier awaited God's deliverance. They could not know how it would come to pass, but they were convinced that God would act in a forceful way to turn the tide of disbelief and religious inattention. To usher in that day, churches throughout the South observed fast days and created prayer groups, with the cumulative effect that the South became "primed for a kind of religious explosion."[40]

As it happened, the explosion came first in Kentucky. After experiencing some persecution in North Carolina, a Presbyterian minister named James McGready migrated in the mid-1790s to Kentucky and became pastor of three small congregations. Eventually, he organized his parishioners into prayer societies. In June 1800 McGready arranged a four-day communion event for the congregants of all three churches. He was assisted in this endeavor by two colleagues, the McGee brothers, one of whom was a Presbyterian and the other a Methodist. On the fourth day of the communion event, a woman began to shout, and John McGee, the Methodist, recognized that the congregation was set for an awakening. Weeping from emotion, he told the congregants that God was nigh, and they came to feel that it was the beginning of God's deliverance. Word spread and a subsequent event was held two months later, which was attended by several thousand Presbyterians, Baptists, and Methodists. Due to the great number of people that had assembled, the preaching was held outdoors among tents and campfires. Once more, there were widespread emotional outbursts and a shared sense of God's presence and activity. The revival service had been born. Similar outdoor events, which came to be known as camp meetings, spread across the South over the next few years, bringing thousands of conversions and helping to establish evangelicalism as the region's favored religion.[41]

The first camp meetings in Georgia were interdenominational. Nevertheless, although Presbyterians and Baptists participated to some degree, it was the Methodists who took charge of the camp meetings in the state. Indeed, some Baptists avoided camp meetings altogether, because they did not favor interdenominational events and preferred to have similar gatherings at their own associational meetings. Presbyterians, meanwhile, tended to disdain the emotional aspect of the camp meetings and therefore acquired few new members from them. All in all, it was the Methodists who gained the most converts through the camp meetings.[42] One of the first camp meetings was held at Rehoboth Chapel, Warren County, in October 1802, and the distribution of ministers present gives a clear indication of the Methodist strength: out of a total of twenty-six ministers who preached to about seven thousand persons, there were eighteen Methodists, but only five Baptists and three Presbyterians.[43]

Over time, the camp meetings became regularized, and manuals were published to address the details of staging them, including instructions regarding advertising, the placement of seats and tents, activity schedules, and how to maintain order.[44] Typically, camp meetings were multiday events, with several ministers giving sermons day and night, both on a stage and among the crowd. Attendees, who represented all ages and generally included both whites and blacks, camped in tents when not listening to the sermons. Those in the crowd who were in need of repentance were asked to come down to the "mourners' bench," where they could feel all eyes upon them. Sometimes camp meeting participants had startling reactions, such as convulsions (the "jerks").

One participant's account of a camp meeting in 1807, held about three miles south of Sparta in Hancock County, gives a representative description:

> The meeting began on Tuesday, 28th July, at 12 o'clock, and ended on Saturday following. We counted thirty-seven Methodist preachers at the meeting. . . . From the number of people who attended preaching at the rising of the sun, I concluded that there were about 3000 persons, white and black together, that lodged on the ground at night. I think the largest congregation was about 4000 hearers. . . . The first day of the meeting, we had a gentle and comfortable moving of the spirit of the Lord among us. . . . On Thursday the work revived more & spread farther than what it had done before; and at night there was such a general stir among the mourners at the Stage that we did not attempt to preach there; and as we had but one Stage it was thought best to have preaching at some of the Tents. . . . Friday was the greatest day of all . . . three of the preachers fell helpless within the altar; and one lay a considerable time before he came to himself. From that the work of convictions and conversion spread, and a large number were converted. . . . I suppose there was about eighty souls converted at that meeting, including white and black people. It is thought by many people that they never saw a better Camp-Meeting in Georgia.[45]

The camp meetings contributed to the development of a simple folk the-ology that cut across evangelical denominational lines and centered on the need for individuals to repent. Instead of a complex set of doctrines or pre-scribed liturgical steps, evangelical preachers emphasized Bible stories that modeled proper or improper behavior, and above all they stressed the need for conversion. According to John B. Boles, these preachers discovered "that vivid, concrete, emotional preaching uncomplicated by much theology or doctrine was the most effective way to move listeners. . . . Sermons told or retold Bible stories. . . . The point of scriptural explication was to show how the Bible addressed the particular situation of individuals, always with the aim of effecting conversions in the end."[46] The upshot of such a folk theology was a rejection of this world as one's true home, with the saved expressing a desire to leave this earthly abode.

A window to this theology is provided by the spiritual hymns sung by camp meeting participants, which were compiled in various songbooks in the first half of the nineteenth century. One of the most prominent and impor-tant, *The Sacred Harp*, was produced in 1844 by Georgians B. F. White of Hamilton and E. J. King of Talbotton.[47] The songs in this collection do not feature the lofty language of the theologian, but instead reflect sentiments that all participants would feel comfortable singing, "the common denomina-tor of plain-folk religious belief."[48] *The Sacred Harp* records many variations on the central themes of repentance, salvation, and rejection of this world, such as "I will believe, I do believe, That Jesus died for me"; "I feel like, I feel like I'm on my journey home"; and "This world's a wilderness below, This world is not my home."

Among the hymns sung by participants at camp meetings, one held that "God is calling ev'ry nation."[49] And certainly camp meetings led many to answer the call, both white and black. While during the colonial period the slaves who had been born in Africa were only slightly touched by the Christian faith, those blacks born into slavery in the young United States of America were more exposed to Christianity and, when revivalism struck, they responded in large numbers. Thus, Albert J. Raboteau has observed that "the gods of Africa gave way to the God of Christianity."[50]

As Raboteau goes on to point out, however, the emerging Afro-Christianity had a hybrid nature, with some lingering African elements, especially relat-ing to the ritual use of music and dance. One particularly distinctive religious expression of slaves along the Georgia coast was a form of collective singing and dancing known as the ring shout. In this context the word "shout" does not refer to loud vocalization, but rather to a dancelike shuffling movement in a counterclockwise direction, accompanied by call-and-response singing and percussive hand clapping. Linguist Lorenzo Dow Turner proposed that this use of the word derives from the Afro-Arabic *saut*, in reference to the counterclockwise movement around the Kaaba in Mecca associated with the Hajj. Art Rosenbaum has written about contemporary practitioners of this long-lived tradition in McIntosh County, and he refers to the ring shout as "probably the oldest surviving African American performance tradition on the North American continent."[51]

In addition to camp meetings, the use of circuit riders, itinerant ministers who served numerous churches along a set course, contributed greatly to Methodist growth.[52] Due to the success of the camp meetings and circuit riders, Georgia Methodists surpassed their previous high water mark of members, reaching 3,702 in 1803, only the second year of camp meetings in the state. Unlike their first brief spurt in the 1780s, this time Methodist growth was sustained. By 1814 there were approximately 10,500 Methodists in Georgia; fifteen years later Methodist membership in the state was close to 19,000. As a result, national Methodist Episcopal Church authorities formed a Georgia Conference in 1831.[53]

Like the Methodists, Baptists enjoyed sustained expansion in the nineteenth century. Baptist growth in Georgia from 1790 to 1850 came not only through participation in both denominational and interdenominational meetings, but also from having a relatively large number of ministers. Charles O. Walker has gathered information regarding Baptist pastors and preachers known to have been active in Georgia during the first part of the nineteenth century, and he has identified more than eighty clergymen.[54] In addition to plentiful clergy, Baptist growth was aided by two broad, internal movements: the creation of various regional associations and organizations, and a heightened interest in missions.

Even before the camp meetings began, several Baptist associations had been formed. The Georgia Association was the first, in 1784, and it was followed by the Hephzibah Association in 1794, the Sarepta Association in 1799, and the Savannah Association in 1802. Three conferences that were held in 1801, 1802, and 1803 at Powelton helped Baptists in these associations maintain unity. Additional expansion led to the creation of the Ocmulgee Association in 1810. With a supportive infrastructure in place, Baptists enjoyed continuous growth. In 1812 alone, the various Baptist associations in Georgia added some 3,800 new members. Two years later, Georgia Baptists could claim approximately 170 churches and 16,000 members.[55]

In May 1814 a national meeting of Baptists was held in Philadelphia, Pennsylvania, to organize support for foreign missions. Among the thirty-three delegates was William Bullein Johnson, then a pastor in Savannah, who would later become the initial president of the Southern Baptist Convention in the 1840s. The delegates formed the first national organization of Baptists, the General Missionary Convention of the Baptist Denomination in the United States for Foreign Missions. Since they decided to meet every three years, the organization became known as the Triennial Convention.[56] In the wake of the creation of this national body, a number of additional local missionary societies sprang up in Georgia and missions work became a key feature of the Baptist faith. Thus, while missions activities were rarely mentioned by eighteenth-century Georgia Baptists, in the nineteenth century support for missions cut across all parts of the Georgia Association.[57]

Further progress was made in 1822 with the creation of a state Baptist body to coordinate missions and other activities, which came to be known as the Georgia Baptist Convention (GBC). To be sure, not every Baptist in Georgia was associated with the GBC. Some who disagreed with centralization of power and money-based agencies frowned on the activities of the GBC and established associations that were independent of it.[58] Foremost among these were Primitive Baptists, who strongly espoused the doctrine of predestination and therefore opposed forceful missionizing. (For this reason such Baptists have also been known at various times as Predestinarian and Antimission.)[59] Nevertheless, it can safely be said that the GBC became the main organizational body for Baptists in Georgia. By 1850 the GBC included more than eleven hundred churches with a combined total of almost seventy thousand members.[60]

Within the GBC, Adiel Sherwood may be singled out as one of the primary contributors to Georgia Baptist growth in the 1820s and 1830s.[61] Indeed, his biographer Jarrett Burch argues that during this period Sherwood was nothing less than "the primary force . . . in Georgia Baptist life."[62] Burch points to Sherwood's use of "altar calls" in the late 1820s, which helped bring in sixteen thousand new Baptist converts in Georgia.[63] Among his many other contributions, in the early 1830s Sherwood started a manual-labor school, which allowed ministerial students the opportunity to work in order to pay for their education, an approach that led to the establishment of Mercer Institute in 1833 at Penfield.[64] The institution, which moved to Macon in 1871, is now Mercer University.[65]

Mercer Institute was named after another key nineteenth-century Baptist figure, Jesse Mercer.[66] Mercer's range of influence in Georgia is difficult to overstate. In 1798, as a delegate to one of the state's constitutional conventions, he wrote the section of the state constitution that secures religious liberty. As a minister, Mercer helped found several churches. He was also very prominent in the GBC, serving as its first president as well as institutional clerk for twenty-one years, and as its moderator for twenty-three years. His monumental history of the organization, published in 1838, remains valuable.[67] In addition to being an influential pastor and denominational leader, Mercer was also a publisher. In 1833 he bought the *Christian Index* and eventually moved its office from Washington, D.C., to Georgia. The *Christian Index* became the voice of Georgia Baptists and an important organ for Baptists throughout the South.[68]

A third important person in the development of the Baptist faith in Georgia was John Leadley Dagg, who was at Mercer Institute in the 1840s and 1850s, serving as both a professor of theology and as president.[69] Dagg hailed from Virginia and held a number of pulpits and educational positions in Pennsylvania and Alabama, culminating in the presidency of Alabama Female Athenaeum from 1836 to 1844. For the next twelve years he was at Mercer. During Dagg's presidency, Mercer experienced impressive growth, including the construction of four brick buildings, and the student body expanded from about 70 to 180. Dagg also became well known beyond the grounds of Mercer due to a series of theological works he published after his retirement from teaching and administration in 1856, when he began to live with his son, also a Georgia minister. They lived at various times in Cuthbert, Madison, and Forsyth while Dagg wrote several influential books, which established him as "the country's first systematic Baptist theologian [and] perhaps the most representative theological figure among antebellum Baptists in the United States."[70]

While Baptists were creating a denominational infrastructure, they were also making inroads both in the backcountry and the low country. A degree of such acceptance came fairly early, since by 1800 Baptists had already established both black and white congregations in Savannah. Methodists, on the other hand, remained on the fringes of polite society for quite some time.

In 1806 Frances Asbury visited Charles Tait, a judge in Elbert County, and the pointed contrast between the two men that he recorded in his journal draws attention to this situation: "I did not present myself in the character of a gentleman, but as a Christian, and a Christian minister: I would visit the President of the United States in no other character; true, I would be innocently polite and respectful—no more."[71] The rustic and simple appearance of many Methodist ministers was a source of open ridicule. When Hope Hull, the "father of Georgia Methodism," tried to preach in Savannah in the 1790s, he encountered hostility, and crowds drove him out of the city. Unlike the Baptists, Methodists were not able to establish a permanent presence in Savannah until after 1810. Christopher H. Owen aptly observes that "before 1820 Georgia Methodism was above all the religion of unlettered up-country whites." Gradually, though, Methodists gained acceptance within polite and educated society as well. Writing in 1827, Nicholas Talley, a Methodist minister, reflected on how far his denomination had come since its beginnings in Georgia. According to Talley, at first "we were without friends, and had to meet the scorn of foes." "But now, thank Heaven," stated Talley, "all hearts bid us welcome, and all doors are open to receive us."[72]

The life of Augustus Baldwin Longstreet offers a good illustration of the new Methodist, who, unlike Asbury, could readily envision and accept being both a Christian and a gentleman.[73] Longstreet, a native of Augusta, was a Yale graduate and an attorney, and he became a wealthy slave owner as well when he married into a plantation family. In the 1820s Longstreet converted to Methodism at a camp meeting and took on still another occupation when he became a Methodist minister.[74] As may be gathered, by this time Georgia Methodists had largely dropped their former antislavery stance.[75] Longstreet became a national figure in 1835 when he published a book titled *Georgia Scenes*, which presents sketches and stories of frontier Georgia.[76]

In addition to his other roles and accomplishments, Longstreet also played a part in the development of Emory University.[77] Presbyterians had long held sway over higher education in Georgia due to their influence in the Franklin College (now the University of Georgia). From 1819 to 1829 the school's president was Moses Waddel, a Presbyterian minister and educator who was particularly accused of Presbyterian favoritism.[78] Longstreet applied for an open professorship at the Franklin College in 1832. Methodists objected when the position was given to a Presbyterian and accused the school of denominational partiality. The experience strengthened the resolve of Methodists to build their own school, with the result that in 1836 Emory College was formed at Oxford, Georgia. Longstreet became its second president in 1840. In a related development, in 1843, when the Macon Female College (which had been founded in 1836) was experiencing financial problems, Georgia Methodists took over the management of the school, after which it became known as Wesleyan Female College. Wesleyan is today widely recognized as the nation's first college to grant degrees to women.[79]

In 1835, a year before Emory College was established, the state of Georgia chartered Oglethorpe University as a Presbyterian institution of higher education.[80] The school now operates in Atlanta, but originally it was located near Milledgeville, which was then the state capital. That the school was created in Georgia not only reflects the state's leadership position in the South, but also the fact that Presbyterians had been able to make some modest gains. We have already observed that because of their insistence on an educated clergy, as well as a reluctance to use emotionalism when proselytizing, Presbyterians grew much more slowly in Georgia than did either the Baptists or the Methodists. As late as 1810 there were only 5 Presbyterian ministers and 218 communicants recorded in the state. Around 1820, however, there began to be some growth in the numbers of Presbyterians under the leadership of a few zealous evangelists, especially Remembrance Chamberlain. As a result, by 1845 there were 5 presbyteries, 53 ministers, 94 churches, and about 3,000 communicants in Georgia. This growth was sufficient to bring about a division of the Presbyterian Synod of South Carolina and Georgia.[81]

While Presbyterianism would remain relatively small in size when compared to its fellow evangelical denominations, a number of individual Presbyterians in Georgia gained regional and national prominence during the nineteenth century, including the writer and composer Sidney Lanier, the celebrated author of "The Marshes of Glynn," who was born in Macon in 1842.[82] The most famous Presbyterian to have lived in Georgia was no doubt Woodrow Wilson, who was born in Virginia in 1856, but whose family moved to Georgia in 1858 when he was just a one-year-old so that his father could serve as pastor of the First Presbyterian Church of Augusta. The future president lived in Augusta until 1870.[83]

A movement that began among Presbyterians in Kentucky and Pennsylvania in the early years of the nineteenth century led to the emergence of a new denomination, now known as the Christian Church (Disciples of Christ). This denomination does not promote a set of particular doctrines beyond traditional beliefs such as the authority of the Bible and the divine status of Jesus, preferring to stress unity and commonality among Christians rather than doctrinal differences. The earliest Christian congregation in Georgia was developed in large measure by Disciples of Christ who had split from Methodists in North Carolina and relocated close to Scull Shoals (Oconee County). In time, the denomination attracted several leading Georgians, including Daniel Hook, a trustee of the Franklin College, who helped to form Christian congregations throughout Georgia.[84]

Perhaps the most well-known Disciple in Georgia was Emily Harvie Thomas Tubman of Augusta, who devoted her great wealth (inherited when she was widowed) to a wide array of philanthropic concerns, including the Christian Church. Among other contributions, she donated the building that housed the First Christian Church in Augusta, established in 1835.[85] Tubman has been recognized by Georgia Women of Achievement for having freed her servants and assisting several of them in moving to Africa, an act that was honored by naming a new community in Liberia "Tubman Hill."[86] Tubman's commitment to the Christian denomination, as well as her wit and resolve, may be gathered from a fabled anecdote about her. When a minister approached Tubman for a donation to help rebuild a church building following a fire, she responded that she would be pleased to contribute on the condition that the church "would honor only Christ in the name it should bear." The minister tried long and hard to convince Tubman that "there is really nothing in a name." Without a word, Tubman gave him a large check, but it was signed with the name of one of her black servants. The minister, delighted by the large sum on the check, did not examine its signature and failed to note that it did not use Tubman's name. When a clerk refused to cash the check, saying "this name is not known by the bank," the minister returned to Tubman to explain the problem, which he thought to be a simple error on her part. Tubman replied: "No, I have made no error. Did you not argue with me long and learnedly that there is nothing in a name. I only wished to convince you of the fallacy of your argument."[87]

Around the time that Oglethorpe University and Emory College were established, and the First Christian Church of Augusta was founded, federal troops were preparing to expel the last Cherokee Indians who remained in Georgia and take them to Indian Territory in present-day Oklahoma. The removal of the Cherokees in the 1830s was brought about by a number of factors, including the desire for more land on which to grow cotton and the discovery of gold in Cherokee territory, as well as the intolerance of many white Southerners toward Indians.[88]

Several missionaries were jailed and abused because of their opposition to removal. Indian missions had existed throughout the first decades of the nineteenth century. As early as the first Powelton Conference in 1801, Georgia Baptists agreed to support two missionaries to the Creeks.[89] Large-scale missionizing among these Indians occurred only after they were forced out of Georgia, though, which took place in stages culminating in the 1820s. By contrast, missions were established by all three evangelical groups, as well as by the Moravians, among the Cherokees in Georgia.[90] Chief James Vann and other Cherokee leaders had invited Moravians to establish a mission, which came to be called Spring Place, near Chatsworth. Vann's home, now a museum, stands close to the site of the mission. As part of the mission, Moravians provided a school for Cherokee children that housed and educated more than one hundred students between 1804 and 1833.[91]

It is most difficult today to judge how thoroughly Cherokees "converted" to Christianity in the early nineteenth century. William G. McLoughlin has pointed out that Cherokees had three approaches to Christian evangelism: they could ignore it, embrace it, or take from it according to their desires or needs. The missionaries sought the second choice, but doubtless most Cherokees ended up adopting the third approach in borrowing aspects of Christianity. This they did in a general way: that is, not by taking on particular doctrinal positions, but rather by professing a broad acceptance of a non-Indian worldview regarding science and history. Accordingly, it seems that some aspects of what remained of the prehistoric Southeastern Indian worldview continued, while other elements receded. "The world might still be flat and suspended from the arch of heaven," concludes McLoughlin, "it might still be animated by all kinds of spiritual beings from above and below, but the Cherokee people were no longer at the center of it."[92]

Whatever their level of success, the work of Christian missionaries in Georgia was cut short by the removal of the Cherokees. Among the missionaries who were jailed by the state for opposing removal was Samuel Worcester, a Congregationalist, who lived among Cherokees at their capital, New Echota (near Calhoun). A case filed against the state, *Worcester v. Georgia*, was heard by the United States Supreme Court in 1832.[93] In its decision, the Court held that Georgia had no jurisdiction over the Cherokee Nation and asserted that the state's actions toward the Cherokees "are repugnant to the Constitution, laws, and treaties of the United States." "They are," stated the Court, "in direct hostility with treaties, repeated in a succession of years, which mark out the boundary that separates the Cherokee country from Georgia; guarantee to them all the land within their boundary . . . and recognize the pre-existing power of the nation to govern itself."[94]

The state of Georgia refused to enforce the Supreme Court's decision, however, and President Andrew Jackson would not support the Court. In fact, Jackson was well known as a strong proponent of the removal of Indians from the Southeast. Hence, the last remaining Cherokees in Georgia were forcibly removed during the intensely cold winter of 1838–1839. At least four thousand persons, fully one-fifth of the entire Cherokee population, died during the forced migration, which became known as the Trail of Tears.[95]

The noted Presbyterian minister Benjamin M. Palmer, who graduated from the Franklin College in 1838 just prior to the Trail of Tears, later gave a celebrated address in New Orleans, Louisiana, that posited a divine historical design. At one point Palmer proclaimed that the displacement of Indians by Europeans was nothing less than an act of God's providence, on a par with acts recorded in the Bible. He drew a parallel between the dislodging of Canaanites and Indians by stating: "It was in the way of a judgment, strictly retributive in character, that [God] swept away the old Canaanites into the pathless deserts surrounding their land, in order to find room for his chosen people; and when the Indians had, for countless centuries, neglected the soil [and] had no worship to offer to the true God . . . the time came at length when . . . in the just judgment of a righteous and holy God . . . the Indian has been swept from the earth, and a great Christian nation . . . rises up."[96] As we will see in the next chapter, such notions of the hand of God acting to exalt white Americans, particularly Southerners, would lead to tragic ends.

The removal of the Cherokees effectively closed the Georgia frontier. Whites streamed into former Indian lands, bringing cotton culture and slaves. Between 1830 and 1850 the state population nearly doubled, going from 516,823 to 906,185, and Methodist and Baptist growth kept pace.[97] Indeed, by 1850 all but a very few counties in Georgia had either a Methodist or a Baptist denominational majority.[98] Thus, evangelicalism had become firmly established in Georgia. But by the middle of the nineteenth century Methodists and Baptists in the South had also split from their northern counterparts, and the nation was pointed toward internecine strife.

Tomochichi was the leader of Indians who lived at Yamacraw Bluff, which would become the site of Savannah, Georgia's first town. His nephew, Toonahowi, is depicted holding an eagle. Birds played an important symbolic role in the religious traditions of Southeastern Indians. (Courtesy of the Hargrett Rare Book & Manuscript Library/University of Georgia Libraries)

A statue of John Wesley (1703–1791), the founder of Methodism, commands Reynolds Square in Savannah. Wesley served as the third rector of the Christ Church congregation. He was forced to leave Georgia under threat of arrest, delaying the introduction of Methodism into the colony until after the Revolution. (Photo by the author)

The Congregationalists who moved en masse with their slaves to Georgia from South Carolina in 1752 were part of the influx of new settlers into the colony after the legalization of slavery. A slave gallery can still be seen in their house of worship, Midway Church in Liberty County. After the first building on the site burned, the present building was erected in 1792, making it the second-oldest church in Georgia. (Photo by the author)

During the late eighteenth and early nineteenth centuries in Georgia, evangelicals were on the periphery of polite society. When wealthy and well-educated figures like Augustus Baldwin Longstreet (1790–1870) joined the fold following the Great Revival (1801–1805), it signaled that evangelicalism was becoming acceptable across all social classes. (Courtesy of the Hargrett Rare Book & Manuscript Library/University of Georgia Libraries)

A bronze statue of Jesse Mercer (1769–1841) is displayed on a bench at the school named for him, Mercer University, in Macon. Mercer's long career of service as an influential minister and publisher helped to establish a strong denominational infrastructure for the Baptist faith in Georgia.
(Photo by the author)

In addition to Christianity, slaves practiced a range of religious traditions, including African traditional religions and Islam. One devout Muslim slave was Bilali, who lived on Sapelo Island during the nineteenth century. Bilali wore a fez and prayed eastward toward Mecca. He also owned a leather-bound booklet containing Arabic religious writings, presumably in his own hand. (Courtesy of the Hargrett Rare Book & Manuscript Library/University of Georgia Libraries)

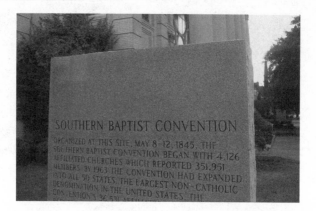

In 1845 the Southern Baptist Convention was founded in Augusta. Although there were representatives at the meeting from eight Southern states, Georgia led the way, with more than half of the registered delegates being from that state. Thus was born a lasting "Georgia Tradition" within the Convention, as Baptists *of* the South became *Southern* Baptists. (Photo by the author)

Some of the oldest Confederate monuments are located in Georgia, such as the pillar in Athens that was unveiled in 1872 and now stands across from the Arch representing the gateway to the University of Georgia. In a graphic illustration of the intermingling of Confederate imagery and Lost Cause religion, the marble pillar resembles a church steeple. (Photo by the author)

Following the Civil War white Baptists largely remained members of the Southern Baptist Convention, and blacks eventually formed the National Baptist Convention. Methodists splintered into several groups. The African Methodist Episcopal (AME) Church, led in Georgia by Bishop Henry McNeal Turner (1834–1915), garnered the most support from black Georgia Methodists. (National Archives photo RG029/RG105/RG393/ NARA)

When Leo Frank, a Jew, was lynched in 1915 in Marietta, it sparked the revival of the Ku Klux Klan. The antisemitism that surrounded the Leo Frank case left Georgia's Jews feeling isolated and marginalized for the next several decades. Frank was only one of close to five hundred persons, the vast majority of whom were black, who were lynched in Georgia between 1880 and 1930. (Courtesy of the Jacob Rader Marcus Center of the American Jewish Archives)

In her books, especially *Killers of the Dream* (1949), Lillian Smith (1897–1966) discussed growing up in a family that was "firmly triangulated on sin, sex, and segregation." Writing from her home on Screamer Mountain, near Clayton, she strongly protested racial bigotry, making the case that it was detrimental to both blacks and whites. (Photo by Hans Namuth; courtesy of the Center for Creative Photography, University of Arizona; © Hans Namuth Estate)

A Southern Baptist minister from Talbotton, Clarence Jordan (1912–1969) created a "demonstration project" of authentic Christian living in Americus with Koinonia, an interracial farming commune. Jordan and Koinonia provided inspiration to the burgeoning civil rights movement. (Photo by Wally Howard)

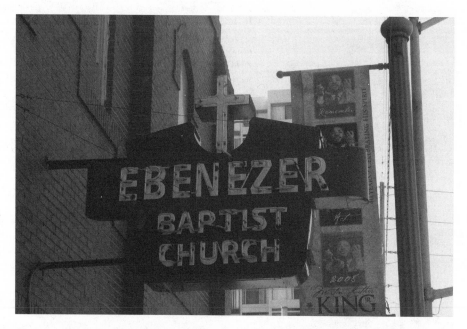

When Martin Luther King Jr. moved back to Georgia from Alabama in 1960 and became copastor of his home church, Ebenezer Baptist, it transformed Atlanta into the headquarters of the civil rights movement, and Ebenezer became, in the words of Andrew Young, "kind of like the mother church, it was the shelter." (Photo by the author)

In 1944, when the Monastery of the Holy Spirit was founded in Conyers, Catholics could consider Georgia a "desert" in regard to their faith. Today Catholics constitute the third-largest religious group in Georgia, behind Baptists and Methodists. The rapid growth of Catholicism has been fueled in large part by the influx of Catholic Hispanics into the state. (Courtesy of the Georgia Archives, Vanishing Georgia Collection; roco19)

A popular slogan before the Olympics were held in Georgia in 1996 was "The World is Coming to Atlanta!" In many respects, world religions had already arrived. Christianity is now one of several world religions being practiced in the state, including historically Eastern religions such as Hinduism and Buddhism, as well as Islam. Al-Farooq Masjid mosque in Atlanta is among the largest Muslim houses of worship in the Southeast. (Photo by the author)

CHAPTER FOUR

The Crucible of Slavery

In the final month of 1860, newly elected president Abraham Lincoln corresponded with Georgian Alexander H. Stephens, with whom he had served during the 1840s in the U.S. Congress.[1] In the course of their communication, each man drew attention to slavery as the main issue dividing the South and the North. On December 22, Lincoln wrote from Springfield, Illinois: "You think slavery is *right* and ought to be extended; while we think it is *wrong* and ought to be restricted. That I suppose is the rub. It certainly is the only substantial difference between us."[2] In his reply, written on December 30 in Crawfordsville, Georgia, Stephens asserted: "We at the South do think African Slavery, as it exists with us, both morally and politically right. This opinion is founded upon the inferiority of the Black race. You, however, and perhaps a majority of the North, think it wrong."[3] Georgia seceded in January 1861, and the following month Stephens became vice president of the Confederacy.[4]

On March 21, 1861, Vice President Stephens gave an address in Savannah that came to be known as "The Corner Stone" speech, in which he outlined what he deemed to be the essential foundation of the new Southern nation. After stating that the issue of "the proper *status* of the negro in our form of civilization" was "the immediate cause of the late rupture and present revolution," Stephens observed that Thomas Jefferson and the other framers of the Constitution had considered "the enslavement of the African . . . in violation of the laws of nature" and thought slavery incorrect as a matter of principle, "socially, morally and politically." According to Stephens, such notions were "fundamentally wrong." He asserted that "they rested upon the assumption of the equality of races. This was an error. It was a sandy foundation." Stephens avowed that, by contrast, the Confederacy was "founded upon exactly the opposite idea; its foundations are laid, its corner-stone rests upon the great truth, that the negro is not equal to the white man; that slavery—subordination to the superior race—is his natural and normal condition." "This, our new government," Stephens said, "is the first, in the history of the world, based upon this great physical, philosophical, and moral truth."[5]

Stephens was certainly not alone in his views regarding slavery and blacks. The *Savannah Republican* newspaper reported that his speech was repeatedly interrupted by applause. More important for our purposes, by the time Stephens gave his address white Southern clergy were overwhelmingly proslavery in their thoughts, sermons, and writings.[6] Southern ministers had provided support for slavery throughout the nineteenth century, particularly from the 1830s on, and they had supplied biblical arguments to defend and justify slavery. The formal separation of both Methodists and Baptists along Northern and Southern regional lines in the 1840s due to differences within the denominations over slavery helped lead to the national rupture of the 1860s.[7]

To be sure, there were some antislavery voices in the South. In a book-length study, David B. Chesebrough discusses notable examples of Southern clergy who opposed slavery between 1830 and 1865. Significantly, though, none of the major figures he refers to were in Georgia.[8] Indeed, as we have already seen, a number of Georgia Baptists were slaveholders from the late eighteenth century on, and Methodists failed to pick up large numbers in the state while their clergy opposed slavery. It was only when Methodist ministers began to drop their criticism of slavery that they gained numbers and prominence; by the time of the outbreak of the Civil War the majority of Methodist ministers in Georgia owned slaves.[9]

As slavery came to be accepted by Southern clergy, it led to a desire to provide religious instruction to slaves.[10] Hoping to build on the upsurge in conversion of blacks that occurred during the heyday of camp meeting revivalism, Southern clergy sought to increase the number of Christian slaves through an active plantation mission movement.[11] Baptists relied less on slave missions due to the fact that there were already ordained black Baptist ministers and independent black Baptist churches. Therefore, instead of missions to slaves, Baptists could largely depend on efforts from local congregations. Methodists and Presbyterians participated more directly in slave missions.[12]

The staunchest individual advocate of slave missions was the Presbyterian minister Charles Colcock Jones, who left the pastorate of the First

Presbyterian Church in Savannah in 1832 to devote himself to mission work among slaves. At the time, pamphlets encouraging plantation missions were circulating throughout the South, and Jones was optimistic about the future of the movement: "As an evidence of the increase of feeling and effort on the subject of the religious instruction of the colored population we state, that *more has been published and circulated* on the general subject, within the last two years [1833–1834] than in ten or twenty years' preceding."[13]

In 1836 Jones organized the Association for the Religious Instruction of the Negroes in Liberty County, and in 1842 he issued a guide book for slave missions, published in Savannah and titled *The Religious Instruction of the Negroes in the United States.* The book has four sections. In the first two, Jones provided a historical sketch of the "religious instruction of the negroes" in America up to his time and commented on their overall status regarding religion. In the third section Jones made his case for giving slaves "benevolent attention" and spelled out what he considered to be the duty of Christians to attempt "the improvement of the moral and religious condition of the negroes." He argued that Christians were obligated by both the providence and word of God, and therefore that they could not disregard their responsibilities to the slaves without forfeiting their "claim to the spirit of Christianity." In the final section, Jones provided guidance for the religious instruction of slaves.[14]

While Charles Colcock Jones and his associates were vigorous in support of slave missions, Presbyterians as a whole were less active, and the overall results of the denomination's efforts were not impressive. Just prior to the Civil War, out of a slave population of close to five hundred thousand in Georgia and Florida, Presbyterians could identify only 577 slave members. One of the impediments to Presbyterian success among the slaves was the fact that their ministers, who were required to have a high level of education, approached the slaves in an overly intellectual manner. In 1833 a Presbyterian committee investigating the subject of the "Religious Instruction of the Colored Population of the Synod of South Carolina and Georgia" found, concerning Presbyterian ministers in the region, that "such is the elevation of their language and thought, such the amount of knowledge that they take for granted in their audiences, that they might as well preach in Hebrew or Greek."[15]

It was the plain-talking Methodists who, as a group, did the most to proselytize slaves, and from 1844 to 1861 Methodist slave mission membership in Georgia expanded from a total of 3,051 to 11,125. For a time, Methodist efforts were hindered by opposition from suspicious slave owners who were aware of the antislavery legacy of early Methodism. But when Southern Methodists made clear in the 1840s that they no longer opposed slavery by splitting from Northern Methodists over the issue (to be discussed below), slave owners could more fully trust the Southern Methodist preachers and even came to welcome them on their plantations.[16]

Still, whatever success Methodist and other Christian missionaries enjoyed, they were reaching only a small portion of the overall slave population. There are various reasons why slaves did not convert to Christianity in larger numbers, but one explanation that at times is overlooked is that many of them were devout Muslims. Scholars estimate that at least 20 percent of African slaves brought to the Spanish, Portuguese, and British colonies in the New World were Muslims, and a number of them had been sufficiently trained in Arabic and Islamic traditions that they were able to maintain aspects of their faith.[17] It may be noted that Charles Colcock Jones himself referred to the existence of "Mohammedan Africans" among Georgia slaves.[18] It is reasonable to suggest that some of these Muslims would have resisted calls for them to convert to Christianity, since several Muslim slaves seem to have continued to maintain their customs and traditions to the extent they could under the circumstances. Rosa Grant of Possum Point, for instance, recalled how her grandmother Ryna, who was from Africa, prayed in a Muslim manner: "Huh membuh when I wuz a chile seein muh gran Ryna pray. Ebry mawnin at sun-up she kneel on duh flo in uh ruhm an bow obuh and tech uh head tuh duh flo tree time. Den she say a prayuh. . . . Wen she finish prayin she say 'Ameen, ameen, ameen.'"[19]

Among others, Allan D. Austin has explored the practice of Islam among slaves and has drawn attention in particular to two Muslim slaves who lived on Georgia's barrier islands during the first several decades of the nineteenth century—Salih Bilali (St. Simons Island) and Bilali Mohammed (Sapelo Island). Much of our knowledge about Salih Bilali comes from a letter written by his master, James Hamilton Couper, to a friend who had asked for some details about the slave out of ethnological interests. Couper related that Salih Bilali "is a strict Mahometan; abstains from spirituous liquors, and keeps the various fasts, particularly that of the Rhamadam [Ramadan]." Austin points out that one of Couper's sons considered Salih Bilali to have been "the most religious man that he had ever known" and related that on his deathbed Salih Bilali declared: "Allah is God and Muhammad his prophet."[20]

Bilali Mohammed, generally known as Bilali, was owned by Thomas Spalding.[21] Bilali, who wore a fez, lived openly as a Muslim and prayed eastward toward Mecca on a prayer rug.[22] Bilali also owned a small, leather-bound booklet containing Arabic writings, presumably in his own hand. This document is now housed in the Hargrett Rare Book and Manuscript Library at the University of Georgia. A number of scholars have examined the manuscript, including B. G. Martin, who reports that the calligraphic style reflects a form of Arabic script formerly used in West Africa, but that the author's hand also suggests someone who did not write routinely in Arabic. Complicating the deciphering of the text is the fact that on nearly every page the ink has seeped through from one side to the other. Nonetheless, Martin was able to make out several passages that demonstrate a high level of piety, with repeated phrases such as, "O God, I bear witness that there is no god but God" and "Muhammad is the Messenger of God." Martin finds no reason to doubt that Bilali produced the manuscript, though questions remain about where and when. Given the likelihood that paper of the kind used in the manuscript was manufactured for the Islamic trade and was only available on the African continent, Martin believes it is reasonable to suppose that Bilali had the manuscript with him when he was brought to America on a slave ship. If so, then the difficulty he would have faced in hiding his book is a further demonstration of his deep personal devotion to Islam.[23]

Even those slaves who did embrace Christianity often reacted negatively to the paternalism expressed by evangelical missionaries and ministers. Throughout his book on the religious instruction of slaves, Charles Colcock Jones indicated that blacks needed special guidance from whites, and he suggested that even Christian slaves "have but *a poor standard of moral character*, and are *indifferent to the general corruption of manners that prevails around them*." Hence, Jones wrote, to hope that they might have as "elevated a morality as obtains among the whites . . . can neither be expected, nor required of them."[24]

Such an understanding helps us put biracial antebellum Christianity in perspective. Several historians have emphasized that biracial church worship was the predominant form of religion for slaves.[25] Certainly, there is a great deal of evidence to support this general notion. The accounts of former Georgia slaves recorded by the wpa Slave Narrative Project during the 1930s, for example, are filled with memories of biracial worship. Tellingly, though, the former slaves recalled attending "the white church" in segregated seating arrangements. Marshal Butler reported: "We went to the white church.

Us . . . sat on one side, and the white folks sat on the other." Olin Williams concurred: "Us went to the white folks' church in Watkinsville. . . . Slaves sat up in the gallery, and us had better be still and listen, elsewise old Marster sure would lay us out." Other accounts record former slaves' recollections of sitting behind partitions or at the rear of the church.[26] Slaves also recalled as sources of irritation the homilies presented specially to them at worship services, which have been compared to today's children's sermons. One former slave bitterly remembered that she "had to set an' listen to the white man's sermon. . . . Always took his text from Ephesians, the white preacher did, the part what said, 'Obey your masters, be good servant.' Can' tell you how many times I done heard that text preached on."[27] In light of such testimony, we should be careful not to overemphasize the extent of biracialism, since whites controlled congregations.[28]

Nonetheless, even though the churches were dominated by whites, blacks were participating in church life. Clarence L. Mohr, who has published a study of slaves and white churches in antebellum Georgia, concludes that "the status of blacks in racially mixed congregations was always a subordinate one, but the subordination was seldom rigid or total."[29] Mohr points out, for example, that congregational disciplinary proceedings, which decided whether congregants deserved punishment for offenses such as public drunkenness or sexual misconduct, were conducted virtually in a color-blind manner.[30] Indeed, it is remarkable that blacks, who could not bear witness against whites in civil courts, were allowed to provide testimony in church disciplinary trials involving whites.[31]

Most important, slaves were sufficiently acquainted with congregational life to gain the necessary background and experience to be able to establish their own churches and denominations after the Civil War. Former slave James Bolton recalled that "we went to the white folks' church and listened to the white preachers." And Robert Shepherd remembered: "Fourth Sundays was our meetin' days, and everybody went to church. Us went to our white folks' church. . . . When they had done given the white folks the sacrament, they called [us] down from the gallery and give [us] sacrament, too."[32] It is clear from later developments that slaves not only heard sermons and took communion, but they also sang the same songs and learned the same Bible passages as whites.

Understandably eager to worship on their own terms, some slaves came to practice dual religious lives, emulating their white masters in church-based worship while practicing their own brand of religion in slave quarters, forest clearings, and brush arbors in what has been described as an "invisible institution" away from the eyes of their white masters.[33] Charlie Hudson, who had been a slave in Elbert County, reported that he and others were given passes so that they could "go round from one plantation to another on Sundays for prayer meetin's in the cabins and under trees." Caroline Ates, who was a slave near Macon, also recalled that "lots of times durin' the week, we'd slip off by ourselves and have prayer meetin'." Similarly, Bob Mobley, who was a slave also near Macon, remembered that "Marster let us clear an oak grove on the plantation, and we'd have prayer meetin's there."[34]

Direct evidence about these clandestine prayer meetings is rare. A particularly interesting account was provided by Neal Upson, who had been a slave in Oglethorpe County, near Lexington. Upson recollected that "slaves was allowed to have prayer meetin' on Tuesday and Friday round at the different plantations." According to Upson, white preachers "done the talkin' at the meetin' houses," but the slaves themselves spoke "at them Tuesday- and Friday-night prayer meetin's." He added: "There weren't many slaves what could read, so they jus' talked 'bout what they done heard the white preachers say on Sunday. One of the favorite texts was the third chapter from John, and most of 'em just 'membored a line or two from that." This biblical chapter contains the well-known verse, John 3:16 ("For God so loved the world, that he gave his only begotten Son, that whosoever believeth in him should not perish, but have everlasting life"), as well as the sentence: "Except a man be born again, he cannot see the kingdom of God" (John 3:3). Perhaps it was these passages that were most remembered by the slaves. Notably, though, the chapter also states, in what can easily be viewed as a commentary on the contrast between slaveholders and slaves: "And this is the condemnation, that light is come into the world, and men loved darkness rather than light, because their deeds were evil. For every one that doeth evil hateth the light, neither cometh to the light, lest his deeds should be reproved. But he that doeth truth cometh to the light, that his deeds may be made manifest, that they are wrought in God" (John 3:19–21). In any case, Upson recalled that the prayer meetings he had known were largely evangelistic in tone: "From what folks said 'bout them meetin's, there was sure a lot of good prayin' and testifyin', 'cause so many sinners repented and was saved."[35]

The idea that white Christians in the South also had a duty to evangelize and save blacks was reinforced by the growth of abolitionism in the North. In May 1835 the Northern-based American Antislavery Society planned to distribute thousands of abolitionist messages throughout the nation, including in the South. Mail bags containing abolitionist literature were seized in Charleston, South Carolina, in July 1835 and were burned in front of an approving crowd of several thousand people. Following this event, anti-abolitionist meetings were held in several Georgia towns, including Waynes-boro and Athens. As a further step, church leaders in the state passed resolutions condemning abolitionism. The Presbytery of Georgia, for instance, issued an announcement that sought to calm fears about Presbyterian ministers by asserting that "they reject the *tenets* and doctrines of Abolitionism and solemnly declare for themselves and their churches, that they never were and cannot be Abolitionists."[36]

In the face of Northern challenges concerning the morality of slavery, white Southerners not only trumpeted their rejection of abolitionism but also came to assert that slavery represented a positive good. Their position was that God favored slavery for blacks so that they could be exposed to the good news of Christianity and rescued from the "heathenism" of Africa. Indeed, Southern clergy members not only defended slavery but also argued that the institution was moral on some grounds and was at least permitted, if not endorsed, by the Bible.[37] No doubt many antebellum white Southerners would have agreed with one Presbyterian minister in Augusta who suggested that slavery presented spiritual benefits for both blacks and whites: "The institution of domestic slavery . . . by saving a lower race from the destruction of heathenism, has, under divine management, contributed to refine, exalt, and enrich its superior race!"[38]

The foremost Methodist apologist for slavery in Georgia was Augustus Baldwin Longstreet. In his *Letters on the Epistle of Paul to Philemon: Or, the Connection of Apostolical Christianity with Slavery*, published in 1845, Long-street asserted that Paul's letter clearly proved "a slaveholder may be a good Christian," since the New Testament figure Philemon was both a highly regarded convert and a slave owner. Longstreet noted that Paul himself held Philemon in esteem and returned Philemon's slave, Onesimus, to him when the slave came to the apostle. Thus it was clear, Longstreet suggested, that slavery was permitted by the Bible, and he felt that four matters were firmly established by Paul's letter: first, "there is no sin in holding slaves"; second, "a Slaveholder may be a very pious man in the sight of God, and worthy of the love, fellowship, and confidence of the best of men"; third, "there is no *moral evil* in slavery"; and, fourth, "slaveholding is no disqualification for the ministry."[39]

Longstreet's position should be viewed together with the Few Resolution, passed in 1837 by the Georgia Methodist state conference, which asserted that slavery was not a "moral evil." Christopher H. Owen points out that the resolution constituted an implicit admission that slavery might be a "social evil," while not holding individual slaveholders accountable for its existence. Owen adds that Longstreet only affirmed that slavery "was a necessary evil allowed by the Bible, not that it was divinely sanctioned as a positive good."[40]

The year before Longstreet issued his study of Philemon, fellow Georgian Patrick Hues Mell wrote a pamphlet whose title reveals that he advocated a more thoroughgoing endorsement of the peculiar institution: *Slavery. A Treatise, showing that slavery is neither a moral, political, nor social evil.* When he published the tract, Mell was a professor at Mercer College; he would go on to become a professor, vice chancellor, and chancellor (president) at the Franklin College. Mell also later served as president of the Southern Baptist Convention for more than fifteen years, both during and after the Civil War (1863–1871 and 1880–1887).[41]

Mell advanced several arguments in his treatise to demonstrate that slavery was both just and necessary. In fact, he boldly proclaimed: "Slavery, under some form or other, by whatever name it may be called, is essential to the existence of civil society." Further, Mell insisted that slavery was not a negative experience for slaves themselves: "*In every respect*, the condition of the slave, in these United States of America, is better than that occupied by his brethren in any part of the world, now, or during any past age. Nothing can be more easy than to prove this. . . . In his *moral, intellectual and physical* condition, he is better off than the race have ever been in *Africa*." Mell cited a contemporary source indicating that African religion "consists only in a stupid worshipping of snakes and animals, or an idol made of wood or stone," and he stated that Africans therefore "have no idea of the true and living God, and Christ and His Gospel are alike unknown to them." According to Mell, African slaves received a positive good by being brought to America, where they could be introduced to Christianity: "No one can deny that the slave, in this christian land, enjoying the benefits of the Gospel, and affected by its influences, is immeasurably superior, in moral condition, to the besotted and depraved African."[42]

Having made clear that he would recognize "no code of morals but that contained in the sacred Scriptures," Mell asserted that slavery "*is an institution which God Himself established*." Mell made this claim on the basis of the story of Noah and the curse that is laid upon Canaan, Noah's grandson: "A servant of servants shall he be unto his brethren" (Genesis 9:25).[43] In the nineteenth century this verse was usually understood to refer more broadly to Canaan's father, Ham, since he was the one who had caused Noah harm, which led to the curse. John Leadley Dagg, for example, wrote that Noah's curse of Canaan was issued "because of a crime committed by his son Ham, the father of Canaan." He added: "[The words of Noah] are a denunciation of God's displeasure at the sin of Ham, and an explanation of the degradation which has fallen on his posterity." And that posterity included not just Canaanites, because Ham was also considered the ancestor of Africans (see Genesis 10:6–20). Dagg affirmed that "the curse of Ham's transgression fell heavily on the Canaanites; but it was not confined to this branch of his family. The enslaved negroes in our midst are his descendants, and their condition agrees with this ancient prediction."[44] Mell concurred with this interpretation: "From Ham were descended the nations that occupied the land of Canaan, and those that now constitute the African or negro race. Their inheritance, according to the prophecy, has been and will *continue to be* slavery." Mell emphasized, therefore, that slavery is "*directly* sanctioned by the letter of the Scriptures" and is "not *indirectly* forbidden by the spirit of the Scriptures." For Mell, since "God, by the mouth of Noah . . . instituted slavery . . . it cannot be an immorality."[45]

The influence of this line of argument can be seen by the fact that Alexander H. Stephens, in the conclusion of his "Corner Stone" speech in 1861, referred to the putative fulfillment of the curse in the enslavement of Africans: "With us, all of the white race, however high or low, rich or poor, are equal in the eye of the law. Not so with the negro. Subordination is his place. He, by nature, or by the curse against Canaan, is fitted for that condition which he occupies in our system." Stephens also took for granted that God had ordained slavery: "The architect, in the construction of buildings, lays the foundation with the proper material—the granite; then comes the brick or the marble. The substratum of our society is made of the material fitted by nature for it, and by experience we know that it is best, not only for the superior, but for the inferior race, that it should be so. It is, indeed, in conformity with the ordinance of the Creator."[46]

Since white Southerners felt that their proslavery position was guided by the Bible, they asserted that Northern abolitionists lacked scriptural support for their position and thus were forced to argue that slavery was immoral as a matter of conscience. Southerners further alleged that by usurping the authority of the Bible in favor of human conscience, the abolitionists were guilty of nothing less than infidelity. One of the foremost voices in articulating this view of the moral superiority of the Bible over the human conscience was Presbyterian Samuel J. Cassels of Georgia, who published an article titled "Conscience—Its Nature, Office and Authority" in the *Southern Presbyterian Review* in 1853. Cassels objected to the notion that the conscience is the greatest source of morality by declaring that "God is our only true moral governor, and his will is our only supreme law. Our subjection, then, is not to be a subjection to conscience, (which, being a part of ourselves, would imply subjection to ourselves,) but a subjection to God, as our moral governor." He maintained that "the very moment we set up conscience as a sort of rival to Jehovah, that moment we become idolators."[47] Mitchell Snay observes that by equating abolitionism with religious infidelity and idolatry, Southern clergy were taking "the first step toward secession and separate nationhood."[48]

The understanding that slavery was ordained by the Bible led many Southern ministers to encourage moral treatment of slaves. The fact that Christian slaves and masters could have an affinity can be demonstrated by the example of Wesley J. Gaines and his owner, Gabriel Toombs, a Wilkes County resident and brother of the well-known Georgia politician Robert Toombs.[49] The nature of their relationship before the Civil War can be gleaned from their interactions following it. First, Gabriel Toombs convinced Gaines that the former slave should become a minister. Gaines did indeed become a minister, initially within the Methodist Episcopal Church, South, denomination, and later in the African Methodist Episcopal Church. As an African Methodist Episcopal minister, in 1881 Gaines was instrumental in the founding of Morris Brown College in Atlanta, "the first educational institution in Georgia under sole African American patronage."[50] In 1889 Gaines, who had become an African Methodist Episcopal bishop, returned to Washington, Georgia, where he had lived when he was a slave, to direct a church conference. He took the opportunity to visit his former owner, and Toombs introduced him to others as "our Bishop Gaines and my friend."[51]

That even ministers were capable of abusing their slaves, however, is demonstrated by the eyewitness testimony of Leah Garrett, who was a slave in Richmond County and was interviewed as part of the WPA Slave Narrative Project. Garrett related: "In dem days, preachers wuz just as bad and mean as anybody else. Dere wuz a man who folks called a good preacher, but he

wuz one of de meanest mens I ever seed. When I wuz in slavery under him
he done so many bad things." Among the instances of cruelty that Garrett
recalled was the following:

> One Sunday mornin' his wife told him deir cook wouldn't never fix nothin'
> she told her to fix. Time she said it he jumped up from de table, went in de
> kitchen, and made de cook go under de porch whar he always whupped his
> slaves. She begged and prayed but he didn't pay no 'tention to dat. He put
> her up in what us called de swing, and beat her 'til she couldn't holler. De
> pore thing already had heart trouble; dat's why he put her in de kitchen,
> but he left her swingin' dar and went to church, preached, and called hisself
> servin' God. When he got back home she wuz dead.[52]

Such events were not rare. Indeed, Albert J. Raboteau observes that "incidents of Christian slaveholders, including clergymen, brutalizing their slaves
abound in the narratives of former slaves."[53] Certainly, as Georgia slave Charles
Ball remarked in 1836: "If there are hard and cruel masters in the South, there
are also others of a contrary character. The slaveholders are neither more nor
less than men." Yet with virtual unanimity, masters viewed slaves as inferiors
and their conduct reflected this fundamental fact.[54] Although Ball went on
to note that some slaveholders were "good," it remained that "very many
are bad."[55]

The extensive diary entries left by one nineteenth-century woman, Frances
"Fanny" Kemble, provide an arresting eyewitness account of the abysmal conditions that slaves often endured. Kemble was a well-known British actress
who retired from the stage when she married Pierce Mease Butler in Philadelphia in 1834. In 1838, after Butler inherited property in Georgia, including
hundreds of slaves, the couple traveled with their two young daughters to
his plantations on St. Simons Island and Butler Island, near Darien. Kemble
had abolitionist leanings, and as she listened to the impassioned voices of the
female slaves she came to know, she recorded their stories and her observations in a diary. She also questioned Butler directly about the treatment of
his slaves, which contributed to disagreements between them, and eventually
they divorced.[56] Kemble went on to publish her diary in England in 1863 as
Journal of a Residence on a Georgian Plantation in 1838–1839, which remains
in print.[57]

In the slave states white men idealized white women, which, as we will see
in a later chapter, would have some very unfortunate consequences following

the abolition of slavery. As a result, many white men ended up using slaves for their physical satisfaction.[58] As a new wife, Kemble observed and commented on this overall situation on the Southern plantations: "Mr. [Butler], and many others, speak as if there were a natural repugnance in all whites to any alliance with the black race; and yet it is notorious, that almost every Southern planter has a family more or less numerous of illegitimate colored children."[59]

What drew Kemble's attention most, though, were the horrible physical conditions and treatment Butler's slaves endured. In early 1839 a slave named Teresa was flogged because she had come to speak to Kemble. Shortly thereafter Kemble listened to "a poor woman called Mile, who could hardly stand for pain and swelling in her limbs." Such women appear again and again in the pages of Kemble's journal. One striking story was related by a slave named Die, who told Kemble that her arms had been tied up and that she had been whipped. Kemble observed that Die did not speak of such punishment as anything strange or unusual. Kemble asked her, "did they do that to you when you were with child?" The slave replied: "Yes, missis." Kemble summarized her own feelings of distress by writing: "And to all this I listen—I, an Englishwoman, the wife of the man who owns these wretches, and I cannot say: 'That thing shall not be done again; that cruel shame and villainy shall never be known here again.'"[60]

If Fanny Kemble felt that she was not in a position to speak out against the inhumane treatment she observed, many Southern clergymen did take concrete steps to admonish masters who failed to treat their slaves in what they considered a moral fashion. In an 1851 essay, Baptist minister A. T. Holmes of Hayneville declared: "The mutual obligations [between master and servant] seem limited by the law of Christ, and the law of Christ is the law of kindness and good will." He further stated that "equity, as well as justice, should regulate all our intercourse with others," and he indicated that he did not consider the relationship of master and servant to be an exception. Pointedly, Holmes urged each master to remember, "with humble reverence and with Godly fear, that he, also, has a master in Heaven."[61]

A decade later, Joseph R. Wilson delivered a sermon in Augusta's First Presbyterian Church titled "Mutual Duties of Masters and Slaves." Wilson argued that as "a fundamental law" there "*must* be . . . inequalities in society" such as those between masters and slaves. Indeed, not only did Wilson consider slavery to be "an organizing element in that family order which lies at the very foundation of Church and State," but, like Patrick Hues Mell, he also held that the institution was ordained by God: "Light cannot shine with greater brightness than does the doctrine of the sinlessness—nay, than does the doctrine of the righteousness—of an institution, which . . . besides being recognized as a prime conservator of the civilization of the world, besides being one of the colored man's foremost sources of blessing, is likewise directly sanctioned by . . . Scripture." Since he thought that slavery as an institution was "a benefit and a blessing," Wilson maintained "if it be a wrong, it is not so *in itself*; it can become so only when masters and servants misconceive and abuse their relationship to one another."[62]

Wilson delivered his sermon in early January 1861, less than two weeks before a Georgia state convention voted 208 to 89 to adopt an ordinance of secession from the Union. Typically, explanations of the events leading to the Civil War focus on political considerations. Nonetheless, two decades prior to secession the two largest evangelical denominations in the United States fractured along regional lines, and the schisms between Methodists and Baptists in the North and the South fostered a distinctive Southern regional identity that in turn helped make secession possible.[63] Georgians were very much involved in both of these schisms.

James O. Andrew, who was born near Washington, Georgia, and served a number of pulpits in the state, was appointed a Methodist bishop in 1832 by the Methodist Episcopal Church, due in part to the fact that he did not own slaves. Beginning in 1834, however, Andrew inherited some slaves through marriage. At that time, abolitionism was spreading among Northern Methodists. It became the case that by 1844 the Methodist Episcopal Church was losing thousands of Northern members over the matter of slavery, primarily to a new, avowedly antislavery group, the Wesleyan Methodists. Therefore, Northern leaders of the Methodist Episcopal Church decided to draw a more firm line against slavery. Following weeks of debate, in June 1844 the national General Conference voted 110 to 69, with a regional split, to approve a resolution asking Andrew to "desist from the exercise of his office" so long as he continued to own slaves. Southern Methodists were incensed by this perceived insult, and, as a result, in May 1845 at Louisville, Kentucky, delegates formed the Methodist Episcopal Church, South.[64]

The schism among Baptists developed along similar lines. Once more the fundamental issue was slavery, which divided the national denomination by region. Like their Methodist counterparts, Northern Baptists were taking an increasingly antislavery stance in the 1830s, which caused great concern in the South. Northern abolitionists created the American Baptist Anti-slavery Society in 1840 and the American Baptist Free Mission Society in 1843. Yet the national Home Mission Society tried to maintain neutrality on the matter and published a statement to that effect. In 1844 Georgia Baptists pressed the issue by requesting that James Reeve, a slaveholder, be appointed a home missionary. The request was denied. In response, the Baptist State Convention of Alabama demanded that the Acting Board of the Triennial Convention issue "the distinct, explicit avowal that slaveholders are eligible, and entitled, equally with non-slaveholders . . . to receive any agency, mission, or other appointment." The board declared that it could "never be a party to any arrangement which would imply approbation of slavery." This led Southern Baptists to meet at Augusta, Georgia, in May 1845 and to withdraw from the Triennial Convention, establishing the Southern Baptist Convention.[65] Though there were representatives at the meeting from eight Southern states, Georgia led the way, with 153 out of 293 registered delegates being from the state, including John Leadley Dagg and Patrick Hues Mell.[66]

These denominational schisms provoked great alarm since they constituted "harbingers of disunion."[67] Former senator Henry Clay of Kentucky, writing in April 1845 just before the Methodist Episcopal Church, South, was formed, commented that he would "not say that such a separation would necessarily produce a dissolution of the political union of these States," but he considered that the example "would be fraught with imminent danger."[68] On July 4, 1845, following the Methodist and Baptist schisms, the Presbyterian paper *Watchman of the South* presciently observed: "The churches once divided, North and South, Demagogues will have but little to do to dissolve the Union of the States. That done, then we shall see war and horrible contests. Brother will slay brother."[69]

Two of the most renowned expressions of concern about the potential impact of the schisms were delivered on the floor of the U.S. Senate in March 1850. On March 4, Senator James M. Mason of Virginia read a speech on behalf of its author, Senator John C. Calhoun of South Carolina, who was ill and near death. Calhoun wrote about the various religious, political, and social "cords" that bound the states of the Union together, and he observed how "the agitation of the slavery question has snapped some of the most important, and has greatly weakened all the others." He felt that "the unity of the great religious denominations . . . formed a strong cord to hold the whole

Union together"; yet as powerful as the ties had been that held the denominations together along national lines, they were not able "to resist the explosive
effect of slavery agitation." After mentioning the recent Methodist and Baptist schisms, Calhoun concluded: "If the agitation goes on, the same force,
acting with increased intensity . . . will finally snap every cord, when nothing
will be left to hold the States together except force."[70]

Three days later, Senator Daniel Webster of Massachusetts delivered his
famous "Seventh of March Speech." Early in his remarks, Webster referred
to Calhoun's speech and commented about the unease he shared with the
Southerner: "The honorable Senator from South Carolina the other day
alluded to the separation of that great religious community, the Methodist
Episcopal Church. That separation was brought about by differences of opinion upon this particular subject of slavery. I felt great concern, as that dispute
went on, about the result. I was in hopes that the difference of opinion might
be adjusted, because I looked upon that religious denomination as one of
the great props of religion and morals throughout the whole country, from
Maine to Georgia." As he built to a conclusion, Webster came squarely to the
issue at hand: "I should much prefer to have heard from every member on
this floor declarations of opinion that this Union could never be dissolved,
than the declaration of opinion by any body, that, in any case, under the
pressure of any circumstances, such a dissolution was possible. I hear with
distress and anguish the word 'secession'. . . . Peaceable secession is an utter
impossibility."[71]

Calhoun and Webster were correct in their dire appraisals, as Southern
states ended up seceding in 1860 and 1861, leading to the Civil War. In April
1861, a week after the shelling of Fort Sumter, which ignited the war, Georgian
Thomas R. R. Cobb, a devout Presbyterian who supported secession, happily
declared: "This revolution has been accomplished mainly by the Churches."[72]
It is worth noting that while Methodists and Baptists had split along regional
lines over slavery during the mid-nineteenth century, Presbyterians had also
broken into two main camps, Old School and New School, as a result of
wrangling over theological issues that had nevertheless brought some regional
conflicts into play.[73] After the Civil War broke out, Presbyterian churches
of both the Old and New schools split according to region. In December
1861 Southern Presbyterians assembled in Augusta, as had Southern Baptists,
and formed the Presbyterian Church in the Confederate States of America,
which eventually came to be known as the Southern Presbyterian Church.[74]

Cobb's sense of the fundamental role played by the churches in the events leading to the war is easily understood. The church schisms had not only prefigured sectional conflict, but the Southern churches had gone on to buttress Southern nationalism, which identified Southerners as God's favored people.[75] Following the schisms, Southern religious leaders no longer had to deal directly with the moderating effects of Northerners at denominational meetings, and they came to sacralize the South.[76] In no uncertain terms, Southern churches loudly announced that God stood with the South, and vice versa. Accordingly, Southern clergy came to articulate what Mitchell Snay fittingly terms a "religious logic of secession" by asserting that Northerners were infidels, while Southerners stood for religious purity.[77] It had become a cliché in Southern sermons that by embracing abolitionism and antislavery positions, Northerners were standing in opposition to God, who had appointed slavery. In such a case it fell to Southerners to uphold God's will by preserving slavery. On December 9, 1860, Presbyterian Rufus K. Porter delivered a sermon in Waynesboro titled "Christian Duty in the Present Crisis," in which he argued both that Northerners "have dishonored the very temple of God" and that secession was about nothing less than "the tremendous question of giving up or maintaining the great principles of eternal justice, righteousness and truth."[78] Given such statements, John B. Boles concludes that secession can be considered a religious as well as a political act: "Secession in a sense was the completion of the separation from the evil, misguided northern society that had been initiated through the church divisions almost two decades before. The most prominent religious leaders of all major denominations— and apparently the great majority of laypeople—supported the creation of the Confederacy as the duty required by their religion."[79]

We can see these themes expressed clearly in what was perhaps the most influential sermon in defense of secession, given by the Presbyterian minister Benjamin M. Palmer, who, as was noted in chapter 3, graduated from the Franklin College in 1838, six years after Alexander H. Stephens. Palmer took his first pulpit at Savannah's First Presbyterian Church in 1842. On November 29, 1860, he delivered a Thanksgiving sermon in his later pulpit at the First Presbyterian Church in New Orleans, Louisiana. From the beginning of his remarks Palmer repeatedly referred to the centrality of slavery, the "one issue before us," and noted that it had already "riven asunder the two largest religious communions in the land." He then asserted his view that the South had been given a "providential trust," which was "*to conserve and to perpetuate the institution of domestic slavery as now existing,*" and underscored that this obligation "touches the four cardinal points of duty *to ourselves, to our slaves, to the world, and to Almighty God.*" Indeed, while Palmer considered abolitionism "undeniably atheistic," the South's responsibility constituted nothing less than "defending, before all nations, the cause of all religion and of all truth."[80]

Palmer's sermon struck a chord throughout the South, as noted by Mitchell Snay: "Contemporaries agreed that Palmer's sermon exerted a powerful influence in enlisting support for secession. The Southern political press rang with praise for the sermon."[81] Palmer's local paper, the *New Orleans Daily Delta*, distributed more than thirty thousand copies of the sermon, and it was printed in full in other papers throughout the South, including the *Southern Field and Fireside*, published in Augusta, Georgia. Eventually, the sermon was printed as a booklet by a newspaper office in New Orleans and by publishers in Milledgeville, Georgia.

In December 1860, shortly after Palmer delivered his sermon, a poll taken of Georgia Methodist ministers heading to their annual conference, one month before the state of Georgia formally seceded, showed that "a large majority favored immediate secession."[82] In all, as Daniel W. Stowell observes, "few, if any, groups could surpass Confederate clergymen in their devotion to the Southern cause. They preached for it, prayed for it, and interpreted God's purposes in it from the beginning to the end."[83] In October 1862, as the Civil War raged, the *Southern Advocate*, a Methodist paper that had relocated to Augusta from Charleston, South Carolina, made reference to the "Holy War" being fought by the South.[84] The sentiment was not uncommon. Methodist bishop George Foster Pierce, for instance, delivered a sermon before the Georgia General Assembly in March 1863 in which he declared that the South had "peculiar covenant relations with God," and therefore that God "is for us and with us."[85]

The South's early victories, such as the First Battle of Bull Run in July 1861, seemed to confirm such faith. Yet the tide of war began to change against the South in 1863, following Confederate losses at the battles of Gettysburg and Vicksburg in July of that year. Revivals had already begun to break out following the Confederate defeat at Antietam in September 1862, which was, with more than twenty thousand combined casualties, the bloodiest day of battle in American history.[86] The Confederate armies experienced the fervor of revivalism to the end of the Civil War. Southerners had felt God's hand at the time of their early victories, and they had to come to terms with the meaning of their defeats. Their clergy responded with jeremiads that called Southerners to confess their sins so that God would again show them favor.[87]

The wartime sermons delivered by Episcopal bishop Stephen Elliott, who held the pulpit at Christ Church in Savannah, illustrate this progression of interpretations.[88] In September 1861 Elliott expressed optimism, based on what was happening in the war effort. He gave all thanks to "Almighty God" for "a series of brilliant victories won by our gallant soldiers over the invaders of our soil" and credited "his presence with us upon those fields of terrible conflict." Yet already in February 1862 Elliott's hopefulness seemed to dim: "It may be that the bloody war in which we are engaged is necessary for our purification. War is a fearful scourge . . . but it may sanctify as well as chasten." By August 1863, immediately after Gettysburg and Vicksburg, Elliott was plainly trying to comprehend what was happening. He asserted: "From the beginning of the revolution . . . we have boldly assumed the position, that we were fighting under the Shield of the Lord of Hosts. . . . We have assumed a very grand but a very solemn position, and we cannot, without utter shame and confusion of face, abandon it. . . . We are compelled to acknowledge this day . . . either that we ourselves have been deceived in supposing that God was on our side . . . or we must declare him to be a Being in whom no reliance can be placed." For Elliott, the answer was clear. The South had been too hasty to assume God's unwavering support, and there was a lesson to be learned. Surely God was turning away from the South because of its sins. If those sins could be identified and corrected, God would deliver the South as before: "In turning ourselves, therefore to God in fasting and prayer, let us truly humble ourselves and beseech Him to show us our own hearts and to convict us especially of those sins which are offensive to him and which have placed us in the wrong way."[89]

Georgia itself was not the scene of ground battles until relatively late in the war. When the Union attacks did arrive, they came with a fury. The destruction accompanying the burning of Atlanta and Major General William Tecumseh Sherman's march to the sea are well known, having been immortalized in lore as well as in books and films such as *Gone with the Wind*. In Savannah, Elliott continued to maintain faith in God's plan for the South even in the face of these dramatic events. In a sermon titled "Vain is the Help of Man," delivered on September 15, 1864, following the fall of Atlanta and just weeks before Sherman would begin his march toward coastal Georgia,

Elliott was certain that in the end the South would be triumphant: "I look to God for His help, and in due time it will come. Meanwhile we must be patient and enduring—patient under his chastisements, and enduring while he is making things work together for good to us. As I have said to you, again and again, this war is never to be ended by any victories of ours; God will give us just enough of them to enable us to keep our enemy at bay; it will be ended by his turning their arms inward upon themselves."[90]

Elliott's faith notwithstanding, the defeat of the South was sealed a little more than six months after his September 1864 sermon. Given the widespread belief in the nineteenth century that God controls historical events, the end of the war in spring 1865 was assumed to have deep theological significance, and Southerners struggled to understand the meaning of what had happened.[91] Ella Gertrude Clanton Thomas, who lived on a plantation near Augusta, no doubt spoke for many of her white contemporaries when she recorded in her diary in the fall of 1865 that "by the surrender of the Southern army slavery became a thing of the past and we were reduced from a state of affluence to comparative poverty. . . . For a time I doubted God. . . . When I prayed my voice appeared to rise no higher than my head. When I opened the Bible the numerous allusions to slavery mocked me. Our cause was lost. . . . I was bewildered—I felt all this and could not see God's hand."[92]

To whatever degree religious Georgians had to struggle to maintain their faith, the underpinnings of what would become a widespread theological interpretation of Southern defeat had been established both before and during the war. Driven by their perceived duty to uphold slavery and their self-understanding as the defenders of true religion, many white Southerners believed that their defeat represented the divine plan for the South, albeit accompanied by paternal discipline.[93] Writing in the *Christian Index* in November 1865, S. G. Hillyer advised: "Let us not falter in our faith, in this time of public and private calamity. Let us accept the chastenings of the Lord with all humility. They are the dealings of a father's hand. His love in the method of its manifestation, may be incomprehensible. But he is too wise to err." The editor of the *Christian Index*, Henry H. Tucker, concurred: "Whether you see the good that is to come of what has happened or not, is immaterial. God will be certain to subserve some grand purpose of mercy by it." Tucker could be sure of such a claim because he felt that "the present result is not of man's doings. God is the author of his own providences. . . . The hand of the Lord is then in this thing. It is God who has done it." Given the conviction of this view, Tucker rhetorically asked: "Will his saints complain? Do they doubt his wisdom? Do they question his goodness?"[94]

On December 1, 1862, one month before he issued the Emancipation Proclamation, emblematic of the end of American slavery, President Lincoln wrote: "In *giving* freedom to the *slave*, we *assure* freedom to the *free*—honorable alike in what we give, and what we preserve. We shall nobly save, or meanly lose, the last best, hope of earth."[95] By contrast, white Southerners and their clergy felt that, in actuality, they were God's last, best hope. In 1862 Georgia Methodist James R. Thomas, who was then president of Emory College, asserted that the Confederate South was no less than "the last hope of Freedom and the last home of a pure Gospel."[96] After the Civil War, although they felt that they had been chastened, religious whites in the South clung to this notion and hoped that the cause of their purifying defeat would be made more clear in time. The South's former slaves, on the other hand, thought that the meaning of the Confederate defeat was plain enough already: God had struck down slavery, which was evil, and had given them their freedom. These conflicting views would lead to a transformation of religion in postwar Georgia.

CHAPTER FIVE

A Racial Pas de Deux

On the morning of November 16, 1864, Union major general William Tecumseh Sherman set out from Atlanta, which he had recently captured, and headed for Georgia's coast with his troops. As they advanced toward Savannah, Sherman and his forces cut a swath through the heart of Georgia.[1] White Georgians reacted with horror to Sherman's march to the sea, "the Civil War's most destructive campaign against a civilian population."[2] Dolly Sumner Lunt, who lived on a plantation near Covington, kept a wartime diary and recorded on November 19 that "Sherman with a greater portion of his army passed my house all day." The soldiers tore down her fencing, drove livestock through her yards, and burned buildings on her land. "Such a day," she wrote, "if I live to the age of Methuselah may God spare me from ever seeing again."[3] Many blacks in Georgia, on the other hand, were overcome with joy at what Sherman's march meant. Shortly after the Union troops marched into Savannah on December 21, an emotional celebration was held at the Second African Baptist Church. The service was filled with expressions of thanksgiving. A prayer in which a deacon thanked God that blacks were "free, and forever free," was met by shouts: "Glory to God! Hallelujah! Praise his name."[4] The differences in the reactions of white and black Georgians to the march to the sea reflect the fundamental divide between the two groups, which involved not only slavery and the Civil War, but, ultimately, the issue of racial equality.

A vivid depiction of the black desire for freedom came during a remarkable event when Sherman and his men stayed in Savannah for a few weeks before pressing on to confront Confederate troops in the Carolinas.[5] On the evening of January 12, 1865, Sherman, together with Secretary of War Edwin M. Stanton, met with a group of twenty black leaders, primarily from the Savannah area, the majority of whom were former slaves. The men chose

Garrison Frazier, a Baptist minister, to speak on their behalf. According to minutes of the meeting, the black leaders were posed the following question: "State what you understand by Slavery and the freedom that was to be given by the President's [Emancipation Proclamation]." Frazier answered as follows: "Slavery is, receiving by *irresistible power* the work of another man, and not by his *consent.* The freedom, as I understand it, promised by the proclamation, is taking us from under the yoke of bondage, and placing us where we could reap the fruit of our own labor, take care of ourselves and assist the Government in maintaining our freedom."[6]

One of the most obvious results of emancipation and the end of the Civil War was the mass departure of blacks from formerly biracial churches. It is unclear to what extent they were seeking to "take care of ourselves," since scholars have debated whether in the main blacks voluntarily withdrew from existing congregations to found new all-black churches or were essentially driven out due to mistreatment by whites.[7] In any case, it is clear that the number of blacks in the established evangelical denominations rapidly dropped after 1865. Black Methodists associated with the Georgia Annual Conference of the Methodist Episcopal Church, South, went from a prewar total of more than 27,000 to only 1,504 in 1870. The Georgia Baptist Convention, which had a comparable prewar black total, could count but 10,354 black members in 1870, and most of those members were gone by 1877, presumably having joined unaffiliated black congregations. The Presbyterian Synod of Georgia had only 643 black members in 1860; after the war many of them joined black Methodist or Baptist churches, leaving virtually no black members by 1870.[8]

Whether blacks withdrew voluntarily or were forced out of the churches, it is important to recall that their experience in prewar biracial worship had prepared them to establish new, all-black churches and denominations after the Civil War. As we observed in the preceding chapter, they had firsthand knowledge of how to conduct services and establish church governance. John B. Boles has pointed out that the postwar black congregations were very similar to the antebellum biracial churches. Generally speaking, after the Civil War black churches had longer services and more emotional worship patterns than white churches, but Boles suggests "it was the white churches that had changed."[9]

White Presbyterian membership in the Synod of Georgia remained somewhat stagnant following the Civil War, with the total number of congregants remaining below ten thousand throughout the 1860s and 1870s.[10] As already

mentioned, there were very few black Presbyterians in Georgia shortly following the war. Methodists and Baptists, on the other hand, were able to make
great strides in the postwar years, when one considers both whites and blacks
together. Indeed, by 1870 there were approximately forty thousand more pew
seats and five hundred more congregations in Georgia than there had been in
1860, with the vast majority representing Baptist and Methodist growth.[11] This
story will be recounted below. For a more complete understanding of religion
in postwar Georgia, however, we must first consider spiritual responses to the
Confederate defeat by white Southerners that went beyond the borders of
the established Christian denominations. Whites did not tend, like blacks, to
view the outcome of the Civil War in terms of freedom and liberation; rather,
they cast their eyes back to the "good old days" of the "Old South."

At the war's end, the women of the Soldiers' Aid Society of Columbus,
Georgia, began to care for the graves of Confederate soldiers. One of them,
Elizabeth "Lizzie" Rutherford, proposed an annual observance to decorate
graves, an act that is credited by some as having inaugurated Confederate
Memorial Day.[12] A generation later, one writer compared the work of the
Columbus women to that of the women who came to Jesus's grave: "Where
were Mary Magdalene and the other Mary after the crucifixion? At the sep-
ulcher with sweet spices. So these women came to the soldiers' graves with
choice plants and bright flowers."[13] If this comparison seems overblown, consider that what the women in Columbus were engaged in was, in part, no
less than a new form of Southern religion. Some scholars refer to this as Lost
Cause religion, which was interdenominational and represented an admix-
ture of evangelicalism and Southern nationalism.[14] David W. Blight explains
that the Lost Cause "came to represent a mood, or an attitude toward the
past. . . . For many Southerners it became a natural extension of evangelical
piety . . . that helped them link their sense of loss to a Christian conception
of history."[15]

The term "Lost Cause" is not a modern invention, having been used by
Southerners soon after the war. The most notable early use of the term was by
Virginian Edward A. Pollard in his postwar books, including *The Lost Cause:
A New Southern History of the War of the Confederates*, which was published
in 1867.[16] One purpose of Lost Cause ideology was to cultivate the sense that
secession had represented heroic and sacred principles, in order for Southern-
ers to maintain a sense of honor despite their defeat. As Georgian Clement A.
Evans, who had served as a Confederate general, stated: "If we cannot justify

the South in the act of Secession, we will go down in History solely as a brave, impulsive but rash people who attempted in an illegal manner to overthrow the Union of our Country."[17]

Beyond serving as an apologetic to maintain the South's honor, the Lost Cause concept also called for a continued sense of the South's special status. In Pollard's closing remarks in *The Lost Cause*, he wrote: "It would be immeasurably the worst consequence of defeat in this war that the South should lose its moral and intellectual distinctiveness as a people, and cease to assert its well-known superiourity in civilization, in political scholarship, and in all the standards of individual character over the people of the North."[18] Thus, while the idea of a separate Southern nation was defeated on the battlefield, the ideal of a distinct Southern people with a noble cultural character remained.[19] Arguably, since Lost Cause advocates sought to maintain the concept of a superior white Southern culture against perceived attacks, it is best to consider expressions of Lost Cause religiosity as exemplifying *culture religion*, which involves self-referential beliefs that a given group of people desire to strengthen or restore.[20]

Major components of religion include myth, symbols, and rituals, and the Lost Cause culture religion manifested all three. When scholars of religion use the term "myth" they do not mean to imply a falsehood. Rather, in religious studies, a myth is a foundational account, a story that explains.[21] The essentials of the Lost Cause myth are easily identified, since they were repeated in writings, lectures, and sermons by scores of postwar Southern figures.[22] First, the prewar South—the putative "Old South"—was a place of nobility and chivalry.[23] Slavery had been a benign, even beneficent, institution.[24] The South had not fought to defend slavery; rather, the war had resulted from conflicts over states' rights and cultural differences between the North and the South.[25] While Southerners were a people of honor and purity, Northerners were invaders, a people consumed by lust for power, "an avaricious 'industrial society' determined to wipe out its cultural foes."[26] Thus the Civil War was recast in Lost Cause mythmaking as a defense of the South against interfering Northerners, and the "War of the Rebellion" (as the federal government called it) became the "War Between the States" or the "War of Northern Aggression."

Some of the key symbols of the Lost Cause are conveniently laid out in a statement published in 1896 by Clement A. Evans, who, in addition to being a Confederate general, was also both a Methodist minister and a commander of the United Confederate Veterans. Evans referred to "a deep and honorable respect for some things which are our own and which we call our mementoes"; they were, he said, "sacred." Limiting himself to "only three, each of which deserves our perpetual commemoration," he listed the song "Dixie," the Confederate battle flag, and the gray uniform jacket of the South.[27] To Evans's list may be added the living symbols of the Lost Cause, the Confederate soldiers themselves and their leaders, especially Jefferson Davis, Robert E. Lee, and Thomas J. "Stonewall" Jackson. Each of these men played a fundamental role in what Charles Reagan Wilson calls "the myth of the Crusading Christian Confederates," and together they provided Moses (Jackson) and Christ (Davis and Lee) figures.[28] (It is worth noting that images of these three men are now carved on the side of Stone Mountain, near Atlanta, constituting the largest Confederate memorial in the country.) There was also a figure of evil in Lost Cause religion. Georgian James Longstreet (nephew of Augustus Baldwin Longstreet), who had served as a Confederate general, was accused by several Lost Cause proponents of having lost the war due to his actions at Gettysburg. In the process, Longstreet became identified as a Judas-like personage. Although Longstreet had been Lee's senior subordinate officer, several groups, including the United Daughters of the Confederacy chapter in Savannah, refused to acknowledge his death with the customary wreaths or statements.[29]

In addition to Confederate Memorial Day, "the Sabbath of the South," other rituals honored Confederate veterans, especially the creation and dedication of Confederate monuments, which served as reminders of the Lost Cause throughout the year and as focal points for cultural memory.[30] Gaines M. Foster has identified ninety-four Confederate monuments that were dedicated in the South by 1885 and notes that more than four hundred others were added by 1912.[31] Some of the oldest of these monuments are to be found in Georgia, such as the pillar in Athens that was unveiled in 1872 and that now stands on a traffic island immediately across from the Arch representing the gateway to the University of Georgia. In a graphic illustration of the intermingling of Confederate imagery and Southern religion, the marble pillar resembles a church steeple.[32]

Three of the best known Confederate monuments in Georgia are in Atlanta, Savannah, and Augusta. A large obelisk some sixty-five feet tall made of granite from Stone Mountain, which stands in Oakland Cemetery in Atlanta, marks a Confederate section of the cemetery containing several thousand graves. When it was dedicated on Confederate Memorial Day in 1874, the monument was the tallest structure in Atlanta.[33] The Confederate memorial prominently located in Savannah's Forsyth Park was dedicated twice, in 1875 and 1879. The first version of the memorial had two statues, one representing "Judgment" at the top and another denoting "Silence" in a cupola. Initial reaction was unfavorable, so the memorial was altered. When it was unveiled for the second time, a Confederate soldier stood on top and the cupola was bricked up.[34] An imposing Confederate monument that stands on Broad Street in downtown Augusta, which was dedicated in 1878, is engraved with the statement: "No Nation Rose So White and Fair: None Fell So Pure of Crime." A Lost Cause sentiment to be sure.

On the day that the Augusta monument was unveiled, one of the speakers was Charles Colcock Jones Jr., the "Macaulay of the South" and son of the previously mentioned Presbyterian minister and missionary.[35] Jones was one of Georgia's most vocal advocates of the Lost Cause, and in his remarks he repeated one of the canards of its standard argumentation by stating that the South had been defeated solely because it had been "overborne by superior numbers and weightier munitions."[36] Thus, said Jones, the war had only reached "a physical solution of the moral, social, and political propositions," so nothing had been absolutely determined "except the question of comparative strength." Therefore, according to Jones, the "vested rights" of white Southerners remained. Such rights were, he said, "in a moral point of view, unaffected by the result of the contest."[37] In these statements, Jones mirrored the earlier conclusion to Edward A. Pollard's *The Lost Cause*: "The war properly decided only what was put in issue: the restoration of the Union and the excision of slavery; and to these two conditions the South submits. But the war did not decide negro equality; it did not decide negro suffrage. . . . And these things which the war did not decide, the Southern people will still cling to, still claim, and still assert in them their rights and views."[38]

Ultimately, due to the widespread influence of such assertions of Lost Cause dogma, although the South lost the Civil War it would win the battle over the way the war was recalled in the national memory. As Robert Lang helpfully encapsulates, "historically the war was lost over slavery and independence, but peace was waged—and won—for states' rights, white supremacy, and honor."[39] Alan T. Nolan has argued that there are now two independent versions of the Civil War. On the one hand is the history of the war, or what actually happened. And on the other there is the "Southern interpretation," or the Lost Cause. Nolan notes that once the Lost Cause had allowed white Southerners to rationalize their defeat and maintain their sense of honor, its concepts spread to the North, becoming a national explanation. Nolan concludes that today the Lost Cause "represents the national memory of the Civil War; it has been substituted for the *history* of the war."[40]

One of the most vigorous activists for the Lost Cause vision was J. William Jones, a Virginian who lived in Atlanta in the 1880s and 1890s.[41] Jones, a Baptist minister, served as a Confederate chaplain among Robert E. Lee's troops. In Jones's mind, to be a Confederate hero and a pious Christian was a guaranteed combination, and he asserted that the Army of Northern Virginia— and by implication the Confederacy itself—produced "the noblest army . . . that ever marched under any banner or fought for any cause in all the tide of time."[42] One of the standard prayer openings Jones used following the Civil War wedded his dual passions of the Confederacy and Christianity: "Oh! God our help in ages past, our hope for years to come, God of Israel, God of Abraham, Isaac, and Jacob—God of the centuries—God of our Fathers— God of Stonewall Jackson and Robert Lee and Jefferson Davis—Lord of Hosts . . . God of our Southland—our God!"[43]

Historian Charles Reagan Wilson regards Jones as the most important person linking Southern religion and the Lost Cause. His own generation knew Jones as "the fighting parson," who became a celebrity because of his close association with Lee and other Southern generals. He also became the author of many books. When Lee died, his family gave Jones some of the general's materials, and in 1874 Jones issued his first book, *Personal Reminiscences, Anecdotes, and Letters of R. E. Lee.*[44] His other books include his remembrance of wartime life, *Christ in the Camp; or Religion in Lee's Army*, which appeared in 1886 and is still in print.[45] Jones was not only an author; for more than a decade he also held the powerful position of secretary-treasurer of the Southern Historical Society. In this role he edited numerous volumes of the *Southern Historical Society Papers*, the primary organ for the dissemination of Lost Cause ideology. At the same time, Jones became an influential leader of the Southern Baptists. Especially notable is his service in Atlanta from 1884 to 1893 as Assistant Corresponding Secretary of the Southern Baptist Convention's Home Mission Board. As Wilson observes, "Jones's connection to his own denomination provided a resonance to his work as a Lost Cause evangelist."[46]

In 1882 the Southern Baptist Convention established headquarters in Atlanta for a reinvigorated Home Mission Board and hired a new leader,

Isaac Taylor Tichenor, who had been, like Jones, a Civil War chaplain. From the outset Tichenor, a forceful and effective administrator, began to unify Southern Baptist churches and state bodies under the Convention's control. The selection of Tichenor reflected some significant concerns of the Convention, which was seeking to strengthen its reach. Under Tichenor's leadership, the Convention aimed to retrieve churches from Northern Baptist influence and to develop new Southern Baptist congregations.[47]

The 1892 report of the Home Mission Board presented to the annual meeting of the Southern Baptist Convention, held that year in Atlanta, reviewed the progress that had been made over the previous decade:

> Ten years ago the Convention . . . resolved to remove the Board from Marion, Ala[bama], to Atlanta. . . . A survey of the field indicated a great defeat and a lost cause. Impressed with the conviction that the existence of this Convention depended upon the resuscitation of its fortunes, the new Board threw itself into the arduous work before it with the determination to use every proper effort to reclaim its lost territory . . . . Such were the earnestness of its efforts and the happy results of its policy, that in five years there was not a missionary to the white people of the South who did not bear a commission from either the Home Mission Board of the Southern Baptist Convention, or one of our State Boards in alliance with it. Its territory had been reclaimed.[48]

The linkage between the Lost Cause and the attempt by white Southern Baptists to reclaim their territory from Northern influence cannot be missed.

While the Southern Baptist Home Mission Board was making great strides among whites, it had a troubled relationship with blacks due to paternalism and assertions of superiority. The 1891 Home Mission Board report claimed that "nothing is plainer to any one who knows this race [i.e., blacks] than its perfect willingness to accept a subordinate place. . . . That is the condition it prefers above all others, and this is the condition in which it attains the highest development of every attribute of manhood."[49] And in its 1892 report, only a few pages away from the assertion that Southern Baptists had reclaimed their lost territory after "a great defeat and a lost cause," the Board commented on the presumed necessity of white supervision of blacks:

> No people since the world began ever had so much or such efficient aid in their struggle from a savage life up to a Christian civilization. Three thousand years of barbarism, in a country rich in natural resources [i.e., Africa], is a practical demonstration of their inability to attain to the blessings of a

civilized life without help from others. Brought to this country and sold as slaves, they were placed in the only relation to the white people in which it was possible for them to exist. The miasma emanating from the vices and corruptions of our civilization is death to any inferior race with which we come in contact, unless that race be subordinated to our control.[50]

Not surprisingly, most black Baptists felt, as one put it, that the conduct of the Home Mission Board "makes the colored people entirely passive and completely unmans us." The intensity of this observation can be felt in what William Heard, a black Methodist, once said after hearing the black Baptist minister William Jefferson White speak in the late nineteenth century: "I determined from that night to be a MAN." White was an outspoken advocate of equal rights for freed slaves and worked to further educational opportunities for them.[51] To that end, in 1867 he was largely responsible for the establishment of the Augusta Institute (now Morehouse College in Atlanta), which met in the basement of the Springfield Baptist Church.[52]

Following the lead of independent churches such as Springfield, black Baptists formed their own congregations. Immediately after the Civil War many of these congregations depended on white help and support, and some white churches donated land and other kinds of assistance to them. But such interracial cooperation was qualified by the demand of whites to retain authority and control over blacks. This paternalistic approach led some black Baptists to set up congregations with little or no guidance or assistance from whites, which eventually came to suit most whites.[53] At the 1869 annual meeting of the Southern Baptist Convention, the delegates arrived at the consensus that there would be no interracial Southern Baptist associations. Clinging to prewar notions about race relations, they proclaimed that the Bible did not "abolish social distinctions." Jesse Campbell, a white minister who had served for many years as a missionary to slaves, declared that he was not "disposed, and never expected to be disposed to be on equal terms of social equality" with blacks. Likewise, members of the white Goshen Baptist Association near Savannah effectively threw their hands in the air and declared: "Let the Yankees and negroes take care of themselves."[54]

Although some black Baptists encouraged continued cooperation with whites, rather than separation, many resented the lack of meaningful black participation in the Southern Baptist Convention, especially on the committees of the Home Mission Board, which ministered to blacks. By the mid-

1890s black separatists had gained the momentum. In 1895, three years after the Home Mission Board asserted the need for blacks to "be subordinated to our control," black Baptists formed the National Baptist Convention in Atlanta, and the National Baptist Publishing Board was chartered the following year. These developments helped to fuel the growth of black Baptist churches. By the turn of the century, black and white Baptists were worshipping almost entirely apart.[55]

Georgia Methodists took a similar, though more complex, path out from the Civil War. Whereas white Baptists largely remained members of the Southern Baptist Convention, and blacks eventually formed the National Baptist Convention, Methodists splintered into several groups that were at times mutually antagonistic. In Georgia, the main bodies immediately after the war were the Northern-based Methodist Episcopal Church (MEC), the Methodist Episcopal Church, South (MECS), and the African Methodist Episcopal Church (AME). As will be explained below, these three organizations were joined in 1870 by the Colored Methodist Episcopal Church (CME). To varying degrees, black Methodists could be found in each of these groups. For a time, it was unclear which organization(s) black Methodists would prefer, but ultimately it was the black denominations, the AME and the CME, that garnered the most adherents. As Christopher H. Owen puts it, this only came after "complex maneuvering, bitter infighting, and byzantine alliances among the different Wesleyan groups."[56]

After the Civil War, the MEC was aggressive in trying to reclaim Georgia and in seeking to add new converts. At first, many blacks joined the MEC, and by 1868 they constituted the majority of the denomination in the state. But overall the MEC found rough going in Georgia because it was generally tied to the North and, more particularly, to the Republican Party and its aim of providing black suffrage. An MEC newspaper that was based in Atlanta, the *Methodist Advocate*, became a virtual Republican Party organ. That it had to fold in 1882 due to financial problems reflects the difficulties faced by the MEC in Georgia. MEC ministers found themselves ostracized by polite white society at best, while at worst they were targets of periodic threats and violence. It is reported that one MEC minister, James L. Fowler, routinely kept a brace of pistols in the pulpit while he preached in case he needed to defend himself. It was clear that the MECS would remain the predominant church for white Methodists in Georgia, and therefore white MECS membership surpassed that of the MEC by a wide margin. Around 1875 there were approximately eighty

thousand white MECS members in Georgia but less than five thousand white
MEC members.[57]

In contrast to the MECS and the MEC, the AME, with a mission "to pro-
claim liberty to the captives" (Isaiah 61:1), was intent on gaining black converts. Thus, the AME, which identified itself as "the church of the negro,"
was from the outset essentially a solely black denomination.[58] The AME in
nineteenth-century Georgia was led by Henry McNeal Turner. Although he
is sometimes remembered primarily as a politician, as a minister Turner was
indefatigable in building up the AME. Turner was born in South Carolina in
1834, but after he became a licensed Methodist preacher in 1853 he spent a
great deal of time in Georgia and participated in revivals in Athens, Atlanta,
and Macon. Between 1858 and 1863 Turner held pulpits in Baltimore and
Washington, D.C. In 1863 he helped organize the First Regiment of U.S. Colored Troops and ministered to them, becoming in the process the first black
chaplain in the U.S. military. After the Civil War, Turner returned to Georgia
and founded scores of AME churches in the state. In 1880 he became the first
Southerner to be elected an AME bishop.[59] When Turner died in 1915, W. E. B.
Du Bois eulogized him as "a man of tremendous force and indomitable courage." Du Bois added: "In a sense Turner was the last of his clan: mighty men,
physically and mentally, men who started at the bottom and hammered their
way to the top by sheer brute strength; they were the spiritual progeny of
African chieftains and they built the African church in America."[60]

For a short time after the Civil War the MECS tried to retain its black
members, yet its leadership also acknowledged that blacks desired to have
their own ministers. Since white ministers would not tolerate equality with
black ministers, they reached the position that racial separation of churches
was the best solution for all concerned. In 1866 and 1867, MECS and AME leaders cooperated in a loose alliance. Those blacks who wished to remain in the
MECS were welcome to stay, but those who wanted their own church organization were free to leave and cross over to the AME. The one expectation was
that the AME would stay out of Reconstruction politics. When AME leaders
such as Turner became vocal supporters of Northern-supported Republicans,
the alliance fell apart.[61]

Things came to a head in the late 1860s and early 1870s. In 1868 white
members of the Georgia legislature expelled newly elected black members,
including Turner, who delivered a forceful protest speech in which he asked:
"Am I a man? If I am such, I claim the rights of a man. Am I not a man,

because I happen to be of a darker hue than honorable gentlemen around me?"[62] Eventually, the expelled blacks were reseated after lobbying the federal government. Georgia Democrats were gathering steam, however, and were able to gain control not only of the legislature but the governor's office as well with the election of James M. Smith in 1871. Reconstruction was giving way to Redemption, the reversion to Democratic rule and the empowerment of Southern white supremacist culture, the "Southern way of life."[63] The *Atlanta Constitution*, in its coverage of Smith's inaugural, told readers: "The occasion recalled the good old days of the State. . . . It was the spontaneous outpouring of the PEOPLE in rejoicing over the advent of the new era. It recalled in salient contrast the sham of inauguration that occurred when [the Republican Rufus] Bullock took the reins of government [following the Civil War]. Those who had the misfortune to witness that spectacle, with its immense concourse of negroes and its small attendance of whites, can realize the contrast between that occasion and one in which the sympathies and convictions of the people are enlisted. . . . The darkness is succeeded by light. Thank God Georgia is redeemed."[64]

Since AME leaders had offered support to the Republicans, MECS leaders sought an alternative form of black Methodism. Thus, in 1870, with financial aid from the MECS, the new Colored Methodist Episcopal Church was formed.[65] The leader of the CME in Georgia was Lucius Holsey, who was made a bishop in 1873. Holsey's background as a slave had brought him into close contact with whites from the beginning of his life, and he considered it foolish to provoke them.[66] He was born in 1842 near Columbus, of a black mother and a white father. After his first master and father, James Holsey, died in 1848, Lucius Holsey was owned by T. L. Wynn, who lived in Hancock County. Wynn himself died in 1857. Before his death, he offered Holsey the choice of two of his friends as his new master. Holsey chose Richard Malcolm Johnston, a planter, humorist, and professor at the Franklin College.[67] When Holsey moved to Athens to serve Johnston he was illiterate. He later wrote that he had "an insatiable craving for some knowledge of books."[68] Holsey was able to purchase some books, including a Bible and John Milton's *Paradise Lost*, and with assistance from some white children he learned to read and write.[69]

In 1898 Holsey published a number of the sermons he had given during the preceding decade, and they strongly reflect an essential characteristic of black Christian religiosity. From its early beginnings, black Christianity has tended to be monistic, blending sacred and secular concerns into a single whole. The title of one of Holsey's sermons illuminates this theme: "The Fatherhood of God and the Brotherhood of Man."[70] It is common to suggest that such a monistic orientation is rooted in African traditional religions. Indeed, indigenous religious traditions all over the world tend to blur the separation between spiritual and secular realms, since all of life is considered to be potentially spiritual. For example, African author Chinua Achebe states that "we talk [now] about politics, economics, religion. But in the traditional society all these things were linked together—there was no such thing as an irreligious man. In fact, we don't even have a word for religion in Igbo. It's simply *life*."[71] Samuel S. Hill Jr. observes that we cannot know how much of the African worldview persisted among African Americans, yet at a minimum "we can note that by post-Emancipation times Afro-Christianity had adopted a functional monism."[72] Thus, under the leadership of clergymen such as Holsey, the "black church" came to serve both religious and social ends, with the black minister playing not only a strong spiritual but also community role.

While eventually more than 90 percent of white Methodists in Georgia belonged to the MECS, the creation of the CME led to black Methodists being split among several groups. The AME had the largest number, but it held less than 60 percent of black Methodists in the state. Around 1875, the AME had approximately forty thousand members in Georgia, while the CME and MEC together had about thirty thousand blacks.[73] In addition, a relative handful of blacks belonged to the African Methodist Episcopal, Zion (AMEZ) church, which, compared to the other denominations, was not very successful in Georgia as a religious organization. One of its members, however, was Tunis Campbell, who served as vice president of the Republican Party in Georgia in the 1860s and was arguably the most influential black politician in the state.[74]

When the last few blacks who remained in the MECS joined the CME, the racial segregation of worship among both Baptists and Methodists in Georgia was essentially complete.[75] To underscore the virtual end of biracial worship in late nineteenth-century Georgia, consider what happened in 1876, when Rev. W. A. Pierce, an AME minister, attended a MECS church in order to visit "white brethren." When one white congregant threatened to walk out unless "that negro" was removed, it created a disturbance and Pierce was forced to leave. He concluded that white Methodists in Georgia now refused to worship with even "well-behaved" blacks.[76] Similarly, the pastor of First African

Baptist in Savannah at the close of the century, Emmanuel K. Love, who had tried to remain a cooperationist with whites, determined by 1897 that "he is both blind and foolish who does not recognize the fact that the color line is already drawn."[77] And in the process, eleven o'clock on Sunday morning had become, as Martin Luther King Jr. was to famously put it, "the most segregated hour in America."[78]

CHAPTER SIX

In the Shadow of Jim Crow

Atlanta audiences were in tears watching heart-wrenching scenes of the Civil War era played out before them on the movie screen, including a nighttime depiction of the city burning. A contemporary review in the *Atlanta Journal* held that "there has been nothing to equal it—nothing. Not as a motion picture, nor a play, nor a book does it come to you; but as the soul and spirit and flesh of the heart of your country's history, ripped from the past and brought quivering with all human emotions before your eyes." The opening night audience was completely spellbound: "It swept the audience . . . like a tidal wave. A youth in the gallery leaped to his feet and yelled and yelled. A little boy downstairs pounded the man's back in front of him and shrieked. The man . . . was a middle-aged, hard-lipped citizen; but his face twitched and his throat gulped up and down. Here a young girl kept dabbing and dabbing at her eyes and there an old lady just sat and let the tears stream down her face unchecked."[1] The *Atlanta Constitution* reported: "Never before, perhaps, has an Atlanta audience so freely given vent to its emotions and appreciation. . . . Spasmodic at first, the plaudits of the great spectacle at length became altogether unrestrained. The clapping of hands was not sufficient, and cheer after cheer burst forth." The review went on to note the profound effect of the film: "It makes you laugh and moves you to hot tears unashamed. It makes you love and hate. It makes you forget decorum and forces a cry into your throat. It thrills you with horror and moves you to marvel at vast spectacles. It makes you actually live through the greatest period of suffering and trial that this country has ever known."[2]

The film that moved Atlantans so was not *Gone with the Wind*. Rather, it was *The Birth of a Nation*, which was brought to Georgia in early December 1915 for a run at the Atlanta Theater. The film depicts blacks seizing power

84

in the South during Reconstruction through inappropriate means, leading to social chaos. Eventually, a white hero organizes the Ku Klux Klan, which an intertitle in the film identifies as "the organization that saved the South from the anarchy of black rule."[3] After the hero's younger sister leaps to her death to avoid being accosted by an ex-slave, the offender is killed by Klan members, and, ultimately, social order is restored. Thus one of the central thrusts of the film is the need for protection of white women from black men.[4] This theme resonated in a powerful way with the Atlantans watching *The Birth of a Nation*, who were "deeply enmeshed in a culture of lynchings, Jim Crow segregation, and widespread antiblack sentiment."[5] Ward Greene, a feature writer for the *Atlanta Journal*, reflected the emotions that the film produced in Atlanta audiences: "The land of the lost cause lies like a ragged wound under a black poison that pours out upon it. Loathing, disgust, hate envelope you, hot blood cries for vengeance. Until out of the night blazes the fiery cross that once burned high above old Scotland's hills and the legions of the Invisible Empire [i.e., the Klan] roar down to rescue." Greene added that viewers of the film had "a deeper and purer understanding of the fires through which your forefathers battled to make this south of yours a nation reborn." He wrote: "That's why they sold standing room only Monday night and why every matinee at 2:30 and every night performance at 8:30 this week will be packed."[6]

At the time when Atlantans were flocking to see *The Birth of a Nation*, Georgians were in the midst of two very significant social trends with important religious repercussions. First, as already mentioned, lynchings were a part of the cultural landscape. Between 1882 and 1930 Georgia followed only Mississippi in the number of lynchings per state, with 458 total victims.[7] Of these victims, some 95 percent were blacks, who were killed in virtually all cases by white mobs.[8] A few months before *The Birth of a Nation* came to Atlanta, however, the most notorious lynching in Georgia's history occurred some twenty miles away in Marietta, where vigilantes hung a Jewish man, Leo Frank, who had been accused of murdering a young Christian girl.[9] The first Ku Klux Klan was dissolved in the 1870s by federal action, but, as will be discussed below, the circumstances surrounding the Frank lynching helped lead to the revival of the Klan just outside Atlanta a few weeks before *The Birth of a Nation* was shown in the city.[10] The Leo Frank case also left an impact on state politics, with Frank's prosecutor, Hugh Dorsey, elected governor in 1916. Dorsey was a Methodist, as were the two preceding governors. It is striking, then, that following Dorsey no fewer than twelve of the next fifteen governors of Georgia were Baptists. This fact signals a second important trend, which is that during the first part of the twentieth century the Baptist denomination was in the process of coming strongly to the forefront in Georgia. In the following pages, we will examine the circumstances that accompanied the rise of the Baptists, as well as the spread, and eventual demise, of lynching.

In 1850 the Baptist and Methodist denominations each had roughly seventy thousand members in Georgia; together they constituted approximately 15 percent of the total state population.[11] Over the next one hundred years Baptists surpassed Methodists by a wide margin and clearly came to dominate religion in the state, accounting for some 35 percent of the state population by 1950.[12] How did this transpire? To begin to address this question, it will be helpful to focus first not on the Baptists, but rather on the Methodists. Observing why Methodist growth was hampered will point to why the Baptists were more successful in Georgia.

At the close of the nineteenth century, the vast majority of Baptists in Georgia lived in rural settings, while Presbyterians lived almost exclusively in cities. Methodists had significant numbers in both environments, but they would suffer from their own success during the 1880s and 1890s as they fractured into subgroups along two main ideological lines. Generally speaking, modernizers were primarily located in cities and traditionalists in rural locations. In his study of nineteenth-century Methodism in Georgia, Christopher H. Owen devotes a great deal of attention to these issues and points out that Georgia's Methodists experienced more conflicts between rural traditionalists and urban progressives than did the state's other denominations. The result was that by the 1890s Methodists had begun to experience significant internal tensions, leading to overall decline.[13]

Immediately following the Civil War, modernizing tendencies among Methodists in Georgia were curtailed due to the continuing influence of strong antebellum Methodist leaders. One such figure was George Foster Pierce, who gained distinction on his own but was also the son of the influential Lovick Pierce. The younger Pierce served in various capacities as a pastor and college administrator, including a six-year stint as president of Emory College, at the end of which he was elected a bishop.[14] One indication of Pierce's traditionalism was that in the 1870s he strenuously opposed the creation of Vanderbilt University and its school of theology. His opposition was not due to concern that Emory would have competition from Vanderbilt;

rather, it was that he feared an overemphasis on education might threaten the essentials of piety. Pierce stated that "the power of the pulpit is not in metaphysics, or logic, or literature, but in love, faith, self-denial, zeal."[15]

By the early 1880s, George Foster Pierce, then in his seventies, became weakened by illness, and his capacity to lead diminished. Several other antebellum Methodist leaders were already dead, including Pierce's father, as well as James O. Andrew and Augustus Baldwin Longstreet. As a result, new progressive Methodist voices were increasingly heard.[16] Atticus Haygood, who had also been a president of Emory College, was particularly prominent.[17] A proponent of the New South vision articulated by his friend Henry Grady, Haygood advocated that Southerners stop romanticizing the past and instead welcome the industrial and scientific future. In a sermon delivered on Thanksgiving Day in 1880, Haygood startled many in attendance by expressing gratitude that the defeat of the Confederacy had brought an end to slavery, with the result that the South's new commercial enterprises could flourish in a way that would not have been possible in the antebellum environment.[18]

Haygood also explicitly called for better race relations. In that vein, he published a book in 1881 titled *Our Brother in Black*, in which he called for racial tolerance. Haygood boldly asked Southern whites to admit that their lives were "inextricably mixed" with those of blacks: "These two races in the South . . . cannot get away from each other. What might have been if history had been different; what we would choose if things were not as they are— these speculations are idle. . . . If we of the South cannot get on with the negro; if the negro cannot get on with us; then we two peoples cannot get on at all. For we are here, both of us, and here to stay. But get on we must, somehow and at some speed."[19] When Haygood was elected a bishop in the MECS in 1882, he declined the position in order to help manage financial resources that were being distributed through a fund established by John F. Slater, a Connecticut Congregationalist, to channel Northern money into Southern schools for blacks.[20]

Warren Akin Candler, who served as president of Emory College after Haygood, may also be considered a modernizer, though in a less thoroughgoing way. Like many others, Candler disagreed with the reunification of the Northern and Southern Methodist churches (which eventually occurred in 1939). In contrast to George Foster Pierce, however, Candler greatly supported Vanderbilt University and served on its board of trustees. After the trustees lost their influence over Vanderbilt, they created two new Methodist schools they could control. The resulting institutions were Southern Methodist University in Dallas, Texas, and a transformed Emory University, which was moved from its former location in Oxford, Georgia, to Atlanta. (Candler convinced his brother, Asa, founder of the Coca-Cola company, to contribute $1 million to fund the expense of moving and developing the school.)[21]

Traditionalist Methodists fought back against what they considered to be wrong-headed modernist thinking. One of the strongest advocates of rural "old-time religion" was Rebecca Latimer Felton, who was born in DeKalb County but moved to Bartow County when she married William H. Felton and the couple took up residence on his farm.[22] Today Felton is best remembered for having served a twenty-four-hour "term" as the first woman in the U.S. Senate, resulting from a special appointment when one of Georgia's senators died in 1922. But Felton was also well known in her day as a defender of simple, rural "Old Methodist" values, which she expressed for more than two decades as a columnist for the *Atlanta Journal*. Felton's traditionalism can be gathered from her insistence that Methodist progressives were "looking after the shell, without examining into the kernel."[23] Her biographer, John E. Talmadge, notes that after she joined the Methodist Church as a young girl, Felton never questioned its basic doctrines and "stood as firmly for the religion of rural Georgia as she did for its racial feeling." It is not surprising, then, that when a friend invited her to hear a lecture given by Robert Ingersoll, a well-known orator and defender of agnosticism, she refused and stated that her faith was "too precious to take any chances with it."[24]

Sam Jones of Cartersville, who became the South's most famous evangelist and preacher in the late nineteenth century, was also a strong proponent of rural religiosity, and he railed in particular about his Methodist denomination becoming, in his mind, preoccupied with education: "We have been clamouring for fifty years for an educated ministry and we have got it to-day, and the church is deader than it ever has been in its history." With a characteristic mix of humor and crudity, he added: "Half of the literary preachers in this town are A.B.'s, Ph.D.'s, D.D.'s, LL.D.'s, and A.S.S.'s."[25] Jones was dismissive of religious doctrine and instead delivered a simple message about living a sin-free life, which he summarized with the slogan, "Quit Your Meanness."[26]

One of Jones's particular interests was prohibition, which he firmly believed would alleviate society's ills. Partly due to pressure from evangelicals such as Jones, Georgia enacted local option in 1883, followed by statewide prohibition in 1907.[27] By the 1880s most Georgia Methodists supported prohibition, but even in this regard there was some degree of internal conflict. When Populists advocated prohibition in 1896, political squabbles led to disagreements about the relative importance of prohibition versus other concerns. During the Populist heyday, several longtime Methodist leaders who did not support the Populists, such as the Democrat Clement A. Evans, were criticized for helping the "whiskey side." The issue of women's suffrage added to the storm. Warren Akin Candler, for instance, asserted that he would rather see "a saloon on every other fence corner with bawdy houses between" than endorse women's suffrage. Accordingly, he strongly recommended that Georgia women avoid the national Women's Christian Temperance Union, which supported women's suffrage, leading to a sharp drop in the state membership.[28]

While there was some degree of moderate and traditionalist wrangling among black Methodists in late nineteenth-century Georgia, the issues were not as well-defined as among whites, and the ideological infighting was not as acute.[29] The Holiness Movement, however, became a shared concern for many black and white Methodists, whether traditionalist or modernist. Holiness advocates in the time between the Civil War and the 1890s were largely, though not exclusively, associated with Methodism and endeavored to propagate their understanding of John Wesley's teachings regarding sanctification and Christian perfection. Holiness preachers held that the process of salvation involves both absolution of sins one has committed as well as liberation from the flaw in human nature that causes sin.[30] In time, conflicts over Holiness led to attempts by Methodist leaders to demean and purge various church members.[31]

The ultimate result of all the bitter infighting among various Methodist groups was a decline in membership.[32] Baptists, who could remain relatively free from denominational interference in their autonomous local churches, were prepared to take advantage of the opening and surged ahead. The trend could be detected as early as 1890, by which time the Baptists were the majority faith in Georgia.[33] By the turn of the century the Baptist advantage was increasing even more dramatically, such that there were far more Baptists in Georgia than members of all other denominations combined. In 1906 the U.S. Bureau of the Census collected information from religious organizations through the Census of Religious Bodies. The denominational data for Georgia indicated that Baptists had 596,319 congregants and Methodists had 349,079. Far behind them were Presbyterians, with 24,040 congregants; Roman Catholics, with 19,273; Christian (Disciples), with 13,749; and Episcopalians, with

9,790. All other groups, including Jews, tallied 16,787 collectively. These figures indicate that in 1906 Baptists outnumbered all other religious groups
combined in Georgia by more than 160,000.[34]

Georgia Baptists were able to flourish for a few very powerful reasons.
First, following the Civil War, Southern Baptists, to a greater extent than the
members of any other denomination, tended to stay out of political squabbles
and instead kept their focus on evangelism and missions. As such, they were
a powerful conservative force helping to maintain the social status quo in the
South; unlike the Methodists, moreover, they tended to avoid internal fights.
One political area they did venture into was prohibition, but no charges of
support for the "whiskey side" were to be heard among Baptists, since they
condemned the use of alcohol with virtually one voice.[35] Additional social
issues that Baptists thought represented immorality, such as gambling, were
denounced with similar unanimity. As J. Wayne Flynt has observed, Southern Baptists considered the South's defeat in the Civil War to be due to the
region's moral failings; thus they were intent on ridding the South of every
form of wickedness, creating, in the process, "a version of American civil religion, baptizing the 'lost cause' in the blood of the lamb."[36]

We have seen already that Baptists also profited from having plenty of
clergy members. Since Baptists did not demand that their ministers receive
much education, formal ordination through a seminary, or high pay, there
were few institutional barriers to becoming a Baptist minister. It is notable
that in the initial decades of the twentieth century there were still a great
many farmer-preachers among Southern Baptists. Indeed, 36 percent of the
active Southern Baptist pastors reporting their salaries in the 1916 census had
full-time secular occupations, and the vast majority of them were farmers.
By contrast, 98 percent of active clergy in the Methodist Episcopal Church,
South, earned their living from their ministerial salaries alone. Roger Finke
and Rodney Stark have observed that these trends help to explain "why
the Southern Baptists had a ratio of one minister for every 1.5 churches . . .
whereas the Methodist Episcopal Church, South, could supply only 1 minister for every 3 churches."[37]

Black Baptists in Georgia benefited from many of the same strengths as
whites, especially the local autonomy of Baptist churches. When we consider
Methodist and Baptist growth along racial lines, it is clear that blacks were
embracing the Baptist denomination far more readily than Methodism. In
1906, for example, there were by large margins more black Baptists in Georgia

than white Baptists, more white Baptists than white Methodists, and more white Methodists than black Methodists: 342,154 black Baptists; 254,165 white Baptists; 190,977 white Methodists; and 158,102 black Methodists.[38]

Thus, during the early part of the twentieth century the Baptist denomination was becoming entrenched in Georgia. It is important to recognize as well that Georgia's Baptists had, as a result of their history, become leading forces in both the National Baptist Convention (NBC) and the Southern Baptist Convention (SBC). As discussed in chapter 5, the NBC was founded in Atlanta in 1895. When members of several different black Baptist groups representing missions and education interests met at the Friendship Baptist Church to form the National Baptist Convention of the United States of America, it set the stage for much of the later development of the civil rights movement.

Unlike the NBC, which was not expressly a Southern institution, the SBC was a regional body during most of the twentieth century.[39] Walter B. Shurden has noted that Georgians played a prominent role in the development of the SBC, both in its formation in Augusta in 1845 and in its growth under the leadership of the Home Mission Board, which was based in Atlanta after 1882. Thus he refers to "the Georgia Tradition" as being among a handful of influences that gave the SBC its cultural identity. Shurden observes that "the Georgia Tradition colored the Southern Baptist Convention with an intense sectionalism," such that "Baptists *of* the South became *Southern* Baptists, a people who for years to come would defend the southern way of life."[40] Since that way of life included well-established notions of white superiority and racial segregation, it would not begin to change until the dramatic civil rights court cases and legislation of the 1950s and 1960s.

Throughout the first half of the twentieth century, while the major focus of Georgia Baptists was on evangelism and they tended to stay out of politics, a few social issues did receive some attention from them. The most pressing social matter confronting Baptists, as well as other denominations, was lynching, which drew negative national and even international attention. It is clear that lynching was, to some degree, part of the legacy of the racial separation of Christian denominations following the Civil War. Since blacks and whites no longer worshipped together and lived in a strictly segregated society, whites developed powerful negative images of blacks. John B. Boles observes that "other factors besides religion were involved in this tragic development, but the absence of a shared religious experience surely contributed to . . . the white image of the black as beast. The huge increase in the number of lynchings of blacks was but one indication of this sad turn in racial relations."[41] Rebecca Latimer Felton no doubt spoke for a host of her fellow white Georgians when she stated that in order to dissuade black rapists she was in favor of lynching such "ravening beasts a thousand times a week if necessary."[42]

White racial contempt for presumed black "beasts" can clearly be seen in the lynching of Sam Hose in Newnan, Georgia, in 1899. On April 12 of that year in the small town of Palmetto, southwest of Atlanta, Hose, a black farmhand, accidentally killed his white employer, Alfred Cranford, following an argument over a wage dispute. In actuality, Hose then fled the scene, but rumors spread that he had entered the Crawford house and had thrown the family's baby to the floor before dragging Crawford's wife, Mattie, to another room where he raped her repeatedly. Georgia Governor Allen D. Candler, a proponent of lynching, described the alleged episode as being "the most diabolical in the annals of crime." The day after the incident, the *Atlanta Constitution*'s front-page headline read: "Determined Mob After Hose; He Will Be Lynched if Caught."[43]

Indeed, after he was found, Hose was lynched at Newnan on April 23, a Sunday, in front of a crowd of approximately two thousand onlookers, many of whom had come from Atlanta by train to observe the event. The violence against Hose was unspeakable. He was chained naked to a tree and mutilated by having his ears, fingers, and genitals cut off, and his face was skinned. Wood was stacked around him, kerosene was poured over him, and he was burned alive. As the flames rose, Hose's body contorted and his eyes bulged out of their sockets. Before Hose's body was cool, it was cut up for mementoes. His bones were crushed into particles, and his heart and liver were cut into small pieces. A slice of his heart was apparently taken by one participant to the governor.[44] Shortly after Hose's lynching, Ida B. Wells-Barnett, who read about it in newspapers in Chicago, published a pamphlet titled "Lynch Law in Georgia," in which she noted that the Hose lynching was the twelfth in a six-week span in the state during March and April of 1899.[45]

Andrew Sledd, a Methodist minister who was then a professor of Latin at Emory College, also felt compelled to write and publish about the Hose lynching. While Wells-Barnett read about the Hose lynching after it happened, Sledd actually stumbled across the lynching itself. He was traveling by train from Atlanta to his home in Covington when the conductor stopped to give passengers a view of Hose's lynching, which Sledd found sickening. In response, he wrote an article, eventually published in the July 1902 edition of the *Atlantic Monthly*, titled "The Negro: Another View." In this article, Sledd advocated a new approach to "the negro problem," one that both Northerners and Southerners could embrace. He maintained that people in each section of the country would have to acknowledge "a certain set of underlying facts." Northerners needed to accept that *"the negro belongs to an inferior race,"* but Southerners would have to recognize that *"the negro has inalienable rights."* According to Sledd, the North had "erred in approaching the negro question with the assertion of the equality of the races," when amalgamation of the races should be "coarse and repugnant" to whites in either section of the country. But Sledd had harsh words for Southerners as well. He asserted that "the South has, much more grievously, erred in precisely the opposite direction." Indeed, Sledd stated that "our section has carried the idea of the negro's inferiority almost, if not quite, to the point of dehumanizing him." For Sledd, lynching was the worst example of this dehumanization, and he bitterly noted that in the 1890s, "the last decade of the last century of Christian grace and civilization, more men met their death by violence at the hands of lynchers than were executed by due process of law."[46]

Sledd's article greatly angered his fellow white Georgians. There were various outcries and written threats, and on at least one occasion he was burned in effigy. Eventually, the president of Emory, James Dickey, approached Sledd and demanded his resignation. After talking it over with his wife, Sledd agreed to step down, thinking, as he later wrote in his autobiography, that "the best thing for the college and the best thing for me was that I should quietly tender my resignation."[47]

It is important to underscore that even though Sledd was considered an extremist by many whites, since he dared to suggest that blacks had rights as human beings, he himself could not contemplate racial equality, insisting that "the negro is lower in the scale of development than the white man. His inferiority is radical and inherent."[48] Conversely, many black religious leaders in the South were preparing the ground for a fundamental change in regard to egalitarianism. As we have already seen, Colored Methodist Episcopal Bishop Lucius Holsey's sermon on "The Fatherhood of God and the Brotherhood of Man," which was published the year before the Hose lynching, reflects the monistic thrust of black theology by fusing theological and social concerns. We may observe now that it also represents a vision of equality. In his study of the preaching of black ministers in the generation following the Civil War, Edward L. Wheeler emphasizes that Holsey was representative of the prevailing views among the leading black clergy at the time. Noting Holsey's use of Acts 17:26 in his sermon, Wheeler comments: "Holsey and the black clerical elite argued that because 'God had made of one blood all nations of men for to dwell on all the face of the earth' . . . the full humanity and value of black people had been divinely affirmed."[49]

Visualizing humans as fellow children of God may seem a familiar and unremarkable concept now, but it was a radical notion to assert in the South in the decades following the Civil War. Such language was used in the North by Unitarians and other liberals, but it could be grating to Southern ears, and the vocabulary of equality was not customary in Southern white churches. Thus we may note a stark difference between Southern white and black theological visions at this stage: whites tended to focus solely on individual conversion, while blacks, who were no less interested in evangelism, also emphasized universalism and "uplift." As Holsey himself put it: "Every man is made by the same hand. . . . Neither can racial distinctions, color, climatic or geographical situation of birth and growth make any difference in the characteristics of his real manhood. This proves the unity of the race of man. . . . What, therefore, is possible for one man is possible for all men under the same conditions and circumstances." Consequently, Holsey and his fellow black ministers believed that if blacks were given the same opportunities as whites, "they could achieve the same results; they could be uplifted."[50]

Wheeler remarks that their preoccupation with uplift gave the theology of the black ministerial elite in the South an eclectic quality. On the one hand, together with Southern white clergy, "they retained the doctrines and images of an older evangelical tradition; they preached of heaven and hell, the blood of Jesus, the atonement on the cross, and the need for repentance and salvation." But they also drew upon the idioms of Northern abolitionist clergy and theologians to assert that common humanity is the logical result of God's fatherhood. This combination of different theological patterns suggests that Southern black clergy "used the rhetoric of other traditions for their own purposes and integrated it with the older rhetoric in their own way."[51] Samuel S. Hill Jr. concludes that the black theology crafted in the late nineteenth and early twentieth centuries represents "one of the epochal theological achievements in American Christian history."[52]

That whites in Georgia were not ready for the black vision of racial equality can be seen by the fact that in 1906, less than a decade after the lynching of Sam Hose, Atlanta experienced a widespread outbreak of racially motivated violence. What is now known as the Atlanta Race Riot occurred in the same year as a gubernatorial campaign during which the landslide victor, Hoke Smith, consistently race-baited, advocated white supremacy, and called for the disfranchisement of black voters.[53] The campaign, and the media coverage it spawned, helped feed white fear and hatred of blacks. Beginning on the afternoon of Saturday, September 22, a large mob of thousands of white men and boys in Atlanta went out in search of some blacks who, according to spurious newspaper reports, had attempted to assault white women. The mob ended up attacking hundreds of blacks.[54]

Informing such episodes of racial violence was the fact that Southern white culture considered white females to be pure and godly; thus, ungodly "black devils" had to be kept away from white women and girls in order to protect them and maintain their untainted status. In line with these views, lynchings constituted, in some measure, religious acts. It is worth noting in this regard that lynchings were sometimes attended by quasi-religious emotions. One reporter, for example, described the observers of the Sam Hose lynching as having watched "with unfeigning satisfaction."[55] Similarly, reporter O. B. Keeler of the *Georgian* used extensive religious language to describe another lynching: "In a terrible way it was like some religious rite. Watching the curiously reverent manner of those people, a manner of thankfulness and of grave satisfaction, it was borne in with tremendous force what the feeling must be on those Cobb County men and women toward the man. . . . 'I couldn't bear to look at another human being, hanging like that,' said one woman. 'But this—this is different. It is all right. It is—the justice of God.'"[56]

Donald Mathews ties lynching to segregation, which he asserts was a religious system common to Southern whites following the Civil War, who thought it had been established by God: "Segregation became consensual among whites. It was right; the order of the universe confirmed it. It was sacred in that it placed certain issues beyond dispute; it approached holiness because it established boundaries that demanded individuals 'conform to the class to which they belong. . . . Holiness means keeping distinct the categories of creation.'" Thus, segregation was marked by a system of boundaries and taboos separating white purity from black impurity.[57] It follows that when the boundaries were crossed (or were thought to have been crossed), as by the putative rape of a white female by a black man, it upset the social and religious order, which then needed to be restored.

Of course, setting white women on a pedestal also limited and circumscribed sexual contact between white men and women, and many writers and scholars have described how this matter informed race relations. Joel R.

Williamson has suggested that "the black beast rapist was the only man on earth who had sex with Southern white women without inhibition, to the exhaustion of desire. . . . Thus black men were lynched for having achieved, seemingly, a sexual liberation that white men wanted but could not achieve without great feelings of guilt. In their frustration white men projected their own worst thoughts upon black men, imagined them acted out in some specific incident, and symbolically killed those thoughts by lynching a hapless black man."[58] It is revealing that, following the lynching of Sam Hose, a placard on a tree near the smoldering ashes of all that remained of him read: "We Must Protect Our Southern Women."[59]

Church membership in the South expanded during the heyday of lynchings and other forms of violence against blacks. Thus, an increase in religiosity and collective violence occurred at the same time. It is notable that at the heart of white Southern Christian notions of atonement was the cleansing blood of Jesus's death, with sin, punishment, and sacrifice as ever-present themes.[60] Certainly, one can find numerous examples of these notions in the common hymns sung by white Southern Christians, such as the venerable "Just As I Am": "Just as I am, without one plea, But that Thy blood was shed for me. . . . To Thee whose blood can cleanse each spot, O Lamb of God, I come, I come."[61] Lillian Smith, about whom more will be said below, grew up in rural Florida and Georgia during the first decades of the twentieth century and described one of the essential childhood lessons she learned as follows: "Belief in Some One's right to punish you is the fate of all children in Judaic-Christian culture."[62]

To be sure, several Christian denominational leaders did issue statements opposing mob violence. In 1906 the Southern Baptist Convention declared that "lynching blunts the public conscience, undermines the foundations on which society stands, and if unchecked will result in anarchy." Yet, at the same time, the Convention indicated it assumed those who were lynched were guilty of raping white women when it affirmed that "our condemnation is due with equal emphasis, and in many cases with even greater emphasis, against the horrible crimes which cause the lynchings."[63]

Even Christians who disapproved of lynching made an important exception in regard to Leo Frank, a Jew. On April 26, 1913, Confederate Memorial Day, a thirteen-year-old white girl named Mary Phagan went to collect her paycheck at the National Pencil Factory in Atlanta, where she worked (child labor was not unusual or illegal in those days). Her corpse was found in the basement of the factory early the following morning by a black night watchman. Soon thereafter, Frank, who was raised in New York but had moved to Atlanta to run the pencil factory, was accused of the murder and arrested. A sensationalized trial followed, with public sentiment aroused by a vigorous antisemitic and anti-Northern press, and Frank was convicted and sentenced to death.[64]

In June 1915, just before his term of office ended, Governor John Slaton commuted Frank's death sentence to life imprisonment, following his own exhaustive review of the evidence. Although he had come to the conclusion that Frank had not committed the murder, Slaton issued a commutation, rather than freeing Frank, because he assumed that Frank's innocence would become recognized and he would be freed via the legal system.[65] Slaton, an attorney, issued a lengthy commentary to accompany his decision, but his position can be easily ascertained by one of his statements at a press conference following the issuance of the commutation: "I would be a murderer if I allowed that man to hang."[66] Predictably, public anger turned on Slaton, who was forced to call on National Guard troops for protection, and eventually he and his wife fled the state. Over time, Slaton's decision has been vindicated. Frank was convicted largely on the testimony of the pencil factory's black janitor, Jim Conley. In 1982 an elderly, dying black man named Alonzo Mann stated that he had been an office boy at the factory in 1913 and had observed Conley dragging Mary Phagan's body. Mann asserted that Conley had threatened him not to tell what he had seen, or Conley would kill him. Based upon this statement and other evidence, it is generally agreed by scholars today that Conley was most likely the murderer of Mary Phagan.[67] In 1986 the Georgia Board of Pardons and Paroles granted Leo Frank a posthumous pardon.[68]

Shortly after Slaton issued his commutation of Frank's death sentence, a group of men who had dubbed themselves the Knights of Mary Phagan decided to take the execution of Frank into their own hands. On August 16, 1915, they arrived at the prison in Milledgeville where Frank was being held and seized him. The men then drove with Frank to Marietta, Mary Phagan's birthplace, northwest of Atlanta. They reached Marietta early in the morning of August 17 and lynched Frank in a grove of trees at Frey's Gin (mill), close to the present-day Cobb County restaurant and landmark, the Big Chicken. Word spread and during the day crowds streamed out to view Frank's hanged body.[69] Photographs were taken at the scene, and for years thereafter souvenir pictures circulated of the lynching. Notably, at the time of Frank's murder, while the *Atlanta Constitution* referred to the act as "Georgia's Shame!" the editor of the Georgia Baptist organ, the *Christian Index*, observed that an "orderly mob" had to "administer the justice which the courts should have administered."[70]

Frank's lynchers had been stirred up in large measure by the unrelenting rhetoric of Tom Watson, a very influential politician and publisher. Watson was elected by Georgians to the state General Assembly in 1882 and the U.S. House of Representatives in 1890, and he was the national Populist candidate for vice president in 1896.[71] During the days following Slaton's decision, Watson issued numerous editorials in the magazines he published that simplistically cast the Frank case as Jews against Christians, Northerners against Southerners. Watson inflamed the already tense situation and called for vigilante justice.[72]

Writing in *Watson's Magazine* just after the commutation of Frank's sentence, Watson concluded a long article titled "The Celebrated Case of the State of Georgia vs. Leo Frank" with the following words:

> Leo Frank is now at the State Farm, an honored guest. . . . His little victim, whose upraised hands—fixed by the *rigor mortis*—proved that she had died fighting for her virtue, lies in Georgia's soil, amid a grief-stricken, and mortified people—a people bowed down by the unutterable humiliation of having been sold out to Jew money. . . . When John M. Slaton tosses on a sleepless bed, in the years to come, he will see a vivid picture of that little Georgia girl [attacked] by this satyr-faced Jew: he will see her little hands put out, to keep off the lustful beast. . . . Are the old lessons lifeless? Are the old glories gone? Are there no feet that tread the old paths? Once, there were *men* in Georgia—men who were afraid of nothing, save to do wrong. . . . The sons of these men carried the Grey lines, and the tattered Stars and Bars farthest up the heights of Gettysburg; met the first shock of battle at Manassas; led the last charge at Appomattox. And the sons of these Georgians are today bowed down with unspeakable grief—for they feel that *our grand old Empire State HAS BEEN RAPED!* . . . *We have been violated, AND WE ARE ASHAMED!*[73]

Lest anyone miss his message, Watson wrote in another of his publications, the *Jeffersonian*: "Let the rich Jews beware! *THE NEXT JEW WHO DOES WHAT FRANK DID IS GOING TO GET EXACTLY THE SAME THING THAT WE GIVE TO NEGRO RAPISTS!*"[74] Watson issued these words on August 12, 1915. Leo Frank was dead five days later.[75]

The antisemitism that surrounded the Leo Frank case profoundly affected Georgia's Jews. Indeed, some scholars claim that more than one thousand Jews left the state in the wake of the lynching.[76] Of those Jews who remained, Melissa Fay Greene writes that "the most awful and lasting legacy of Frank's murder . . . was the sense of isolation: they were marginal, they were dispensable, they were still 'the other'. . . . Upper-crust white Christian Atlanta had looked the other way when mobs and demagogues went after the Jews. It was a civics lesson not easily forgotten."[77]

Another lasting impact of the Frank case was that it helped lead to the reemergence of the Ku Klux Klan. Shortly following Frank's lynching, William J. Simmons, a former Methodist minister, became interested in reviving the then defunct Ku Klux Klan. Leonard Dinnerstein observes: "Had it not been for [the lynching of] Leo Frank, Simmons would probably have had to wait before launching his venture. But he found in the Knights of Mary Phagan, already organized but with its sense of purpose vanished, a suitable nucleus for the new Klan."[78]

On the evening of Thanksgiving in 1915, a group that included Simmons and some members of the Knights of Mary Phagan stood atop Stone Mountain, the future site of the Confederate memorial carving, and officially ushered in the second Klan by burning a cross and reading aloud from the Bible.[79] A few days later, the *Georgian* quoted an attendee who described the scene: "The ceremony began around an altar made of stones contributed by each klansman. On this altar was erected a fiery cross in the halo of whose light the men, with uncovered heads, assumed the oath of the klan, and upon bended knees were dedicated with pure water to the service of country, homes and humanity."[80]

This new version of the Klan, essentially "a social club for [Protestant] white supremacists," was to direct its energies against not only blacks but also other groups that the members found objectionable and un-American, including immigrants, Jews, and Catholics.[81] The second Klan received a Georgia state charter very shortly after its founding, and within a few years it claimed between three and six million members nationwide. The national headquarters of the Ku Klux Klan was located on Peachtree Road in Atlanta.[82]

Following the rise of the second Klan, efforts to prevent lynchings became a key focus of some Christian leaders in Georgia. Among the most important organizations were the Commission on Interracial Cooperation (cic) and its offshoot, the Association of Southern Women for the Prevention of Lynching (aswpl). The cic, which was established in Atlanta in 1919 and remained based in the city until the 1940s, grew in part out of an interracial group known as the Atlanta Christian Council. This group was composed of both white and black ministers who sought to ease racial friction. Among those who would go on to prominence in the CIC was Will W. Alexander, a Methodist, who became the organization's director.[83]

Individual and collective religiosity influenced the activities of the CIC to a great extent. In particular, Alexander's motivation to work for better race relations derived from his own religious beliefs. He stated that no white Christian should accept overt discrimination against "the colored brother in our midst." Thus, under Alexander's guidance, an early CIC declaration of principle only a few hundred words in length used the terms "Christ" or "Christian" ten times, and one of the CIC's conferences asserted as a "profound conviction" that "the real responsibility for the solution of interracial problems in the South rests directly upon the hearts and consciences of the Christian forces of our land."[84]

At its inception, the national CIC included only white men, but several black men were invited to join in February 1920.[85] It took longer for women to be welcome in the CIC, even though church women had been working to better race relations for some time. In spite of the contributions they had already made, there was opposition within the CIC to inviting women to join. Alexander favored their inclusion, but the idea was not embraced by many CIC members. Undaunted, Alexander pressed on and at a white Methodist Women's Missionary Council (WMC) meeting in Kansas City, Missouri, in April 1920 he urged the women to align their efforts with those of men. As a result, a female Commission on Race Relationships was established, and Carrie Parks Johnson of Griffin, Georgia, served as its initial leader. The group floundered initially, however, discovering that they did not know how to reach out to "the best of the Negro race" since they knew only the "cook in the kitchen" and the "maid in the house." Alexander assisted by helping the group connect with Lugenia Burns Hope, a black woman in Atlanta whose husband, John, was president of Morehouse College.[86]

Hope, believing that the time was at hand for cooperation between white and black women, invited Johnson and another leader of the WMC to attend a conference of the National Association of Colored Women held in July 1920 at Tuskegee Institute in Alabama. The white women were initially dismayed when they were not treated with the deference to which they were accustomed. In turn, several of the black women were suspicious that the white women sought only to obtain help in finding good domestic servants. The mutual distrust was overcome as the women fell back on their common religious bond. Johnson later reflected: "The discussion, which was most painful at times, was held in a frankness which could have come in no way save in the course of the constraining love of Christ." Hope told the white visitors that "we can achieve nothing . . . unless you . . . are willing to help us find a place in American life where we can be unashamed and unafraid." In response, Johnson asked the group for a platform statement, which she presented at a conference in October 1920 in Memphis, Tennessee, for white women who were leaders in Southern Christian agencies. These women were receptive to the statement and called for an array of improvements in domestic conditions, educational facilities, and the judicial system. The women also pledged to foster public sentiment to assist law enforcement officers in preventing lynchings. As a result, efforts to combat lynching became a common rallying point of the state-level women's groups associated with the CIC. In 1930, the ASWPL was created with funding from the CIC and went on to attack lynching in various ways. These organizations did much to affect the public acceptance of lynching, and they deserve a great deal of credit for the decline in the number of lynchings in the South during the 1930s.[87]

To a limited degree, antilynching efforts such as those of the CIC and the ASWPL represent an expression of social conscience in the South, and certainly some Christians can be singled out for their laudable contributions. Yet, since their main concern was with the conversion of individuals, overall the Southern white evangelical churches retreated from society at large. As such, they failed to address social ills in a rigorous way, as John B. Boles notes: "No significant Social Gospel movement emerged to critique the institutions of society that produced poverty and injustice. The white churches sanctified the memory of the Lost Cause, called for personal conversion, and mostly ignored the very real problems of society. . . . Few were challenged to address the societal ills that afflicted the region and its people. That was the central tragedy of southern white Protestantism in the century after the Civil War."[88] It is in keeping with the general white evangelical posture, then, that in 1905 the Southern Baptist Convention announced: "It is no affair of this Convention to solve the so-called negro problem."[89] Even the CIC and ASWPL did not attack segregation itself, which would have been considered too radical a goal given the nearly universal acceptance among Southern whites of the necessity of racial separation.[90]

That white supremacy and black inferiority had become foundational beliefs for white Southerners can be seen in a set of racial concepts published in 1914 by Thomas P. Bailey. Bailey, who had served in educational positions from California and New York to Tennessee and Mississippi, detected a clear "racial creed" among whites in the South: "The race attitude of the Southern whites is not a code of cases but a creed of a people,—a part of their morality and of their religion." Bailey provided a list of fifteen elements of this creed, including: "the white race must dominate"; "the negro is inferior and will remain so"; "no social equality"; "only Southerners understand the negro question"; and "the status of peasantry is all the negro may hope for, if the races are to live together in peace."[91] The experience of Rev. Clinton Lee Scott, a native of Vermont, underscores the pervasiveness of such notions. Scott recalled that when he came to Atlanta in 1926 to serve the Unitarian-Universalist congregation, he discovered that "every institution, including all churches, was Jim Crow. There was an elaborate system of intercolor relations baffling to a Yankee. . . . I found all such superficial but deeply rooted formalities difficult to live with, and I never could explain them to my children."[92]

The "deeply rooted formalities" of the Southern way of life were eloquently described by the author Lillian Smith, who was born in Florida in 1897 but moved with her family in 1915 to Clayton, Georgia. In her autobiographical work, *Killers of the Dream*, Smith captured well the interconnected instructions concerning religion, race, and sex she had been taught in her youth. She wrote: "I do not remember how or when, but by the time I had learned that God is love, that Jesus is His Son and came to give us more abundant life . . . I also knew that I was better than a Negro, that all black folks have their place and must be kept in it [and] that sex has its place and must be kept in it." She added: "I had learned that God so loved the world that he gave His only begotten Son so that we might have segregated churches in which it was my duty to worship." In what has become perhaps her most well-known passage, Smith related: "From the day I was born, I began to learn my lessons. . . . I learned it is possible to be a Christian and a white southerner simultaneously; to be a gentlewoman and an arrogant callous creature in the same moment; to pray at night and ride a Jim Crow car the next morning and to feel comfortable in doing both. I learned to believe in freedom, to glow when the word *democracy* was used, and to practice slavery from morning to night." Smith wrote that she had learned her lessons "the way all of my southern people" did: "By closing door after door until one's mind and heart and conscience are blocked off from each other and from reality."[93]

Cracks in those doors would come but slowly. One mark of the Baptist triumph in Georgia was the fact that the Baptist World Alliance came to Atlanta in July 1939 for a weeklong convention. Historian James Adams Lester has recorded the excitement surrounding this occasion, referring to 1939 as a banner year for Georgia Baptists and noting that the *Christian Index* issued a 178-page special edition to honor the event.[94] Georgia Governor E. D. ("Ed") Rivers, himself a Baptist, welcomed the assembled leaders of his denomination to Atlanta. By this time Baptists were beginning to cement their leadership position in Georgia, from the state house to the local community level. That Georgians of all stripes had a long way to go in regard to racial issues is evidenced not only by the fact that Governor Rivers, like many other Georgia politicians, had once been active in the Ku Klux Klan, but also by the scene in Atlanta at the end of the year during the events associated with the premiere of the film version of *Gone with the Wind*.[95] On December 14, 1939, the evening before the premiere, the Junior Chamber of Commerce hosted a "Gone with the Wind Ball": "The guest list was truly remarkable, representing an eclectic group of Americans . . . as long as you were a Hollywood celebrity, a southern politician or wealthy. . . . Noticeably absent were Hattie McDaniel (Mammy) and Butterfly McQueen (Prissy), black actresses with major roles who were not welcome in the white side of the segregated Atlanta society." Notably present, however, through the lens of history, was a young man known as Mike King, who sang in a "negro boys choir" from his Atlanta church, Ebenezer Baptist, where his father served as pastor.[96] At the time of the premiere of *Gone with the Wind* European powers were at war, and the United States entered the conflict a short time later. Segregation would die a slow death following World War II, forcing racial and religious relations in Georgia to modulate.

CHAPTER SEVEN

Things Are Stirring

In the mid-1930s, a young black boy in Atlanta discovered the existence of a race problem in America. When he and a white friend he had known for three years entered the city's segregated school system, the friend's father would no longer let the two boys play together. "I never will forget what a great shock this was to me," he later recalled. He discussed the matter with his parents and they told him about some of their own negative racial experiences. He later recounted: "I was greatly shocked, and from that moment on I was determined to hate every white person." Although his parents told him he "should not hate"—that it was his "duty as a Christian to love"—he was not satisfied. "The question arose in my mind," he recollected, "how could I love a race of people [who] hated me and who had been responsible for breaking me up with one of my best childhood friends?" Shortly before this experience, the young black boy, who was named Michael at birth, was renamed Martin by his father. His attitudes toward the race problem and whites would eventually change as well, leading to his role as the foremost leader of the civil rights movement.[1]

In January 1971, three years after the assassination of Martin Luther King Jr., the newly elected Georgia governor, Jimmy Carter, surprised many members of the audience during his inaugural address by declaring that racial intolerance in the state should end. Reg Murphy, a columnist for the *Atlanta Constitution*, wrote the next day: "He said for everybody to hear that 'the time for racial discrimination is over.' Some of the crowd standing under the thin winter sun in Washington Street applauded, and others groaned."[2] Carter's words led to him being featured on the May 21, 1971, cover of *Time* magazine, accompanied by the heading, "Dixie Whistles a New Tune."[3]

Between the childhood of Martin Luther King Jr. and Jimmy Carter's gubernatorial inauguration lay tumultuous and momentous years. Speaking generally, during this time period there were three broad phases of the civil rights struggle in Georgia: an upsurge of protest in the 1940s, followed by white supremacist backlash in the 1950s, capped by the direct action protests of the 1960s.[3] The upsurge of the 1940s was linked to the impact of black soldiers returning from a war to defeat a racist ideology, who understandably looked at their own situation back home through new eyes. Black ministers took up the postwar call for civil rights. J. Pius Barbour, editor of the *National Baptist Voice*, a newsletter for black Baptist ministers, described a meeting in Pelham, Georgia, in 1948 by saying that "not only was there no compromise but rather an intensifying of the demands that Negroes would take no back ground in their fight for their rights." He added: "Things are stirring in the South and don't you forget it." In the same year, William Holmes Borders, president of the black Georgia Baptist Missionary and Educational Convention, declared that ministers would need to provide leadership: "The Negro preacher must take the lead in fighting for the civic rights of the Southern Negro and he must not flinch before the . . . Klan or any other race hating group. We must serve notice . . . that we will not be intimidated."[4]

One of the most important leaders of the quest for black civic rights was Ralph Mark Gilbert, pastor of First African Baptist Church in Savannah from 1939 to 1956. Gilbert, who had been educated at the University of Michigan, was very familiar with Northern activities of the National Association for the Advancement of Colored People (NAACP), and he reinvigorated the Savannah branch upon his arrival. He served as branch president from 1942 to 1950, during which time he also organized and became the first president of a Georgia state conference of the NAACP. When he came to Georgia the NAACP was nearly defunct in the state, but under Gilbert's leadership it thrived, with more than forty chapters by 1950.[5] While in some rural areas NAACP meetings had to be held in secret, in Savannah membership in the NAACP became a public badge of honor, with window stickers proudly announcing, "I am a member of the NAACP."[6] In addition to Gilbert's leadership in the NAACP, Charles J. Elmore highlights Gilbert's work in the Citizens Democratic Club in Savannah, through which he challenged the all-white Democratic primary by initiating a drive to register black voters. This effort led to the election of a white mayor and city council that were open to reforms.[7] Stephen G. N.

Tuck concludes that, in many ways, such as broad-based community involvement and a confrontational protest posture, "the Savannah movement of the early 1940s presaged the city movements that were to sweep the South during the 1960s."[8]

In stark contrast to postwar calls by blacks for equal rights, white supremacy was deeply rooted in and among Georgia's whites. This situation makes all the more remarkable the progressive stances taken by a few whites, such as the journalist Ralph McGill and the social activist Frances Pauley. Perhaps most noteworthy in their unflinching opposition to segregation were the author Lillian Smith and the Southern Baptist minister Clarence Jordan. Smith was among the earliest white Southerners to condemn segregation, which she felt had a harmful effect on both blacks and whites. As will be explained below, Jordan also considered segregation immoral and faced grave personal danger to actively oppose it.

Smith's upbringing in a family that, she later recalled, was "firmly triangulated on sin, sex, and segregation" was discussed in the preceding chapter.[9] In 1922, when she was twenty-five years old, Smith moved to China to become a music instructor at a Christian missionary school. She returned home in 1925 because her parents' health was declining, and she then took over the management of a girl's camp they had established near Clayton, Georgia.[10] In the ensuing years, Smith increasingly turned her attention to exposing and combating bigotry. Margaret Rose Gladney observes that Smith ended up challenging some fundamental assumptions of her culture: "That by divine decree whites are superior to blacks and males are superior to females, that a racially segregated political and economic power structure must be maintained at all cost, and that nothing about the system of segregation should be questioned." Gladney further notes that Smith's boldness cost her the critical attention that she deserved for her writings.[11] Even Ralph McGill, the editor and publisher of the *Atlanta Constitution*, who has been lionized for his moderate racial stance, decried Smith's gall. In a review of one of her books, McGill wrote: "Miss Smith is a prisoner in the monastery of her own mind. But rarely does she come out of its gates, and then, apparently, seeing only wicked things to send her back to her hair shirt and the pouring of ashes on her head and salt in her own psychiatric wounds."[12] Eugene Talmadge, who served multiple terms as governor of Georgia (he was elected four times between 1932 and 1946), was characteristically more blunt about Smith. He suggested that her writing was fit for use in Southern outhouses, referring to her novel *Strange Fruit*, which depicts an interracial relationship, as a "literary corncob."[13]

In 1942, two years before *Strange Fruit* appeared, Clarence Jordan founded a cooperative farming community called Koinonia (from the Greek word for "fellowship") near Americus.[14] Jordan's nephew, Hamilton Jordan, former chief-of-staff for President Carter, captures the audacity of what his uncle dared to create: "While Martin Luther King Jr. was in the seventh grade, Clarence Jordan founded an interracial commune in rural South Georgia. It was . . . years before the Supreme Court declared the 'separate but equal' doctrine unconstitutional and more than two decades before blacks could drink from a public water fountain or use a public bathroom."[15]

The progressive racial values of the black church suffused and motivated Martin Luther King Jr. but Clarence Jordan had to buck the then-prevailing racist attitudes expressed within the Southern Baptist Convention. Jordan was a native Georgian, having been born in Talbotton in 1912. As an adult, he recalled various childhood experiences that led him to question what he considered to be a hypocritical streak in Southern white evangelicalism. In short, Jordan came to feel that if one truly believed the message that God loves all people, then one's conduct must conform to that message. Thus Jordan had no hesitation in engaging in interracial relations, even on the most social of levels. Following his graduation from the University of Georgia in 1933 with a degree in agriculture, Jordan moved on to the Southern Baptist Seminary in Louisville, Kentucky.[16] Jordan's openness to preaching among and working with African Americans there prompted mixed feelings within his denomination, but his willingness to eat with blacks clearly crossed a line, and he was criticized severely for it.[17] Nevertheless, Jordan remained resolute about his desire to foster authentic interracial relations, since he had decided that he "was going to try to live my faith . . . not act it."[18]

Jordan met a kindred spirit while he was in Louisville, Florence Kroeger, and they married. Soon after his ordination, the couple developed a plan to return to Jordan's rural roots, and Koinonia was the ultimate result.[19] A black farmer who lived near the commune, Corranzo Morgan, recalled his surprise at Jordan's daring when he first arrived: "I almost fell off my chair when Mr. Jordan came over the first time, shook my hand, and invited me and my family for Sunday dinner. I hemmed and hawed and finally said we wuz busy. I'm athinking, this young white boy must not know that coloreds and whites eating together jest isn't done. . . . He is going to get his-self kilt. My next thought was that we might get ourselves kilt too . . . living cross the road from him."[20] Jordan described his initial vision of Koinonia as follows: "At first, we'll set up simply as farmers, trying to win the confidence of the people and establishing ourselves as good neighbors and citizens. When we feel that we are a part of the community, and are accepted as such, we'll try to bring in some of the principles we cherish."[21] As we will see, Jordan's high hopes for Koinonia never quite materialized in the way he envisioned.

Lillian Smith and Clarence Jordan clearly represent one end of a spectrum regarding white responses to segregation in Georgia. A more characteristic white intransigence was displayed in the 1950s by a backlash against assertions of racial equality. There is no better example of white resistance to integration than Eugene Talmadge's son, Herman, who himself served as governor briefly in 1947 and again from 1948 to 1954. (He was elected by Georgians to the U.S. Senate in 1956, and served through reelection until 1980.)[22] As an apt summation of his approach to racial matters, one may note that the *New York Times* referred to Herman Talmadge as the "all-time Georgia champion of white supremacy."[23]

Stephen G. N. Tuck observes that with Eugene Talmadge's election as governor in 1946, the upsurge in black activism in Georgia ended, but that the election of Herman Talmadge in 1948 brought a decade of aggressive white supremacy. Indeed, Herman Talmadge's gubernatorial election led to the expression of white backlash at all levels of the state government, and the Ku Klux Klan was strongly linked to his administration. Following Talmadge's election Klan membership in Georgia surged, with approximately one hundred thousand members by 1949. Tuck points out that, far from there being continual growth of black protest from the 1940s to the 1960s, as a result of white backlash the 1950s brought setbacks. One striking result was that while Klan membership in Georgia was soaring, the state NAACP system was collapsing. Georgia membership in the NAACP, which had been in excess of eleven thousand by 1948, fell rapidly to a low of three to four thousand after Talmadge was elected, with the majority of this membership in Atlanta and Savannah, where there were relatively moderate race relations. By his own account, Talmadge had run for governor on a platform of making voting in the state "as white . . . as possible," and almost overnight after his election some twelve thousand black voters were purged from state records. Many more were intimidated into not voting. The end result was that Klan membership in Georgia was almost equal to the number of registered black voters. In short, concludes Tuck, the "white supremacist backlash succeeded in dismantling the nascent statewide civil rights movement."[24]

In 1951 Talmadge proclaimed: "As long as I am governor in Georgia, Negroes will not be admitted to white schools."[25] In 1955, in between his service as governor and senator, and following the controversial 1954 *Brown v. Board of Education* Supreme Court decision that eliminated racial segregation of public education facilities, Talmadge published a slim volume titled *You and Segregation*, in which he made his case for segregation and attacked the NAACP. Addressing himself to "Americans," he wrote: "We have a tradition of segregation in the South. It has proven itself to the best interest of both races. Its continuance is of extreme importance." The reason it was important for the racial status quo to continue, Talmadge argued, was that "regardless of where you live, more than segregation is at stake." To Talmadge, segregation and freedom were interrelated: "Important as segregation is to us, the far reaching and all embracing May 17, 1954 'decision' of the United States Supreme Court has even more important implications. They directly affect every citizen of this nation. Make no mistake about it. The issue is your freedom."[26]

Talmadge was convinced that the end result of desegregation would be the strengthening of "the Communist party and its fellow-travelers," among whom he included the leadership of the NAACP: "The ultimate aim and goal of NAACP leaders in the present segregation fight is the complete intermingling of the races in housing, schools, churches, public parks, public swimming pools and even in marriage." Under the heading *God Advocates Segregation*, Talmadge asserted: "Ethnology teaches that there are five different races: white, black, yellow, brown and red. God created them all different. He set them in families and appointed bounds of habitation. He did not intend them to be mixed or He would not have separated them or segregated them." Talmadge continued: "Certainly history shows that nations composed of a mongrel race lose their strength and become weak, lazy and indifferent. They become easy preys to outside nations. And isn't that just exactly what the Communists want to happen to the United States?" He concluded his book with a plea to his fellow citizens "to preserve . . . our traditional way of life" by opposing "the mixing of the races."[27]

That God had established racial segregation was not an uncommon notion among Southern whites when Talmadge wrote. In keeping with the way that

Southern antebellum church figures had cited scripture to support slavery, in the 1950s many religious whites in the South claimed that segregation had a biblical mandate. Whereas the curse of Ham/Canaan (Genesis 9) was thought to justify the lower status of slaves, the biblical verse that Talmadge drew upon, Acts 17:26 ("And [God] hath made of one blood all nations of men for to dwell on all the face of the earth, and hath determined the times before appointed, and the bounds of their habitation"), was the primary proof text for segregationists. Mark Newman observes that since interpretation of the Bible was a widespread linchpin of the segregationist worldview, "if the civil rights movement was a religious movement, opposition to it was, at least in part, a kind of religious movement as well."[28]

Segregationists who cited Acts 17:26 considered that the phrase "all nations of men" represented races, whom God meant to have separate living spaces. Since historical developments caused different races to inhabit the same geographic regions, it followed that they needed to be segregated in order to conform to the divine will.[29] The reader will recall that, in a poignant irony, Acts 17:26 was also a text that opponents of segregation relied on to foster a conception of common humanity, crossing—even eradicating—racial distinctions. We have seen that, following emancipation, Southern black clergy such as Lucius Holsey accentuated the Fatherhood of God. Such figures emphasized the first words of the verse, "And [God] hath made of one blood all nations of men for to dwell on all the face of the earth," while segregationists pointed to the following assertion that God had also "determined . . . the bounds of their habitation." One is reminded of Abraham Lincoln's statement in his Second Inaugural Address: "Both read the same Bible, and pray to the same God. . . . The prayers of both could not be answered; that of neither has been answered fully."[30] While Lincoln had in mind Northerners and Southerners, it is clear that his words are also applicable to those who opposed and favored segregation.

Just as the concept that God had established segregation was a common notion among Southern whites, the idea advanced by Talmadge that desegregation was a tool of Communism was also prevalent. Segregationists held that integration was tied to Communism for several reasons, including the notion that racial intermarriage would cause the white race in the United States to weaken, setting the stage for a Communist takeover. In 1957 Baptist minister William T. Bodenhamer, who was a leader in the Georgia Baptist Convention and an officer in the segregationist States' Rights Council of Georgia, linked racial conflict in the United States and the threat of Communism. Bodenhamer sent a letter to Atlanta ministers who had signed a statement supporting positive race relations and declared: "The Communists planned over thirty years ago to inflame 'the Negro minority against the whites' and 'to instill in the whites a guilt complex for their exploitation of the Negroes.' How they have succeeded!"[31]

Herman Talmadge was himself a Baptist, and an influential one at that. During the 1954 meeting of the Georgia Baptist Convention, soon after the *Brown* decision, a resolution was offered that called for "justice and calmness" regarding race issues. Before a vote was taken on the resolution a delegate from Augusta announced that he was opposed to it, and he claimed that the majority of Georgia Baptists would agree with him. After voicing his support of Talmadge's opposition to integration, he asserted that approving the resolution would constitute a rejection of Talmadge's policies. The resolution eventually passed, but only after James P. Wesberry, a leading Atlanta minister who was a friend of Talmadge, said that he did not think the resolution opposed the anti-integration program Talmadge advocated.[32]

As resistance to the *Brown* decision increased among Southern whites during the second half of the 1950s, the Southern Baptist Convention remained silent and did not adopt any resolutions concerning race until 1961. Mark Newman has pointed out that, conversely, other denominations issued "increasingly progressive resolutions and pronouncements" concerning race relations. Newman observes that in 1956, for instance, the Methodist Church affirmed that there was no room within its ranks for "racial discrimination or enforced segregation." The following year, the Southern Presbyterian General Assembly issued a document that formally rejected the Ku Klux Klan and racial discrimination. In 1958 the Roman Catholic Bishops of the United States advocated equal economic and educational opportunities.[33]

It is important to recognize that official statements like these had little impact on lay people.[34] The experience of Robert B. McNeill, pastor of First Presbyterian Church in Columbus, illustrates the tension that was present at the local, congregational level. In May 1957 McNeill published an article in *Look* magazine titled "A Georgia Minister Offers a Solution for the South." In the article, McNeill called for "creative contact" between whites and blacks, by which he meant that representatives of both groups should be on city councils, grand juries, school boards, and the like. The month after the article appeared, the Southwest Georgia Synod received complaints about McNeill, and several members of his congregation demanded his resignation or dismissal. When McNeill refused to step down, a special judicial commission was convened. At first the commission ruled in his favor, but when reports circulated that *Look* was going to issue a follow-up story about the case, McNeill was dismissed.[35]

Cutting against the flow, Atlantan Dorothy Tilly tried to counter racism directly at the lay-person level. In 1946 Tilly, who had served as Georgia's state representative in the Association of Southern Women for the Prevention of Lynching, was appointed by President Harry S. Truman to a national Committee on Civil Rights. Partly due to her experience on this committee, Tilly formed in 1949 a biracial group of Southern female leaders of religious organizations, which became known as the Fellowship of the Concerned (FOC). Tilly's father had been a Methodist minister when she was a child, which revealed to her the challenging circumstances that poor black and white Southerners endured.[36] She recalled later that "throughout my youth . . . I saw and heard the troubles of the community, both Negro and white, pour over the doorstep of the parsonage. . . . Regardless of color, people were people first."[37] This upbringing left a lasting impression on Tilly, stimulating her to want to help those less fortunate than she.[38] As Tilly herself put it: "Brotherhood is the basis for peace, and brotherhood must begin with the church."[39]

At first, the FOC concentrated on matters involving racial injustice in courtroom proceedings and voter registration. In 1953, just prior to the *Brown* decision, Tilly redirected the focus of the FOC to helping white Southern society come to terms with the inevitability that segregation would end. Tilly thought that women could attack racism most effectively by teaching and modeling tolerance to their husbands and, especially, to their children. Such an approach would have the effect, over time, of alleviating racial problems. In short, Tilly felt that if white women raised more tolerant children, this would ultimately lead to a society that would offer more equality.[40] Tilly's deeply felt faith is clear in the way she handled the crank and threatening phone calls that she received: she would often play a recording of the Lord's Prayer in their ears. "It always helps me," she said, "and it silences the one at the other end of the phone."[41]

Tilly's fellow Atlantan, Rabbi Jacob Rothschild, sounded a similar voice of tolerance from his synagogue pulpit at The Temple, where he ardently called for better race relations and the demise of segregation. Because of The Temple's long history and prominence, Rothschild was a visible figure in 1950s Atlanta.

The Temple is the direct continuation of the earliest synagogue in the city, The Hebrew Benevolent Congregation, which was chartered in 1867 as "the first official Jewish organization in Atlanta."[42] Among its members was Morris Rich, who opened a small dry-goods business in Atlanta in the same year, which evolved into Rich's Department Store (now associated with Macy's), the largest in the Southeast.[43] The Rich family's success is emblematic of the elite German-Jewish retailers, business owners, and physicians who attended The Temple.[44] As Melissa Fay Greene observes, The Temple "served as the hub of the religious, social, and philanthropic operations of an old and august Jewish community."[45]

Rabbi Rothschild was motivated to speak out against segregation not only by black and white racial concerns, but also by the precarious situation of Southern Jews. Indeed, from the *Brown* decision until the end of the 1950s, some 10 percent of bombings of religious buildings in the South were directed at Jewish targets, including synagogues, the homes of rabbis, and Jewish community centers.[46] As noted previously, the Atlanta Jewish community felt especially vulnerable due to the lasting legacy of the Leo Frank lynching.

In spite of the evident risk, Rothschild denounced racism in his weekly sermons, drawing on biblical calls to "aid the oppressed" as well as his favorite passage from rabbinic literature: "It is not incumbent upon thee to finish the work, but neither are thou permitted to desist from it altogether." In a sermon he delivered in May 1958 titled "Can This Be America?" Rothschild reviewed a recent spate of bombings of Jewish targets throughout the South, and said: "We'd like to ignore the whole thing. We think, 'Maybe if we talk about it, we'll be bombed too.' But we must face the facts." For Rothschild, the simplest fact was that "hate is hate, and violence is directed against all minorities when it becomes possible and fashionable." Thus, there was no avoiding the problem, even if one remained silent: "We are a vulnerable minority. What we do makes no difference in how we are treated. Whether we speak our conscience, or hide and remain silent—we will be attacked." And for Rothschild, silence was unthinkable to begin with. When one Southern rabbi asked him to tone down his remarks about racial injustice, Rothschild shot back: "If this is dangerous, then I shall have to live dangerously. Because, I firmly believe, that this is my responsibility as a rabbi. And even if I weren't a rabbi, it would be my responsibility as a human being."[47]

As had been feared, The Temple was indeed attacked. On October 12, 1958, the congregation's building was bombed, causing massive damage.[48] Ralph

McGill, who would win a Pulitzer Prize in 1959 due in large measure to his editorials following the bombing, famously observed the next day: "This is a harvest. It is the crop of things sown. It is the harvest of defiance of courts and the encouragement of citizens to defy law on the part of many southern politicians. . . . It is not possible to preach lawlessness and restrict it." McGill continued: "To be sure, none said go bomb a Jewish temple. . . . But let it be understood that when leadership in high places in any degree fails to support constituted authority, it opens the gate to all those who wish to take law into their own hands." According to McGill, religious figures were also to blame: "This, too, is a harvest of those so-called Christian ministers who have chosen to preach hate instead of compassion. Let them now find pious words and raise their hands in deploring the bombing of a synagogue. You do not preach and encourage hatred for the Negro and hope to restrict it to that field. It is an old, old story. It is one repeated over and over again in history. When the wolves of hate are loosed on one people, then no one is safe."[49]

The bombing of The Temple sent moral shockwaves through the city of Atlanta and beyond. Just after the bombing, President Dwight D. Eisenhower remarked: "I think we would all share in the feeling of horror that any person would want to desecrate the holy place of any religion, be it a chapel, a cathedral, a mosque, a church, or a synagogue." An outpouring of support came from numerous Atlanta churches, including telegraphs, cards, and financial gifts. This response from Christians in Atlanta led Rabbi Rothschild's wife, Janice, to label the crime "The Bomb that Healed."[50]

There were troubles at Koinonia too after the *Brown* decision, but there was no public outcry for support in this case. Fittingly, Hamilton Jordan labels 1955 to 1965 "the difficult years" for his uncle Clarence.[51] In 1956 Clarence Jordan offered assistance to two black students who were attempting to apply to an all-white business school in Atlanta, which brought an angry backlash against Koinonia. The commune's egg market in Americus experienced a boycott, and their farm land was vandalized. When a roadside market was bombed in July 1956, the Koinonians responded by placing an ad in a local paper stating: "We pledge ourselves to respect the rights of those who differ with us. We believe the citizens of this county [i.e., Sumter] will give us the same consideration." That this plea fell on mostly deaf ears can be judged from the reaction of the solicitor general of Sumter County, who said: "Maybe . . . what we need now is for the right kind of Klan to start up again and use a buggy whip on some of these race mixers. . . . I had rather see my little boy dead than sit beside a Negro in the public schools."[52]

Given such official sanction, hostility against the Koinonians increased. In late January 1957 a machine gun sprayed bullets into several houses at Koinonia, but fortunately no one was hit. In the evening a few days later, two cars fired shots at commune children who were playing volleyball at a lighted playground.[53] When crosses began to be burned near Koinonia property, and the Knights of the Ku Klux Klan held a rally against Koinonia in Americus, it was not hard to guess who was responsible for much of the violence.[54]

At one point, Jordan wrote to President Eisenhower telling him that "a community of nearly sixty men, women, and children is facing annihilation unless quick, decisive action is taken by someone in authority." Jordan noted that "we welcome into our fellowship any person of any color or race. . . . Until the Supreme Court's decision on desegregation of schools . . . we were not molested. Since then our life together has become increasingly difficult and our very existence more precarious." He concluded: "We have been told that the end is near. We shall not run, for this is America. It is a land where free men have the right—and the duty—to walk erect and without fear in their pursuit of peace and happiness. Should this freedom perish from our land, we would prefer to be dead. We gladly offer our lives for its preservation."[55]

Apparently, Jordan's letter never reached the president's desk; instead, it made its way to the Georgia governor's office. Eventually, there was an investigation of Koinonia by a Sumter County grand jury. Jordan was called to testify before its members, and afterward he told a reporter that he had "tried to explain to them the difference between Christ and Marx but it soon became clear that they didn't know anything about either one of them." The grand jury concluded that the Koinonia community had committed violence against itself.[56]

Clarence Jordan receives only a brief mention in John Egerton's massive book *Speak Now against the Day: The Generation before the Civil Rights Movement in the South*, where he is merely listed among those who started interracial communes in the United States.[57] He is not referred to at all in many other pertinent scholarly works. Jordan also downplayed his own significance. Hamilton Jordan recalls asking his uncle, during a visit to Koinonia: "Haven't you accomplished a lot here?" He was taken aback by Clarence's answer: "'We have made progress, but not much.' And holding up his large, rough hands, he put his thumb and forefinger almost together. 'Every inch, every centimeter has been so hard . . . and at such a great price. But we have survived and persevered. We have survived,' he repeated. 'A tiny light in a sea of hate.'" Clarence Jordan died in 1969, at age 57, of a heart attack. According to his nephew, his family considers that Jordan died of a "broken heart."[58] Indeed, Jordan never saw his initial dream of true community come to fruition, and today Koinonia is better known as the birthplace of Habitat for Humanity than it is as an interracial commune.[59]

Still, while Clarence Jordan did not feel that Koinonia had made much progress, his own resolve and Koinonia's endurance influenced many blacks in the burgeoning civil rights movement. Mabel Barnum, one of the leaders of the movement in Americus, commented: "When people saw that [the Koinonia community] wasn't going to let the Klan run them off, they knew from that time on that you don't have to be scared of the Klan." Charles Sherrod, a field worker with the civil rights group, the Student Nonviolent Coordinating Committee, agreed that "much of the spade work has already been done by the Koinonia farm people. . . . This is a good start even if it is emblazoned with bullet fringes."[60]

Hamilton Jordan notes that Martin Luther King Jr. referred to Clarence Jordan as "my friend, my mentor, and my inspiration." He also writes that King recalled inviting his uncle to speak at Dexter Avenue Baptist Church in Montgomery, Alabama, which was King's pulpit in the early 1950s: "Clarence told us about his interracial commune in rural South Georgia. It was shocking and inspiring . . . and sounded too good to be true. Here was a son of the old South, a white Baptist preacher doing what we were just talking about doing." According to Andrew Young, one of King's closest aides: "Clarence did not spend all his time telling others what to do or making a fuss about it. . . . He just kept living his faith. And Clarence put all the rest of us to shame until we did something about it." Young adds that "when we first heard about Clarence Jordan and Koinonia we considered it too radical, too dangerous. Martin and I were trying to get folks the right to ride on the bus and to shop where they wanted . . . huge challenges back then. But here Clarence was—smack dab in the middle of Ku Klux Klan country—going for the whole loaf."[61] Indeed, after King became involved with civil rights work, it would take some time before he was calling for "the whole loaf."

One may trace the beginning of King's civil rights career to December 1, 1955, when a black woman named Rosa Parks refused to give up her seat on a Montgomery city bus to allow a white passenger to sit there, as she had been told to do by the driver. After Parks was arrested, some activists formed a Montgomery Improvement Association (MIA) and King agreed to lead it. A bus boycott coordinated by the MIA continued for more than a year.

Eventually, the U.S. Supreme Court ruled that the practice of segregation on the Montgomery buses was unconstitutional. The Montgomery bus boycott made King a national figure, catapulting him into an unexpected career as a civil rights leader and setting the course of the rest of his life.[62]

In January 1957 a regional meeting of activists, the Southern Negro Leaders Conference, was held in Atlanta. The conference was hosted by King's home church, Ebenezer Baptist, where his father served as minister. The meeting was prompted by the realization that, in the words of Bayard Rustin, an advisor to King, there needed to be "a sustaining mechanism that could translate what we . . . learned during the bus boycott into a broad strategy for protest in the South."[63] Thus the new group would lead a regional movement, and this would set it apart from the national NAACP. An additional distinguishing feature of the emerging regional movement was the fact that it was led by black clergy such as King and a fellow Baptist minister, Ralph David Abernathy, who would become King's chief partner in the civil rights struggle.[64] In fact, Roy Wilkins, the executive secretary of the NAACP, initially referred to the new movement as "the ministers group."[65] In February 1957 the movement adopted the name Southern Leadership Conference, and King, as the group's president, announced that its activities would be "rooted in deep spiritual faith." In August 1957 King proposed a name change for the organization, to Southern *Christian* Leadership Conference (SCLC), to underscore that the foundation of the movement was the black church.[66]

Though the SCLC was based in Atlanta, initially King retained his position at Dexter Avenue Baptist in Montgomery. In 1960, however, he moved back to Atlanta with his family so that he could better manage the activities of the SCLC. Gary M. Pomerantz has observed that "King's return to Atlanta would transform the city into the headquarters of the civil rights movement."[67] In addition to overseeing the SCLC, King shared the pastorate of Ebenezer Baptist with his father. King, who grew up in the congregation and in a house near the church, was now quite literally at home.

After King's death, civil rights activist Ella Baker observed that "the movement made Martin rather than Martin making the movement." In any case, it was King's deeply engrained faith that made the man. As King himself once observed: "I grew up in the church. I'm the son of a preacher. . . . My grandfather was a preacher, my great grandfather was a preacher, my only brother is a preacher, my daddy's brother is a preacher."[68] Two of the men he referred to had been ministers at Ebenezer. King's maternal grandfather, A. D. Williams, served there from 1894 until 1931, at which time his son-in-law, King's father (also known as "Daddy King"), took the pulpit.[69] Andrew Young recalls the central role that King's home church played not only in his life but in the life of the civil rights movement. Young states: "[Ebenezer] was kind of like the mother church, it was the shelter. We had an office down the street, but whenever there was an important meeting, we usually went to Daddy King's study."[70]

At the time King returned to live in Atlanta, the state of Georgia was in the midst of a crisis involving public schools. In the wake of the *Brown* decision, state leaders had passed legislation that would cut off state funding to white public schools accepting black students.[71] White social activist and Methodist Frances Pauley was instrumental in helping to end the school desegregation crisis. Pauley mobilized support for integration through the Help Our Public Education (HOPE) campaign, which Stephen G. N. Tuck regards as "by far the most significant single contribution of white liberal organizations to Georgia's race relations in the history of the state."[72]

Pauley herself suggested that the traditional social conscience of Methodism was a major part of her inspiration.[73] Like Dorothy Tilly before her, Pauley's life and work underscore the suggestion, made by one Southerner in the 1950s, that "if you do not know what social action to take, watch the Methodist women, and where they lead, follow." Contemporary scholars have also noted that while in general women have been more forward thinking regarding matters of religious conscience than men throughout the United States, Methodist women in particular became, as one historian puts it, "the most progressive element in the white South."[74] Alice G. Knotts, the author of a book on the role of Methodist women in changing American racial attitudes, suggests that "Methodist women worked for race relations earlier than other mainline denominational groups . . . because they adhered to a gospel message which some of them interpreted as transcending race, class, and gender. . . . Consequently, because Methodists were concerned about social issues, Methodist women accepted as their Christian and civic responsibility the task of influencing the quality of human relations of their communities."[75] In short, many Methodist women followed through on John Wesley's view that "the ideal Christian life [is] one of ceaseless, cheerful activism."[76]

The Georgia school crisis peaked when two black students, Hamilton Holmes and Charlayne Hunter, applied for admission to the University of Georgia. In January 1961, following extended court battles, a federal judge

ordered their admission to the school, which ultimately led the state legislature to repeal its antidesegregation legislation.[77] In the fall of the year, a
direct-action protest began in Albany that was intended to achieve more widespread results: "It was the first mass movement in the modern civil rights era
to have as its goal the desegregation of an entire community."[78] Although King
and the SCLC became involved, the campaign encountered numerous problems and was widely considered to have been a failure since it did not lead to
any major concessions from the city's white power structure. (Taylor Branch
observes that, at the time, "most reporters took a sportswriter's approach and
billed the [Albany] events essentially as Segregation 1, King 0."[79])

After concluding the Albany campaign, King convened SCLC leaders at
Dorchester Academy in Liberty County, close to Midway Church, so that he
and his aides could review what they had learned from the Albany experience.
After determining that they needed to have specific goals and a more coher-
ent strategy, the SCLC leaders chose their next target carefully: Birmingham,
Alabama, which King later indicated he considered "probably the most thoroughly segregated city in the United States," with an "ugly record of police
brutality."[80] There, the new SCLC strategies worked well, especially when,
as expected, Birmingham police, under the orders of Chief Eugene "Bull"
Connor, broke up demonstrations with brutal force, using police dogs and
high-power water hoses. This heavy-handed approach brought national news
attention and federal intervention. Both in turn led local white leaders to the
negotiating table.[81]

King's national prominence increased not only due to the success of the
Birmingham protest but also because of his eloquent "Letter from Birmingham City Jail," which he wrote to several white ministers while imprisoned
during part of the campaign. Responding to their suggestion that he and his
fellow protesters show more patience, as well as the general criticism that
his activities were "unwise and untimely," King wrote: "I am in Birmingham because injustice is here. . . . I am cognizant of the interrelatedness of
all communities and states. I cannot sit idly by in Atlanta and not be concerned about what happens in Birmingham. Injustice anywhere is a threat to
justice everywhere. We are caught in an inescapable network of mutuality,
tied in a single garment of destiny. Whatever affects one directly, affects all
indirectly."[82]

The years from 1963 to 1965 mark the apex of King's career and trace the
familiar arc of the successes of the civil rights movement. In August 1963

came the March on Washington for Jobs and Freedom, the largest single event of the civil rights era, with hundreds of thousands in attendance. King was awarded the Nobel Peace Prize in 1964. That same year brought passage of the federal Civil Rights Act outlawing segregation in public facilities. The following year saw a prominent SCLC campaign in Selma, Alabama, that led to the Voting Rights Act of 1965, which abolished legal impediments to voting rights for blacks.[83]

Arguably, King's own high point was his triumphant "I Have a Dream" speech, delivered on the steps of the Lincoln Memorial on August 28, 1963, during the March on Washington. His prepared text did not contain what became its most famous passage. A few months later King recalled: "I started out reading the speech . . . and all of a sudden this thing came to me that I have used—I'd used it many times before, that thing about 'I have a dream'— and I just felt that I wanted to use it here. I don't know why."[84] Perhaps by liberating himself from his prepared words, King was better able to speak from his heart that day.[85] Whatever the case, though King had used some of his extemporaneous wording before, the setting provoked a more powerful delivery and reception than ever: "I still have a dream. It is a dream deeply rooted in the American dream that one day this nation will rise up and live out the true meaning of its creed—we hold these truths to be self-evident, that all men are created equal. I have a dream that one day on the red hills of Georgia, sons of former slaves and sons of former slave-owners will be able to sit down together at the table of brotherhood. . . . I have a dream my four little children will one day live in a nation where they will not be judged by the color of their skin but by content of their character. I have a dream today!"[86]

After pleading for America to "let freedom ring" across the land "from every mountainside," including "Stone Mountain of Georgia," King concluded: "And when we allow freedom to ring, when we let it ring from every village and hamlet, from every state and city, we will be able to speed up that day when all of God's children—black men and white men, Jews and Gentiles, Catholics and Protestants—will be able to join hands and to sing in the words of the old Negro spiritual, 'Free at last, free at last; thank God Almighty, we are free at last.'"[87]

While King and the SCLC received national and international attention, some local civil rights efforts in Georgia relied on other leadership. In Savannah, with a history of a strong local NAACP dating back to Ralph Mark Gilbert, one NAACP leader openly stated that "we want to keep this thing among

Savannahians, we don't want to have to bring Martin Luther King here." The undisputed head of the black community in the city was W. W. Law, who led the Savannah NAACP.[88]

By contrast to Savannah, what marked civil rights efforts in Rome was a dedicated biracial council, the Council on Human Relations, which eventually included a wide array of black and white professionals. In addition, Berry College in Rome admitted black students a year before other colleges in Georgia. It has been suggested that, as a general phenomenon, "the presence of a college significantly increased the likelihood of racial cooperation in towns across Georgia."[89]

Aldon Morris has asserted that the black church was "the institutional center" of the civil rights movement.[90] It was certainly the fountainhead of the regional work of the SCLC. Yet it is clear that in Georgia additional organizations, such as the NAACP, local councils, and colleges, were also key factors in addition to the black church and the church-based SCLC. Therefore, while he acknowledges that the church was important, Stephen G. N. Tuck concludes that in Georgia it did not play a paramount role.[91] Yet if the church was not of utmost importance for all those involved in the civil rights struggle in the state, it was supremely important for Martin Luther King Jr. himself.

To the end of his life, King relied on his faith. At the beginning of his civil rights career, King had a transformative religious experience from which he drew strength until his death. He had, he later said, "an experience with God in the way that you must . . . if you're going to walk the lonely paths of this life." On the night of January 27, 1956, King was in the throes of a crisis of confidence. He had been receiving disturbing phone calls, and one making a death threat had come on that Friday evening. Unable to sleep, King made his way quietly to his kitchen and found himself sitting at a table with an untouched cup of coffee before him. He recalled later that he was "ready to give up" and remembered trying "to think of a way to move out of the [leadership] picture without appearing a coward."[92]

Around midnight, King sat thinking about the caller who had threatened his life and about the danger to his family. Ultimately, he reached a point where he felt he "couldn't take it any longer." Then King experienced his life-changing moment. Although he had been accustomed to Christianity from birth, King reported that he "discovered then that religion had to become real to me, and I had to know God for myself." Thus he "bowed down over that cup of coffee" and prayed. He recorded later that he then sensed "the presence of the Divine" as never before, and it seemed to him as though he could hear "the quiet assurance of an inner voice saying: 'Stand up for righteousness, stand up for truth, and God will be at your side forever.'" He returned to bed and woke the next morning with a renewed sense of calm and courage: "My uncertainty disappeared. I was ready to face anything."[93] Though he would occasionally become physically and emotionally exhausted, King's faith did not waver. On the very day he was murdered, April 4, 1968, he told his aides: "I'd rather be dead than afraid. You've got to get over being afraid of death."[94]

At the heart of King's Christian faith was a vision of what he called the "beloved community." Kenneth L. Smith and Ira G. Zepp Jr. have written about the centrality of this concept in King's thought, and they note that it ran like a leitmotif throughout King's career as a civil rights leader, from his earliest to his last speeches and sermons. They summarize the beloved community as "a vision of a completely integrated society, a community of love and justice wherein brotherhood would be an actuality in all of social life."[95]

King's vision of the beloved community remains unfulfilled. In one of his last books he wrote: "A genuine revolution of values means in the final analysis that our loyalties must become ecumenical rather than sectional. Every nation must now develop an overriding loyalty to mankind as a whole in order to preserve the best in their individual societies. This call for a world-wide fellowship that lifts neighborly concern beyond one's tribe, race, class and nation is in reality a call for an all-embracing and unconditional love for all men."[96] In light of the contemporary era of domestic and international culture conflicts, the title of the book in which this statement is found raises a question that could well be imagined to be hanging over us all: *Where Do We Go from Here: Chaos or Community?*[97]

CHAPTER EIGHT

Culture and Worship Wars

A twenty-two-year-old indigent Georgia woman, who came to be known by the pseudonym "Mary Doe," applied to the Abortion Committee of Atlanta's Grady Memorial Hospital in March 1970. She was nine weeks pregnant and already had three children, the youngest of whom she had given up for adoption, while the older two were in foster care. She had received advice that "an abortion could be performed on her with less danger to her health than if she gave birth to the child she was carrying." After her application to have a therapeutic abortion was denied, she sued the attorney general of Georgia, Arthur K. Bolton, "on her own behalf and on behalf of all others similarly situated." Her case, *Doe v. Bolton*, was eventually argued before the U.S. Supreme Court. On January 22, 1973, the Court decided *Doe v. Bolton*, as well as the better known *Roe v. Wade* case, which involved a woman from Texas.[1] The decisions in *Roe v. Wade* and *Doe v. Bolton* sparked a rancorous national debate, which has persisted ever since, over whether or when abortion should be legal, and over the role of religious views in the political and legal spheres.

In 1991 James Davison Hunter gave a name to this debate when he published a book titled *Culture Wars: The Struggle to Define America*. Hunter argued that debate over the abortion issue has expanded to include other controversial issues, such as women's rights, homosexuality, and multiculturalism. According to Hunter, these issues do not register with most people until their lives come into contact with the touchstone issues, such as when a friend has an abortion. Then suddenly an abstraction becomes quite real. As a result, wrote Hunter, "the contemporary culture war touches virtually all Americans; nearly everyone has stories to tell."[2] The concept of culture wars gained national exposure when, in a speech given at the 1992 Republican National

Convention in Houston, Texas, political commentator and erstwhile presidential candidate Pat Buchanan declared: "There is a religious war going on in our country for the soul of America. It is a cultural war, as critical to the kind of nation we will one day be as was the Cold War itself."[3]

Georgia has certainly not been immune to the culture wars, and in fact it has sometimes taken center stage in them. Indeed, the twenty-first century opened with Cobb County in the national spotlight about the teaching of evolution in schools, when the Cobb School Board had a sticker placed in science textbooks that advised students: "This textbook contains material on evolution. Evolution is a theory, not a fact, regarding the origin of living things."[4] Also drawing national attention was the action taken in October 2000 by former president Jimmy Carter to break his ties with the Southern Baptist Convention (SBC). Carter, a longtime member of the SBC, left the Southern Baptists in large measure over the issue of women's rights. He stated: "For me, being a Southern Baptist has always been like being an American. I just have never thought of making a change." Nonetheless, referring to an "increasingly rigid" Southern Baptist creed, Carter asserted that "the Bible says all people are equal in the eyes of God. I personally feel that women should play an absolutely equal role in service of Christ in the church."[5] Carter was reacting in part to the 2000 SBC Baptist Faith and Message statement, which declared: "A wife is to submit herself graciously to the servant leadership of her husband. . . . [She] has the God-given responsibility to respect her husband and to serve as his helper in managing the household."[6] Rev. James Merritt of Snellville, who was then president of the SBC, defended the denomination's positions and said of Carter's departure: "With all due respect to the president, he is a theological moderate. We are not a theological moderate convention."[7]

By the time Merritt declared that the SBC was not theologically moderate, a very contentious debate had been waged within the denomination about that very point. Several books have been written to chronicle this debate, and some of the more provocative titles suggest the tone of the conflict, such as *Baptist Battles*, *The Southern Baptist Holy War*, and *The Struggle for the Soul of the SBC*.[8] Given the Baptist tradition of local autonomy, no central authority could decide the issues at hand, and therefore the debate had to be settled by the side that could garner more support across the denomination. The conflict began in the late 1970s, when two Texas Baptists, Paige Patterson and Paul Pressler, led an effort to convince fellow members of the SBC that the denomination had lost its way and had compromised essential theological truths, especially the concept of an inerrant Bible. Some Southern Baptists, who turned out to be a minority, argued in response that theological diversity is a part of the Baptist faith and charged that the fundamentalists led by Pressler and Patterson were seeking to control the SBC. Labeled liberals by the fundamentalists, those opposed to the fundamentalists eventually became known as moderates. Each side found it difficult to accept the other's position, and the conflict became divisive. Eventually, a moderate organization developed within the SBC, the Cooperative Baptist Fellowship (CBF).[9]

The formation of the Atlanta-based CBF was guided by minister Daniel Vestal, who was serving at First Baptist Church in Midland, Texas, when the Baptist conflicts began but left to pastor Dunwoody Baptist Church in Atlanta from 1988 to 1991. In 1985 Vestal was elected to the Peace Committee of the SBC because, in his words, he was "theologically conservative but politically nonaligned" at that time. While he had opposed "the fundamentalist takeover," he had not taken part in any organized attempts to stop it. Instead, Vestal believed that there remained a chance for reconciliation within the SBC. He has related, however, that during the 1987 SBC meeting in St. Louis, Missouri, he sat next to a friend and looked over to see him crying. When the friend told Vestal, "This is not the SBC I have always known," he felt that his friend was right: "Shared decision making, open communication, acceptance of diversity were gone. In its place was a political machine that governed committee appointments, trustee selection, platform speeches, and even floor debate."[10]

Following the 1987 SBC meeting, Vestal appeared in a Public Broadcasting System documentary on *God and Politics*, after which he received hundreds of responses. He came to the conclusion that "something must be done," and he decided to run for president of the SBC at the 1989 convention in Las Vegas, Nevada. He was not elected. He tried a second time in 1990 at the SBC convention in New Orleans, Louisiana, and was again defeated. Following the second defeat he determined that it was the "end to the moderate political effort," meaning an end to attempts by Vestal and his supporters to reform the SBC from within. He then issued a call for "a convocation of concerned Baptists."[11] As a result, the CBF was formed by some six thousand moderates meeting in Atlanta in May 1991. The organization continues to have its primary office in the city, the Atlanta Resource Center, with Vestal serving as coordinator. By 2003 the group had approximately eighteen hundred "partner churches," while the SBC has some thirty-eight thousand member churches. The CBF does not consider itself a separate denomination, yet in many ways it functions as one, with a budget of more than sixteen million dollars supporting numerous church programs, as well as partnerships with several seminaries.[12]

The SBC annual meeting was also slated for Atlanta in 1991, and it met in June, just after the formation of the CBF. The contrast with the emerging CBF could not have been more stark. By this point the SBC had a more or less open alliance with the Republican Party, and the featured speakers at the convention included President George H. W. Bush, Oliver North, and Charles Colson. The tone of the meeting led one speaker to quip, "I have never spoken to a Republican convention before." As David T. Morgan succinctly puts it: "The 1991 SBC meeting in Atlanta demonstrated that the fundamentalists had little regard for the concerns of moderates. It resembled a conservative political rally more than a convention for doing a religious denomination's annual business."[13] In short, by 1991 the fundamentalists were fully in command of the SBC.

In addition to the issue of women's roles, which provoked the departure of President Carter from the SBC, one of the culture war issues of great interest within the SBC has been homosexuality. The SBC Position Statement on Sexuality is straightforward: "We affirm God's plan for marriage and sexual intimacy—one man, and one woman, for life. Homosexuality is not a 'valid alternative lifestyle.' The Bible condemns it as sin."[14] The SBC has not simply drawn this line in words, but has also taken significant action to oppose accepting homosexuality as a "valid alternative lifestyle." In 1996 the delegates to the SBC annual meeting instigated a boycott of the Walt Disney Company. They gave various reasons for the boycott, including that Disney purportedly had an employee policy "which accepts and embraces homosexual relationships for the purpose of insurance benefits" and had hosted "homosexual and lesbian theme nights at its parks." Such actions, said the delegates, "represent . . . a gratuitous insult to Christians," and they concluded that "the Disney Company has given the appearance that the promotion of homosexuality is more important than its historic commitment to traditional family values."[15] The boycott lasted until 2005.[16]

Two Atlanta-area Baptist churches, Virginia-Highland and Oakhurst, came into especially sharp conflict with the Georgia Baptist Convention (GBC) during the late 1990s. Both churches openly accept homosexuals and allow them to participate in church life, including holding leadership positions such as deacon. Their affiliation with the GBC ended in 1999 when the convention voted to expel the two congregations, the first dismissal of churches in the history of the GBC.[17]

Homosexuality has been a point of contention not only among Baptists. Instead, the issue cuts deeply across denominational lines. In 1992 Catholic priest John Adamski asked his congregation at the Shrine of the Immaculate Conception in Atlanta to sponsor a gay and lesbian support group. According to one observer, the resulting controversy "split the congregation." Yet the majority of the congregation decided to "weather the storm and do the ministry," leaving those who disagreed to find other places to worship.[18] Methodists clashed in 1997 over whether to allow same-sex unions to be performed at Emory University. When Emory president William M. Chace decided to allow such ceremonies on campus, the North Georgia Annual Conference of the United Methodist Church expressed "strong disagreement and extreme displeasure" with his decision.[19] Eventually, a compromise was reached whereby same-sex union ceremonies could be performed at Emory by religious groups that recognize and allow them, such as the Unitarian Universalist Association, but they could not be performed by Methodist clergy.

While Christian groups were experiencing internal culture war debates throughout the latter part of the twentieth century, a new phenomenon of religious pluralism was emerging. During the buildup to the 1996 Summer Olympics, there was a common slogan associated with the games: "The world is coming to Atlanta!" In his introduction to a book published to coincide with the Olympics, *Religions of Atlanta: Religious Diversity in the Centennial Olympic City*, Gary Laderman wrote: "In many ways, the 'world' has already arrived."[20] Laderman cited the increasingly international nature of religious life in Atlanta and the growing number of Muslim, Buddhist, and Hindu communities in the metro area. Additional such communities, along with Sikh, Baha'i, and other religious groups, can be found in urban areas throughout Georgia, including Columbus, Macon, Augusta, and Savannah. According to data collected by the Pluralism Project at Harvard University, by 2000 there were at least sixty-five Muslim, thirty-five Buddhist, and twenty Hindu communities in Georgia.[21] The 2001 American Religious Identification Survey conducted by researchers at the City University in New York suggested that there were as many Muslims and Buddhists combined in Georgia as either Lutherans or Episcopalians.[22]

The presence of these new groups has provided opportunities for both cooperation and conflict. When the Reverend Bob Hudak, then at the Episcopal Church of the Nativity in Fayetteville, held an adult education forum soon after the terrorist attacks of September 11, 2001, he found that his parishioners knew little about Islam other than what they saw on TV or read in newspapers. Hudak later said that he "went home that night determined to get in touch with the Islamic community." Thus he began to foster relations with members of the local Muslim Community Center in Fayette County. Yet there was a less welcoming attitude toward Muslims on display in Fayetteville as well. Some letters appeared in the *Fayetteville Citizen* that Hudak found particularly disturbing. "A number of the letters were vitriolic," he said. "One condemned Islam, and suggested that the next attack might come from [the local mosque]." Hudak responded with his own letter to the editor, in which he defended local Muslims and referred to their mosque as "the new house of prayer in Fayetteville."[23]

Some members of the Church of the Nativity backed Hudak, while others were less receptive to his efforts. Some congregants, for instance, did not wish to support a joint remembrance service with Muslims to mark the anniversary of the terrorist attacks. "I know this sort of ministry isn't everybody's cup of tea," Hudak stated. "The present political climate of our country doesn't favor this sort of ministry. . . . I sense that it's not 'fashionable' these days to be associating with Muslims." But, he added, "It's what Jesus would do." Hudak concluded: "We are a witness to an alternate way of being, that Christians and Muslims can not only live together, but work together toward deepening our hearts in service to others."[24]

Other ministers have been less sanguine about interfaith cooperation. In an interview with the Public Broadcasting System in 2002, James Merritt, who was at that time still president of the SBC, was asked about Baptists participating in interfaith dialogue. He replied: "Historically, we have not. . . . As a Christian, believing that Christ is not just a good way to heaven or the best way to heaven or even the baddest way to heaven [but] that he is the only way to heaven, we can't compromise that singular belief. So we have tended as Baptists not to engage in many of those types of activities." Instead, as Merritt underscored, evangelistic concerns are at the heart of the SBC: "Quite frankly, as president, that is a concern I have—that we keep our focus on evangelism. That's been one of our hallmarks. One of the distinctive marks of Southern Baptists is our emphasis on evangelism and sharing the gospel, the belief that Christ is the only way to Heaven." Merritt added that this key focus on evangelism was made more difficult by the presence of new religious groups: "When I was growing up, you were either Baptist or Methodist. Today, that's no longer true. There are Muslims here, Buddhists here, Hindus here—every ilk and every type of religious persuasion that you could imagine. Even here in the buckle of the Bible Belt, I have seen a trend in that direction." Merritt concluded: "It's more difficult now, I believe, to reach people for Christ. . . . Number one, obviously, is the challenge of reaching over [to] people of other religions and other faiths, such as Islam or Buddhism, for example, and winning them over to Christianity, to faith in Christ."[25]

To aid in proselytizing persons of other faiths, the North American Mission Board, an sbc agency based in Alpharetta, developed a series of pamphlets titled Belief Bulletins for use in "Interfaith Evangelism." The Belief Bulletins for Hinduism and Buddhism are representative of the tailored approaches taken in these documents. The Hinduism Belief Bulletin states that "Hindus hope to eventually get off the cycle of reincarnation," and suggests that there are various paths for doing so: "The way of works (*karma marga*), the way of knowledge (*jnana marga*), or the way of love and devotion (*bhakti marga*)." Therefore, when at the close of the Belief Bulletin several suggestions are made for bearing witness to Hindus, one is to make sure to "communicate that your assurance [of salvation] is derived from God's grace and not from your good works or your ability to be spiritual." On the other hand, asserting that Buddhism is "an impersonal religion of self-perfection, the end of which is death (extinction)—not life," the Buddhism Belief Bulletin recommends that, when bearing witness to Buddhists, Baptists should avoid terms "such as 'new birth,' 'rebirth,' 'regeneration,' or 'born again.'" Recommended substitutes include "endless freedom from suffering, guilt, and sin," "new power for living a holy life," "promise of eternal good life without suffering," and "gift of unlimited merit." It is also recommended that Baptists should comprehend Buddhism sufficiently "to discern weaknesses that can be used to make the gospel appealing."[26]

The sbc Belief Bulletins represent a clear desire to convert persons of non-Christian faiths. It is evident, however, that maintaining peaceful relations in contemporary Georgia may require parties on various sides to be open to change. The case of a Muslim cemetery in Gwinnett County is illustrative. In 2001 a zoning dispute arose between Muslims belonging to the Georgia Islamic Institute of Religious and Social Sciences, who wished to build a cemetery on a five-acre lot in the county, and their neighbors, property owners in the Grayson Oaks subdivision. The subdivision residents expressed concerns about some traditional Muslim burial practices, including wrapping the unembalmed body in a shroud and burying it without a casket or a vault. This practice, it was claimed, might lead to groundwater contamination. The Grayson Oaks residents were also alarmed that the cemetery might lower their property values.[27] The Gwinnett County Commission eventually worked out a compromise that required the Muslims to use caskets and to erect an eight-foot wooden fence surrounding the cemetery.[28] Gary Laderman has noted how each side in the conflict was confronted by the necessity of change. As religious newcomers, the Muslims were required to compromise on burial practices, but ensuring the rights of this religious minority meant that Christians among the residents also had to adjust their attitude toward others in the community.[29]

Such openness did not come easily, and passions ran high during the debate that preceded the commission's decision. In a county with more than one hundred Baptist and Methodist churches, the Muslim burial practices seemed strange to many inhabitants of Grayson Oaks. Contrasting the practices with those at a nearby Methodist cemetery, one subdivision resident said: "I didn't see a man in a sheet being toted around on someone's shoulders. I mean it was a coffin, it was very discreet."[30] The attorney for the Muslims, Dennis Still, reacted by observing that the subdivision residents were approaching Islam as if it were a bizarre cult. "This is a major world religion," he said, noting that Muslims "value their dead no less than you or I." Moreover, Still stressed that the Muslims "are a part of this county [and] are not some outside force." Thus the debate exposed a core conflict arising from the new religious pluralism. On one hand, some Grayson Oaks residents expressed that, as one put it, the cemetery would violate "the values of America."[31] Conversely, Commissioner John Dunn said of the Muslims: "These are all Americans and they should have all the rights and privileges afforded American citizens."[32]

This exchange brings to mind the subtitle of James Davison Hunter's *Culture Wars: The Struggle to Define America*.[33] In this regard, it is important to observe that the new pluralism has contributed to one of the most dramatic changes in the history of religion in the United States, which stands to have a profound effect on how America is viewed from both within and without. While Protestantism has long been the majority form of religion in the country, research by the General Social Survey of the National Opinion Research

Center (NORC) at the University of Chicago shows that the percentage of Protestants is falling precipitously. NORC estimates that Protestants comprised approximately 63 percent of the national population in the early 1990s, but had declined to about 52 percent by 2002. A 2004 NORC paper titled "The Vanishing Protestant Majority" stated that, as the result of "an array of social forces," the United States will soon no longer be a majority Protestant country: "The Protestant share of the population will continue to shrink and they will soon lose their majority position in American society."[34] Some of the main trends contributing to this national phenomenon are at work in Georgia as well, including large-scale immigration from the Middle and Far East, bringing new faiths; a rise in the number of persons having no religious affiliation; and an increase in immigration by Roman Catholics.

Given our concerns in this book, persons without any religious affiliation have been largely ignored to this point. However, that does not mean their numbers are insignificant. According to data collected for the 2001 American Religious Identification Survey, 37 percent of Georgians in 2000 were Baptists, while Methodists, at 11 percent, were the second largest religious affiliation. But the designation of "No religion" was the second-highest grouping overall, at 12 percent. This indicates that there are more Georgians who are unaffiliated with any organized religion than the sum of Presbyterians (3 percent), Pentecostals (3 percent), Episcopalians (2 percent), Lutherans (2 percent), and Jews (less than 1 percent) together. Catholics, at 8 percent, were the third most numerous religious affiliation, and the fourth highest grouping overall. In sum, four groupings—Baptists, No religion, Methodists, and Catholics—accounted for more than two-thirds of Georgians (68 percent) in 2000.[35]

One way of grasping the recent decline in the percentage of Protestants in Georgia, as well as the growth of Catholicism, is to track the proportionate strength of these groups among those persons having a Judeo-Christian religious affiliation. In Georgia in 1890, Baptists held a proportionate Judeo-Christian denominational strength of 52.6 percent, Methodists 40.6 percent, and Catholics only 1.7 percent. One hundred years later, in 1990, the proportionate strength of Baptists was still strong, at 60.9 percent, but Methodists had declined to 14.4 percent, while Catholics had risen to 5.6 percent. By 2000, only ten years later, Baptists had fallen to 48.7 percent proportionate strength, while Methodists held steady at 14.5 percent, and Catholics continued to climb, to 10.5 percent.[36]

When one recalls that Catholicism was the only faith forbidden in the Georgia colony, it is remarkable to note that it has become the third most prominent religious identification in the state, and that it is rapidly closing in on Methodism. The colonial ban on Catholicism was due in part to fears of collusion between Catholics in the British colony and those in Spanish Florida. Therefore, the first Catholic church in Georgia was not founded until long after the War of Jenkins' Ear concluded in 1743, which helped bring an end to the conflict in the New World between England and Spain. In fact, it was not until 1792, after the American Revolution, that a humble log cabin church was built at Locust Grove, near modern-day Sharon (Taliaferro County), to house the first Catholic congregation in Georgia.[37] By 1850 the number of Catholics was sufficient to form a Savannah diocese, which covered all of Georgia. The seat of the diocese, the Cathedral of St. John the Baptist, one of the most beautiful churches in the South and a popular destination for tourists in Savannah, was dedicated in 1876.[38] In 1956, a separate Diocese of Atlanta was established, serving northern counties in Georgia. By 1962 the Atlanta diocese had grown enough to become an archdiocese, overseeing the Diocese of Savannah as well as dioceses in the Carolinas.[39]

Although Catholicism is clearly growing in contemporary Georgia, the state's Catholic community struggled for several decades following the Civil War. Owing in part to an upsurge of anti-Catholicism in Georgia fueled by the rhetoric of Tom Watson and the rise of the second Ku Klux Klan, Catholics could feel strange and out of place in many parts of Georgia as late as the mid-twentieth century.[40] The circumstances surrounding the founding of the Monastery of the Holy Spirit in Conyers in 1944 illustrate this situation. The monastery belongs to the worldwide Order of Cistercians (also known as Trappists), which was formed in 1098 when a small group of monks established the Order in the forested wilderness of Cîteaux, France. The Monastery of the Holy Spirit is a direct descendant of that first Cistercian monastery and is an offshoot of a Cistercian monastery in Kentucky, Our Lady of Gethsemani, which was founded in 1849. The abbot of Gethsemani in the 1940s was Frederic Dunne, who chose the site of the offshoot monastery. Dewey Weiss Kramer, a historian of Holy Spirit Monastery, notes that the selection of rural Georgia was not accidental: "Dom Frederic's choice of Rockdale County, Georgia, was similar to that of the 1098 Cistercian Founders. It, too, was isolated, a 'desert' or 'wilderness.' . . . The abbot deliberately chose a site which was a desert in terms of the Catholic Church. The new foundation would be a witness to the faith in a foreign, perhaps even hostile territory."[41]

While Conyers drew the eyes of Frederic Dunne in the early 1940s, the city attracted the attention of Catholics throughout the world in the 1990s when it became recognized as a Marian apparition site. A Conyers woman named Nancy Fowler claimed that the Virgin Mary appeared to her and she conveyed public messages of the appearances from 1990 through 1998. The crowds that gathered to hear the messages grew over the years from several hundred to as many as several tens of thousands.[42] Though pilgrims came from a wide array of backgrounds, a great many were Hispanics, since devotion to the Virgin is especially important in their Catholic tradition.[43]

For a variety of reasons, including economic considerations, Hispanics flocked to Georgia to take up residence in the 1990s. According to data collected by the Small Business Development Center at the University of Georgia, in 1990 there were approximately 109,000 Hispanics in Georgia, representing 1.7 percent of the state population. By 2000 this number had grown to close to 435,000, or 5.3 percent of Georgia's population. Thus, between 1990 and 2000 the Hispanic population grew by 300 percent, while Georgia's total population grew by just over 26 percent (still a considerable amount, leading to Georgia becoming the ninth most populous state).[44] Many Hispanics were drawn to jobs in the construction, poultry, and carpet industries of north Georgia, including those in and around Atlanta, Cartersville, Rome, Dalton, and Gainesville.

Studies suggest that with increased acculturation to the United States, a number of Hispanics leave Catholicism for Protestantism. Nevertheless, a sizable number remain Catholics, as reported by *Christianity Today*: "Specifically, Hispanic immigrants to the United States are about 74 percent Catholic, 18 percent Protestant. Their children are 66 percent Catholic, 25 percent Protestant. By the third generation, the split is 59 percent Catholic, 32 percent Protestant."[45] In response to what has been described as both a "gift" and a "challenge," the Atlanta archdiocese created a Hispanic Ministry Office to assist parishes and missions in serving the needs of Hispanics in their areas.[46]

In addition to the growth of Catholicism, another major change in Georgia during the twentieth century was the efflorescence of Pentecostal groups. According to the American Religious Identification Survey, in 2000 approximately 3 percent of Georgians identified themselves as Pentecostal.[47] While there are several definitions of Pentecostalism, arguably the most distinguishing characteristic is belief in being "baptized with the Holy Spirit" (see Acts 1:5), which is manifested by spiritual gifts, especially *glossolalia* or "speaking in tongues."[48] Most generally, one may locate the origins of the Pentecostal movement in the late nineteenth-century Holiness groups that emerged within Methodism.[49]

One prominent Pentecostal leader who lived in Georgia was Joseph H. King, who was born in 1869 in South Carolina but moved early in life with his family to Franklin County in northeast Georgia. King became a Methodist minister and for a time served several northern Georgia churches. He became disappointed with the Methodist Church, however, because he thought it opposed Holiness teachings, which he came more and more to embrace. In 1898, therefore, King left the Methodist Church and joined a Holiness group, the Fire-Baptized Holiness Church, becoming president of the new denomination in 1900. In 1908, having had the experience of speaking in tongues, he became interested in the emerging Pentecostal movement. In 1911 King brought his denomination into the Pentecostal ranks when it merged with the Pentecostal Holiness Church. Franklin County (especially the town of Franklin Springs) remains strongly identified with Pentecostalism and is the location of both Emmanuel College, which is associated with the International Pentecostal Holiness Church, and the Pentecostal Advocate Press. Due to the large volume of Pentecostal material published in Franklin Springs, the town is known to Pentecostals throughout the world.[50]

The Pentecostal movement gained much of its focus and steam in Los Angeles, California, at the beginning of the twentieth century with the Azusa Street Revival, conducted from 1906 to 1909 by the black Holiness evangelist William Joseph Seymour. The success of the revival led to the growth of Pentecostal churches throughout the country. Seymour baptized blacks and whites alike at his small church, and within Pentecostalism it is said that "the color line was washed away in the Blood." Yet, while almost all Pentecostal movements and churches were interracial in the immediate aftermath of the Azusa Street Revival, this situation did not last. By 1925, most Pentecostal churches had separated into racially segregated congregations.[51]

In the 1990s a concerted effort was made to rebuild the bridge between black and white Pentecostals. A meeting in Atlanta in 1993 that outlined plans for racial reconciliation was one of a series that led to the "Memphis Miracle" meeting in 1994, which produced a Pentecostal "Racial Reconciliation Manifesto." The preamble to this statement proclaims: "Challenged by the reality of our racial divisions, we have been drawn by the Holy Spirit to Memphis, Tennessee . . . in order to become true 'Pentecostal Partners.'" The statement concludes by affirming: "At the beginning of the twentieth century, the Azusa

Street Mission was a model of preaching and living the Gospel message in the world. We desire to drink deeply from the well of Pentecost as it was embodied in that mission. We, therefore, pledge our commitment to embrace the essential commitments of that mission . . . and in the reconciliation of all Christians regardless of race or gender."[52]

In 1995 the SBC, meeting in Atlanta, issued a similar "Resolution on Racial Reconciliation on the 150th Anniversary of the Southern Baptist Convention." In this statement, the SBC acknowledged that "our relationship to African-Americans has been hindered from the beginning by the role that slavery played in the formation of the Southern Baptist Convention. . . . Many of our Southern Baptist forbears defended the right to own slaves, and either participated in, supported, or acquiesced in the particularly inhumane nature of American slavery." The statement added that "in later years Southern Baptists failed, in many cases, to support, and in some cases opposed, legitimate initiatives to secure the civil rights of African-Americans." Admitting that racism "has divided the body of Christ and Southern Baptists in particular, and separated us from our African-American brothers and sisters," the SBC resolved to "unwaveringly denounce racism, in all its forms, as deplorable sin."[53]

Among Pentecostals, the "Memphis Miracle" manifesto is widely considered a success. Many white SBC ministers have expressed a belief that their resolution has also helped pave the way for improved race relations. In 2003 Jack Graham, the minister of a Dallas, Texas, church and president of the SBC, stated that "it's definitely getting better," and he concluded: "It's a brand-new day in terms of our attitude, desire and heart." That same year, however, in a story titled "An Unfulfilled Promise?" reporter John Blake of the *Atlanta Journal-Constitution* described widespread skepticism among black Baptists belonging to the SBC. According to Blake, "several of the SBC's best-known black leaders say they're still being treated as if they're on the plantation— that white Southern Baptists refuse to see them as equals or share power." Blake quoted James Coffee, minister of the first black church admitted to the SBC, Community Baptist Church of Santa Rosa, California: "If they're going to accept black people and their churches, they're going to have to get rid of the slave master's mentality that's so prevalent in the convention."[54]

Such comments suggest that Nibs Stroupe, senior pastor of Oakhurst Presbyterian Church in Decatur, is right when he says that, despite the advances of the civil rights movement, "the great divide of race remains with us."[55]

Stroupe and his colleagues, including his associate pastor and wife, Caroline Leach, have tried to help bridge this gap at Oakhurst Presbyterian, which has received national recognition as one of the most successful multicultural churches in the country. The congregation has been featured in *Time* magazine, as well as on *NBC Nightly News*, CNN News, and CBS Radio. National Public Radio's *All Things Considered* stated: "Oakhurst Presbyterian Church is unremarkable on the outside, but the congregation inside is quite remarkable . . . middle class professionals, blue collar and pink collar workers, welfare recipients, old, young, and very young, black, white, Asian, gay and straight. All seem to feel comfortable there, and speak their minds."[56] Indeed, Oakhurst Presbyterian's mission statement asserts that the church embraces "a community of diversities."[57]

Oakhurst Presbyterian is a relatively small church, with roughly three hundred members, but it is located only ten miles from the largest Presbyterian church in the nation, Peachtree Presbyterian, which has approximately ten thousand congregants. Such numbers are not unique. In fact, the largest church in Georgia is New Birth Missionary Baptist Church in Lithonia, which has more than twenty-five thousand members.[58] The church received international attention in 2006 when it served as the location for the funeral of Coretta Scott King, the widow of Martin Luther King Jr. These large-scale churches point to the fact that Georgia has been in the forefront of a growing new phenomenon that cuts across racial as well as denominational lines—megachurches, which emerged after 1955 and began to flourish in the 1980s.[59]

Recent research concludes that there are at least twelve hundred churches in the United States that have more than two thousand weekly worshippers, the minimum amount to be considered a megachurch, and suggests that the number of such churches increased by nearly 50 percent between 2000 and 2005.[60] Despite such growth, megachurches still represent only a small fraction of the total number of congregations in the country. Nevertheless, they account for a staggering number of weekly attendees. One researcher, Mark Chaves, asserts that "the largest 10 percent of congregations [in the United States] contain about half of all churchgoers."[61] With close to seventy-five megachurches, Georgia has the fourth-highest number of any state (behind California, Texas, and Florida), and it has the highest proportion of megachurch members of any state.[62]

What is drawing so many people to these congregations? While the most evident characteristic of megachurches is their number of congregants, their size is the result of several other factors, including "a dynamic senior pastor, emphasis on conservative values, and building small groups to offset [overall] size."[63] In April 2003 the *Atlanta Journal-Constitution* ran a lengthy series on metro-Atlanta megachurches, and these characteristics recur in the series' descriptions of the congregations. By way of example, World Changers Church International is a multiethnic but largely African American megachurch in College Park, with more than twenty thousand members. It is led by the popular evangelist Creflo Dollar and his wife, Taffi, who spread their "prosperity gospel" message through TV broadcasts, recordings, and books. World Changers has approximately sixty weekly programs, from sports leagues to business networks.[64]

World Changers is nondenominational, as are many other megachurches, but Georgia holds several denominational megachurches as well. Peachtree Presbyterian and New Birth Missionary Baptist Church have already been mentioned. Other Atlanta-area megachurches include Ben Hill United Methodist Church, Mount Bethel United Methodist, and St. Catherine of Siena Roman Catholic Church. Several Georgia megachurches are Baptist, such as First Baptist Church of Atlanta, First Baptist Church of Jonesboro, First Baptist Church of Woodstock, and Roswell Street Baptist (Marietta). Yet the Atlanta area is not the only home to megachurches in Georgia. They may also be found in Gainesville, Savannah, Macon, Warner Robins, Columbus, and Valdosta. It is not surprising that Metro Atlanta holds so many megachurches, however, since research suggests that they tend to cluster around fast-growing "sprawl cities" such as Atlanta.[65]

As this suggests, scholarship is emerging that attempts to grasp the sociocultural dynamics of the megachurch phenomenon. Some of the results may seem surprising. Indeed, one study notes that "misconceptions about megachurches abound. . . . [The] data does not confirm many of the stereotypes Americans have of megachurches."[66] For instance, it is widely assumed that there is a connection between megachurches and the political power of the religious right. Yet this notion is not supported by the data on megachurches. In fact, Matthew Dowd, a campaign strategist for President George W. Bush's 2004 election campaign, estimates, based on exit polls from that election, that "about half of those who attend megachurches identify themselves politically as Democrats or independents, not Republicans."[67] To be sure, this observation applies to national trends, rather than specifically to Georgia, which has become a solid Republican "red state." It would not be a surprise, therefore, to find the congregants of megachurches in the Atlanta area largely self-identifying as Republicans, since the "Atlanta doughnut" counties, such as Cobb and Gwinnett, have voted heavily Republican in recent elections and several Atlanta-area megachurches are located in these counties. Yet it remains notable that political associations are not as useful as might seem to be the case in understanding the widespread growth of megachurches.

Indeed, it is problematic to regard megachurches as representing something entirely new. While the multiwatt sound systems and stadium seating of some megachurches suggest altogether contemporary modes of Christian worship, a number of scholars argue that the ritual programming of the mega-churches represents an updated version of patterns of worship that character-ized camp meeting revivalism.[68] Certainly, the extensive marketing practices once used to publicize camp meetings are seldom appreciated today. Yet as we have already seen, George Whitefield, the first great American revivalist, set the pattern for a well-coordinated approach to revival campaigns, complete with months-in-advance publicity.[69]

Perhaps it is best at present to understand megachurches as in large measure representing an attempt to reach, as a billboard advertising one Atlanta-area church put it, "people who don't DO church." Conrad Ostwalt has helpfully identified the essence of megachurches as "a way of conceiving church that focuses not on the churched but on the unchurched, that ministers not so much to the believer as it pitches to the nonbeliever." As he also notes, mega-churches welcome nonbelievers by "sponsoring elements of secular life, includ-ing technology and media-produced presentations and entertainment, within the walls of a church."[70] Here we may detect a crucial difference between early revivalism and megachurches. Whereas "Whitefield demonstrated the immense market opportunity for more robust, less secularized religion" in his day, the reflection of today's popular culture that can be glimpsed in mega-churches signifies "the secularization of traditional religion."[71]

One observer of megachurches finds that "their target audience consists of baby-boomers who left the church in adolescence, who do not feel comfort-able with overt displays of religiosity, who dread turning into their parents, and who apply the same consumerist mentality to spiritual life as they do to everything else. The mega-churches are using the tools of American society to spread religion where it would not otherwise exist."[72] Such "tools" can include a wide range of programming—from book clubs and dance classes to groups pooling tax advice—designed to provide a "one-stop shop" for busy American families and make them feel comfortable and at home. This customer-service approach to a congregant's needs in weekly programming has led one church historian to refer to the megachurch movement as the "Wal-Martization of American religion."[73] Even megachurch practitioners trumpet this aspect of their approach. Rod Pearcy, who runs the media center at The Calvary Chapel, part of a California-based evangelical "franchise," has been quoted as saying: "We are in the age of the superstore, like Home Depot, Lowe's and Super Target. The reason people go to them is there is so much more to offer. It is the same thing with mega-churches."[74]

Increasingly, research supports the notion that what megachurch participants primarily seek is relevance, not reverence.[75] A 2006 survey of hundreds of congregations of varying sizes in the United States, titled "FACTS on Growth," identifies important recent trends regarding congregations that are experiencing growth. Out of more than twenty survey items, the only one that *negatively* affected congregational growth was "it is reverent." Those congregations reporting that "reverent" describes their worship patterns "very well" or "quite well" are more likely to be experiencing decline than those who say that "it is reverent" describes their worship either "somewhat," "slightly," or "not at all." On the other hand, the survey found that exciting worship and the use of certain musical instruments making worship more stimulating are "strongly related to growth": "Over half of the congregations that use drums often or always in their worship services have experienced substantial growth from 2000 to 2005, as compared to less than a quarter of congregations that use drums seldom or never."[76] Leading the pack of growth congregations are the megachurches, whose "philosophy hinges on the assumption that affluent baby boomers, [the] target audience, were weaned on television and, therefore, cannot respond . . . without visual and auditory stimulation." Thus, "in order to capture the short attention spans of contemporary churchgoers molded by sound bites, commercials, and half-hour TV spots, megachurches use the arts and contemporary programming and entertainment styles to reach the seeker."[77]

As mentioned above, megachurches tend to cluster in urban areas like Atlanta since they are "predominantly a phenomenon of the suburbs of very large cities."[78] Research performed in 1996 by Mark R. Bell provides a counterweight to such topics. According to Bell, his examination of rural Bartow County, about an hour's drive north of Atlanta, was designed to offset studies focusing on urban areas. In contrast to reports asserting that religion in the contemporary South is becoming increasingly diverse, Bell found Bartow to be characterized by homogeneity instead of religious pluralism. In fact, Bell declared that the diversity that other researchers have seen in American religion is absent from Bartow. To be sure, there are several denominations represented in the county, including Lutheran, Presbyterian, Episcopalian, and Catholic churches, as well as Mormon chapels, Jehovah's Witness Kingdom Halls, a Seventh-Day Adventist church, and a chapter of the Salvation Army. However, the churches of Bartow are overwhelmingly Baptist; taken together, Baptist and Methodist churches account for more than 60 percent of the congregations in the county. Furthermore, Bell observed a striking degree of similarity in the religious expressions in the county. In his review of Bartow's newspaper, the *Daily Tribune News*, Bell concluded: "No issue is published without some talk of religious matters. But the religion that is discussed is always the same. The numerous articles on religious themes assume that the reader and the author have a common understanding of religion. There is never the need to justify or explain their religious paradigm, and diversity is conspicuously absent."[79]

Bell intentionally conducted his research thirty years after the publication of a landmark book by Samuel S. Hill Jr., titled *Southern Churches in Crisis*, and he stated that his overall aim was to explore changes in Southern religion in the years following the publication of Hill's book.[80] Hill had observed that at the foundation of Southern religion was the "central theme" of individual salvation, which he thought permeated every aspect of Southern Christianity: "The southern church . . . regards the conversion of [persons] as virtually the whole task of the church. . . . All the affirmations of popular southern Protestantism grow out of one concern, the salvation of the individual. . . . This is the foundation upon which assumptions are made, doctrinal systems are constructed, and church programs based. . . . Overriding everything else is consideration of the ancient question, 'What must I do to be saved?'"[81]

What Bell found in Bartow County in 1996 was a situation "as Hill might have expected to find it in 1966." Bell observed in Bartow a continuation of the "central theme," finding that the issue of being saved is of central importance. Further, he found that Bartow residents seemed not to care about what kind of church someone attends, so long as he or she is "born again." One Bartow resident interviewed by Bell helped him appreciate the uniformity cutting across the various religious institutions in the county by responding, when asked to explain the differences among the churches in his area of the county, that it came down to food: "The Baptists have the best cooking, the

Methodists are a close second, [but] I never knew a Presbyterian [who] could cook. That's about the only difference." Another person interviewed by Bell explained that salvation was tied to a single, datable occurrence, and she drew a distinction between her perceptions of the born-again rural experience and urban religiosity: "Some of my cousins that live in Atlanta don't believe 'once saved, always saved,' but we do."[82]

Hill has written in recent years that a new focus on doctrinal purity has developed in Southern religion, which has replaced individual salvation as "today's central theme." Hill explains that the theme of doctrinal purity is expressed through commitment to a certain lifestyle, with greatest emphasis being given to monogamy, the singular legitimacy of heterosexuality, and a pro-life position regarding abortion.[83] We may recognize in these matters the backdrop of the contemporary culture wars. Bell indicates, however, that his research in Bartow County does not corroborate Hill's new central theme. Instead, according to Bell, while Hill's new analysis suggests a way to understand the battles between Baptist fundamentalists and moderates over the past several decades, it is not helpful in describing Bartow County. Bell acknowledges that he occasionally encountered culture war topics such as abortion, monogamy, and homosexuality during his research, but such matters were secondary to a prevailing concern about salvation. Thus, he concludes that "the new central theme has yet to reach Bartow." Bell suggests that the new theme of doctrinal purity might be more relevant in an urban locale, given the number of seminary-trained clergy in such settings, who have to assert a standard orthodoxy to win over congregants. For Bell, rural Bartow County exists beyond such a setting, and thus "the future . . . seems to offer more of the same."[84]

Nevertheless, demographic data suggest that if the concerns of the new central theme are characteristic of urban areas, then they might be on their way to Bartow County sooner than Bell realizes. Bell is correct to point out that the scholarly focus when speaking of diversity and pluralism has typically been on mostly urban areas, but he seems to underestimate the rate of change in rural Georgia. Admittedly, as he notes, the motto of the Cartersville/Bartow County Convention and Visitors Bureau at the time he conducted his research was "Just 45 minutes north, but 100 years away from Atlanta." Yet in the decade during which Bell studied Bartow County it was in the midst of a growth spurt: in the 1990 census the county population was 55,915, but that figure had climbed to 76,019 by the time of the 2000 census.[85] In addition, the urban pockets surrounding Bartow County are expanding, with accompanying jokes that "Atlantanooga" is on its way. The 1960 census was the first to record that a majority of Georgians were living in urban areas, but by the 2000 census approximately 80 percent of the state population was urban.[86] A CNNMoney.com study of the one hundred fastest-growing counties in the United States by percentage growth between July 2004 and July 2005, based on Census Bureau statistics, showed that eight of the top thirty fastest-growing counties in the nation are in Georgia, including some that neighbor Bartow, such as Paulding, Cherokee, and Forsyth.[87] The conclusion is inescapable: as sprawl continues, urban issues may spread as well, producing more and more sites of religious conflict and negotiation.

Nancy Eiesland has provided a valuable study of one such conflict by investigating how small churches struggle in the shadow of megachurches. Eiesland examined dramatic changes taking place in Dacula, a city with a population of only three thousand, but located in a rapidly growing county, Gwinnett. In 1990 Gwinnett's population was 352,910 but by 2000 it had grown to 558,448, and the county was home to several megachurches, including Hebron Baptist in Dacula.[88] Eiesland studied how the appearance of Hebron put the old-style rural religion studied by Bell at risk. Eiesland reported that members of Hinton Memorial United Methodist Church "were affronted by regularly being 'hebroned'—the term they gave to door-to-door evangelistic campaigns done by the local megachurch, Hebron Baptist." The pastor of New Hope Baptist Church, Dana Alsop, told Eiesland: "Now, I'm not saying it's bad, but sometimes it seems that Hebron can act without considering anyone else in the community. . . . When they have their Starlight Crusades they don't seem to care that other churches are having revivals, too. Our people can't even get through the crowds to come." While some of the longtime local congregations were reluctant to make changes in their worship patterns in response to the presence of Hebron, some did try to emulate aspects of the megachurch. Eiesland reports, however, that such attempts were rarely successful. As a result, most of the congregations experienced serious decline because they were unwilling or unable to change sufficiently "to fit within an altered and denser ecology."[89]

Demographic studies repeatedly suggest that Georgia will become increasingly urbanized during the twenty-first century. One analysis, published just after the 2000 census, dramatizes a possible bleak future: "Georgia's population growth is among the most rapid in the nation. . . . This explosive growth is transforming the Georgia renowned for its history, distinctive charm, and ancient, sweeping magnolias into a Georgia whose roots may soon be unrecognizable—a Georgia of clogged highways, razed fields, and sprawling cities."[90] The report goes on to note that every day in Georgia some fifty acres of farmland and open space are lost to development. In 2002, following a three-year study by professors at Rutgers and Cornell universities, a Washington-based group, Smart Growth America, ranked Atlanta as the fourth most sprawling area in the nation.[91] Several additional studies, such as *USA Today's* Sprawl Index, which ranks Atlanta as the metro area with the fifth-most urban sprawl in the country, support this finding.[92] According to U.S. Census Bureau statistics released in April 2007, Atlanta added more new residents from 2000 to 2006 than any other metro area in the country.[93]

Georgia is not only becoming increasingly urban. It is also experiencing a dramatic increase in racial and ethnic diversity. Indeed, Georgia is close to joining a small number of states that have a "majority-minority" population. An August 2005 news release from the U.S. Census Bureau announced that Texas had joined Hawaii, New Mexico, and California as a majority-minority state, along with the District of Columbia, and it noted that five states, including Georgia, "are next in line with minority populations of about 40 percent."[94]

It is well known that the largest minority group in Georgia is African Americans, who comprise just under 30 percent of the state's inhabitants. But there are a significant number of other minority groups in the state as well. Janice Morrill, who has written about the range of ethnic celebrations in Georgia, notes how economic prosperity and successful refugee resettlement programs have made the state "a magnet for new settlers." She spotlights Vietnamese, Cambodian, and Laotian refugees who began to come to Georgia in the 1970s, as well as more recent immigrant groups such as Somalians, Ethiopians, Eritreans, Ukrainians, Russians, and Arabs. Morrill also mentions groups that have been in Georgia for generations, including Portuguese along the coast, Chinese in Augusta, and Greek and Middle Eastern groups in Atlanta.[95] In addition, as was discussed above, one of the most notable results of the 2000 census was the remarkable increase in Hispanics in Georgia since 1990. The full impact of all these groups across economic, political, and religious spheres of interest cannot be known. As Gary Laderman has expressed, "the kind of pluralism we're seeing is unheard of, and we don't know what the response is going to be."[96]

It is clear then, that, in addition to culture war issues such as abortion, the role and status of women, and sexual orientation, in the future Georgians will have to grapple, more and more, with diversity of all kinds (racial, ethnic, and religious) as well as increasing urbanization. In 1903 W. E. B. Du Bois wrote that "the problem of the Twentieth Century is the problem of the color-line."[97] We may anticipate that the problems of the twenty-first century will be more complex, as Georgians will need to navigate the profound issues presented by dramatic increases in population and pluralism.

Epilogue

The Civil War stands almost at the midpoint between James Oglethorpe's colony and today's state of Georgia. It also represents a dividing line for Georgia's churches. Before the war, black slaves worshipped with whites in biracial settings, albeit ones controlled and dominated by whites. After the war, free blacks established their own churches and denominations. Segregation of worship mirrored the segregation of society. Following the demise of enforced societal segregation in the 1950s and 1960s, selective segregation of worship largely continues.

Prior to the founding of the colony of Georgia, English-sponsored Indian slaving had developed, which in time gave way to the Atlantic slave trade. While Oglethorpe was still in Georgia, some religious groups, especially the Presbyterians in Darien and the Lutherans at Ebenezer, openly argued that enslavement of Africans was morally wrong. After Oglethorpe returned to England and slavery was deemed lawful by the colonial trustees in 1751, however, religion and slavery in Georgia began to be intertwined. When the Congregationalists who founded Midway arrived from South Carolina in 1752, they came as a community and brought their slaves with them. By the time of the Revolution there were almost equal numbers of free whites and enslaved blacks in Georgia.

As evangelicals came to the fore in the nineteenth century, their rise was accompanied by increasing acceptance and defense of slavery on religious grounds. We have seen that the opposition to slavery voiced by some Methodists hindered the growth of Methodism in Georgia during the early 1800s. But when slave owners such as Augustus Baldwin Longstreet joined the Methodist fold, the denominational numbers soared. Longstreet was joined by such fellow Georgians as Patrick Hues Mell, a Baptist, and Samuel Cassels, a Presbyterian, in defending slavery before what they collectively considered the impudence of Northern abolitionists. In their eyes, to oppose slavery was blasphemous, and the defense of slavery was evidence of piety.

Not only did Southern clergymen consider slavery to be in keeping with biblical command; they also came to view it as a key component of God's plan for human salvation. In a sermon delivered in Savannah in 1862, as the Civil War was being waged, Episcopal bishop Stephen Elliott argued at some length that God's purpose was manifest in slavery as practiced in the South. According to Elliott, God's design was to have the gospel preached throughout the world as a prelude to the final days and the return of Christ. But, said Elliott: "If we examine the religious condition of the world, keeping this purpose in our view, we will perceive that paramount Christian influences are steadily at work every where else except in Africa. . . . Africa alone is uninfluenced by Christianity." Elliott acknowledged that missionaries had gone to Africa, yet he asserted that they had made "no impression upon that vast interior which swarms with life and knows no religion save that of Nature, or the fraudulent devices of man."[1]

In Elliott's view, God was using Southern slavery to ensure the Christian education of a limited number of Africans, through whom salvation would eventually come to their continent:

> How, then, is that dark spot upon the world's surface to be enlightened? . . . Whence, then, is their regeneration to come, for come it must, if the Bible be the word of God, ere the present economy of things shall terminate? We are driven to look for it from some agency which shall be able, through national affinities . . . through a oneness of blood and of race, to bear the burden of this work, and ultimately, in God's own time, to plant the gospel in their Father-land, after they themselves shall have been prepared, through a proper discipline, for the performance of this duty. And I find this agency in the African slaves now dwelling upon this Continent and educating among ourselves.

For Elliott, the Civil War "certainly turns upon this point of slavery, and our future destiny is bound up with it."[2]

The enduring legacy of the Civil War can be seen in Georgia in many ways, from monuments and historical markers to bumper stickers and license plates. Although it is probably unknown to most Georgians, a vivid reminder of the Civil War can also be seen daily at the Capitol and other government buildings throughout the state. For, while it is doubtful that most voters realized it at the time, a statewide referendum in 2004 made the current state flag of Georgia essentially equivalent to the first flag of the Confederacy, the Stars and Bars, with the addition of the state coat of arms and the words, "In God We Trust." The Civil War literally hangs over Georgia.

Assertions of black inferiority more than survived the Civil War in the South, and paternalistic white supremacy contributed in some measure to a black exodus from formerly biracial denominations and churches. Christopher H. Owen observes that "in the 1880s and 1890s most . . . churches, as a practical matter, removed their galleries since few blacks attended services" with whites, and he concludes: "The physical evidence of segregation disappeared . . . but only because segregation was near total. For Georgia and the rest of the South, this development was perhaps the key religious consequence of the Civil War and Reconstruction."[3]

Presumably, the largest physical evidence of segregation remaining in Georgia is Oakland Cemetery, a sprawling space of some eighty-eight acres in downtown Atlanta, the first six-acre section of which was created in 1850.[4] The cemetery expanded to its present size by 1872, largely due to increases necessitated by the Civil War. Those sections that were added serve as a stark reminder of the thoroughly segregated society that then existed, for they feature a section used for the burial of blacks and a separate section for the graves of Confederate soldiers. As might be expected, the sections differ noticeably. The African American section has no marker, while the Confederate section has an imposing sixty-five-foot obelisk memorial. In addition, inside the Confederate section is an impressive statue, the fifteen-ton "Lion of Atlanta," which depicts a fallen lion on top of a Confederate flag in memory of the unknown Confederate soldiers buried nearby. Just a few hundred yards away from one another, on either side of the lion, are the grave sites of former slave Wesley J. Gaines, who became an African Methodist Episcopal bishop, and Clement A. Evans, a Confederate general who became a Methodist Episcopal Church, South, minister and an advocate of the Lost Cause.

Less than three miles to the west of Oakland Cemetery is Clark Atlanta University, where at the beginning of the twentieth century W. E. B. Du Bois wrote: "Negro problems have seemed to be centered in this State."[5] Contemporary scholar Stephen G. N. Tuck counters that "no doubt this claim is applicable to many states."[6] If racial problems have not been centered in Georgia, however, certainly one may safely say that Georgia has played a central role with regard to them. For example, we have seen that the church schisms of the 1840s, which foreshadowed secession and the Civil War, involved Georgia and Georgians to a great degree. The Methodist split came as a result of Georgian James O. Andrew's ownership of slaves, and the Southern Baptist Convention was founded in Augusta, as was the Southern Presbyterian

Church. We may further note that the national headquarters of the second Ku Klux Klan was located in Atlanta after the organization was revived atop Stone Mountain in 1915.

Yet Oakland Cemetery offers an additional strong reminder that Georgia has taken a pivotal role not only in fostering racial problems, but in providing solutions to those problems as well. For the entrance to Oakland Cemetery stands at the end of Martin Luther King Jr. Drive, and the cemetery is bounded by the King Center to the north and Ralph David Abernathy Freeway to the south, noteworthy indicators of the centrality of Atlanta and Georgia in the civil rights movement. Further underscoring this centrality is Andrew Young International Boulevard, located nearby. A few miles to the northeast of Oakland Cemetery, on Freedom Parkway, is the Jimmy Carter Presidential Center and Library, representing the work of the man who as governor announced that the time had come for racial discrimination to end, and who is now widely considered a proponent of worldwide peace. To the names of King, Abernathy, Young, and Carter may be added those of other notable Georgians who have attempted to ameliorate racial tensions, including several figures discussed in the pages of this book, such as Will W. Alexander, Ralph Mark Gilbert, Lugenia Burns Hope, Carrie Parks Johnson, Clarence Jordan, Frances Pauley, Jacob Rothschild, Lillian Smith, and Dorothy Tilly.

It is striking that two native Georgians, King and Carter, are among the five Americans to be Nobel Peace Prize recipients. (It might be noted as well that Woodrow Wilson, also a Nobel Peace Prize laureate, lived in Georgia during his youth.) The addresses delivered by King and Carter when they received their Nobel prizes attract attention, for they offer reflection drawn from lifelong experience.[7] It is not surprising that in these remarks, each man took notice of the fundamental role of race in his background. In 1964 King noted the ongoing racial conflicts in America: "The struggle to eliminate the evil of racial injustice constitutes one of the major struggles of our time. The present upsurge of the Negro people of the United States grows out of a deep and passionate determination to make freedom and equality a reality 'here' and 'now.'" Carter, in 2002, had the benefit of looking back on gains made after the time of King. In a moving fashion, he also highlighted the words of his fellow Georgian: "On the steps of our memorial to Abraham Lincoln, Dr. King said: 'I have a dream that on the red hills of Georgia the sons of former slaves and the sons of former slaveowners will be able to sit down together at a table of brotherhood.'" Carter added: "The scourge of racism has not been vanquished, either in the red hills of our state or around the world. And yet we see ever more frequent manifestations of his dream of racial healing. In a symbolic but very genuine way, at least involving two Georgians, it is coming true in Oslo today."

Carter's words acknowledge that some distance has had to be crossed for racial healing to take place. In describing his own religious stance, Carter expressed a message of inclusiveness that bridges gaps between persons of differing faiths and perspectives: "The unchanging principles of life predate modern times. I worship Jesus Christ, whom we Christians consider to be the Prince of Peace. As a Jew, he taught us to cross religious boundaries, in service and in love. He repeatedly reached out and embraced Roman conquerors, other Gentiles, and even the more despised Samaritans. Despite theological differences, all great religions share common commitments that define our ideal secular relationships."

In a justly celebrated section of one of his last books, King presented a comparable vision of an interrelated global community:

> Some years ago a famous novelist died. Among his papers was found a list of suggested story plots for future stories, the most prominently under-scored being this one: "A widely separated family inherits a house in which they have to live together." This is the great new problem of mankind. We have inherited a large house, a great "world house" in which we have to live together—black and white, Easterner and Westerner, Gentile and Jew, Catholic and Protestant, Moslem and Hindu—a family unduly separated in ideas, culture and interest, who, because we can never again live apart, must learn somehow to live with each other in peace.[8]

While in his day King could only view such a range of human expression on a global scale, over the past several decades an impressive array of immigrants have come to Georgia. As one mark of the change this represents, it may be noted that in 1959 King traveled to India to study about Gandhi and the teachings of nonviolence in Indian religion. Such direct experience is irreplaceable, yet were he alive today King might very well profit from also visiting the Hindu Temple of Atlanta in Riverdale, Shree Shakti Mandir of Atlanta in Lake City, or the Greater Atlanta Vedic Temple in Lilburn. Indeed, all of the groups that King spotlights—blacks and whites, Easterners and Westerners, Gentiles and Jews, Catholics and Protestants, Muslims and

Hindus—are today present in impressive numbers in contemporary Georgia, together with many additional communities.

In addition to ethnic and cultural pluralism, we have noted an increasing diversity of expression of religion in Georgia, such as the emergence of mega-churches alongside traditional, smaller congregations. And the large group of Georgians who identify themselves as having "No religion" must be taken into account as well. Finally, culture war issues such as abortion and homosexuality cross all boundaries, threatening to divide families and communities. All of these factors make living together in a "large house" ever more trying.

In the end, the challenge for Georgians in the future will be to live by something Jimmy Carter related that he learned as a child. In the conclusion to his remarks in Oslo in 2002, Carter said that during his years as president he often thought of an admonition he had received in his small school in Plains from his beloved teacher, "Miss Julia" Coleman.[9] According to Carter, she said: "We must adjust to changing times and still hold to unchanging principles." Then, drawing upon his lifetime of experience, from schoolhouses and sanctuaries in rural Georgia to the world stage, Carter emphasized what is surely an undying principle dear to all people of good faith: "The bond of our common humanity is stronger than the divisiveness of our fears and prejudices."

Notes

Prologue

1. Davis, *Fledgling Province*, insert between pp. 192 and 193.
2. Hence the title of a volume edited by Harvey H. Jackson and Phinizy Spalding, *Forty Years of Diversity: Essays on Colonial Georgia.*
3. Davis, *Fledgling Province*, 14.
4. Mixon, "Georgia," 291.
5. See Gaustad and Barlow, *New Historical Atlas*, 367, figure C.11.
6. Barnes, "Foreword," v: "Although Georgia may be renowned for its red clay . . . the hues that have determined her history are black and white."

CHAPTER ONE. *Before Georgia*

1. Elias Cornelius, "On the Geology, Mineralogy, Scenery," 214, 322–24. There are actually six mounds at the Etowah archaeological site, designated Mounds A–F. However, Mounds A, B, and C, which Cornelius observed close to the river, are much larger than Mounds D, E, and F. Had he noticed these latter three mounds at all (he recorded that he was unable to see Mound A, the largest, for some time after arriving at the site due to "thick forest trees"), Cornelius might have taken them for natural rises in the topography. Cf. Larson, "Etowah Site," 133.
2. Cornelius's experience, however, was not unique, as Charles Hudson (*Knights of Spain*, 437) points out: "By the end of the eighteenth century, many Southeastern Indians professed to have no knowledge of who had built the platform mounds. The naturalist William Bartram traveled extensively in the Southeast in 1765–66 and 1773–77, and he noted many mounds. . . . He concluded that the mounds had been built by an ancient 'nation' who inhabited the land before they were conquered by Cherokees and Creeks. The mounds were so ancient, wrote Bartram, 'that the Cherokees, Creeks, or the nation they conquered, could render no account for what purpose these monuments were raised.'"
3. For example, the Web site for Grayson, Georgia, proclaims: "The rich lands of Gwinnett County, Georgia were home to the Lower Creek and Cherokee Indians many thousands of years before the first European settlers set foot on them." http://www.cityofgrayson.org/graysonhistory.htm (accessed June 16, 2004). The errors in this statement will become clear in what follows in this chapter.
4. Charles Hudson (*Knights of Spain*, 425).

5. John E. Worth, "Before Creek and Cherokee: The Colonial Transformation of Prehistoric Georgia," http://web.archive.org/web/20031002215627/members.aol.com/jeworth/gbotxt.htm (accessed April 18, 2006).

6. David G. Anderson, "Paleoindian Period: Overview," *New Georgia Encyclopedia*, http://www.georgiaencyclopedia.org/nge/Article.jsp?id=h-810&sug=y (accessed December 9, 2006).

7. Lisa D. O'Steen, R. Jerald Ledbetter, and Daniel T. Elliott, "Archaic Period: Overview," *New Georgia Encyclopedia*, http://www.georgiaencyclopedia.org/nge/Article .jsp?id=h-580 (accessed May 28, 2006); DePratter, "Archaic in Georgia."

8. Thomas J. Pluckhahn, "Woodland Period: Overview," *New Georgia Encyclopedia*, http://www.georgiaencyclopedia.org/nge/Article.jsp?id=h-811&hl=y (accessed January 10, 2006).

9. White, *Archaeology and History*, 9–62 (especially 9, 15, 21, 31, 37, 42, 47, 56–58, and 62). Also very useful and authoritative is the online material developed by John E. Worth, "Georgia before Oglethorpe: A Resource Guide to Georgia's Early Colonial Era, 1521–1733," originally housed at SpanishFlorida.net and now available at http://www .lostworlds.org/ga_before_oglethorpe.html (accessed March 22, 2006).

10. Thomas J. Pluckhahn, "Kolomoki Mounds," *New Georgia Encyclopedia*, http:// www.georgiaencyclopedia.org/nge/Article.jsp?id=h-574&hl=y (accessed August 31, 2006). See also Pluckhahn, *Kolomoki*.

11. White, *Archaeology and History*, 58.

12. Mark Williams, "Rock Mounds and Structures," *New Georgia Encyclopedia*, http://www.georgiaencyclopedia.org/nge/Article.jsp?id=h-2867 (accessed May 11, 2006). A number of presumably Woodland-era stone and rock structures (such as mounds, piles, and walls) appear throughout Georgia, including Fort Mountain near Cartersville, which features a stone wall that extends for nearly one thousand feet. A similar wall once stood atop Stone Mountain but was destroyed in the early twentieth century by workers who used the rocks as road fill. On these stone structures, see White, *Archaeology and History*, 52–54; Philip E. Smith, *Aboriginal Stone Constructions*; and Gresham, "Historic Patterns."

13. Regarding the rise of chiefdoms as a general phenomenon in the Americas, see Redmond, *Chiefdoms and Chieftaincy*, and Carneiro, "What Happened at the Flashpoint?" A helpful overview of various theoretical issues about Mississippian chiefdoms may be found in Adam King, *Etowah*, 1–25.

14. See Adam King, "Mississippian Period: Overview," *New Georgia Encyclopedia*, http://www.georgiaencyclopedia.org/nge/Article.jsp?id=h-707&hl=y (accessed May 14, 2006). See also Widmer, "Structure of Southeastern Chiefdoms," 125–55. Max E. White (*Archaeology and History*, 91) describes Mississippian period Indian settlements as follows: "A typical pattern late in this period was a large riverside ceremonial center that served as the capital town, with attached towns, settlements, and farmsteads spread out for miles along the river and its tributaries. . . . Large towns with ceremonial centers, subsidiary towns and villages, and richly furnished burials in or near the mounds suggest a level of society more complex than any seen up to this time in the Southeast."

15. Worth, "Before Creek and Cherokee." For a thorough overview of a Mississippian chiefdom in Georgia, see Marvin T. Smith, *Coosa*.

16. White, *Archaeology and History*, 64.

17. National Park Service, Ocmulgee National Monument Site, http://www.nps .gov/ocmu/ (accessed May 11, 2006); Lewis Larson, "Etowah Mounds," *New Georgia Encyclopedia*, http://www.georgiaencyclopedia.org/nge/Article.jsp?id=h-577&hl=y (accessed May 12, 2006); Adam King, *Etowah*.

18. See White, *Archaeology and History*, 68–69.

19. See Adam King, *Etowah*, 79.

20. Marvin T. Smith, *Coosa*, 65. Smith states: "It is probable that they symbolized the mythical founding ancestors of . . . towns. Adair apparently viewed one of the last vestiges of this aspect of Mississippian religion during the eighteenth century." See also Knight, "Institutional Organization of Mississippian Religion," 681.

21. Worth, "Before Creek and Cherokee." See also Mark Williams, "Lamar Period," *New Georgia Encyclopedia*, http://www.georgiaencyclopedia.org/nge/Article .jsp?id=h-2551&hl=y (accessed May 12, 2006).

22. See Mark Williams, "Languages of Georgia Indians," *New Georgia Encyclopedia*, http://www.georgiaencyclopedia.org/nge/Article.jsp?id=h-2752&hl=y (accessed June 6, 2006). For a convenient overview of languages used among prehistoric Indians in Georgia, see the "Indigenous Chiefdoms of Georgia" section of Worth, "Georgia Before Oglethorpe."

23. Hudson, *Elements of Southeastern Indian Religion*, 6–7.

24. See Waring and Holder, "Prehistoric Ceremonial Complex," 1–34; and Waring, *Waring Papers*. See also Howard, *Southeastern Ceremonial Complex*; Galloway, *Southeastern Ceremonial Complex*; Fundaburk and Foreman, *Sun Circles and Human Hands*, 38–55; Knight, Brown, and Lankford, "On the Subject Matter"; and Power, *Early Art*, 63–105, 109–60.

25. For discussions of concepts of anomalous beings among Southeastern Indians, see Hudson, "Uktena," 62–73; and Hudson, "Meaning in Mississippian Art," 21.

26. Joel W. Martin, *Sacred Revolt*, 30, 31.

27. For overviews of the belief system of Southeastern Indians, see Hudson, *Elements of Southeastern Indian Religion*; Hudson, *Southeastern Indians*, 120–83; and Hudson, *Conversations*, in which Hudson presents a fictionalized account of a historical Spaniard, Domingo de la Anunciación, who encounters an Indian religious practitioner at Coosa and learns about the Mississippian worldview.

28. Mooney, *Myths of the Cherokee*, 239.

29. See Grantham, *Creation Myths*, 89–105.

30. Hudson, *Knights of Spain*, 22–23. Joel Martin (*Sacred Revolt*, 24) adds: "This tripartite division was immensely important for it delineated three classes of sacred beings, three basic kinds of sacred power, and three modes of symbolizing the sacred. . . . The division encouraged [Southeastern Indians] to see reality as fundamentally dynamic. Reality was always being pulled simultaneously in opposite directions by contrary powers."

31. Hudson, *Southeastern Indians*, 127–28; and Martin, *Sacred Revolt*, 24–25, 27.

32. Mooney, *Myths of the Cherokee*, 304–5.

33. On the importance of birds in Southeastern thought, see Hudson, *Southeastern Indians*, 128–30. Hudson (128–29) observes: "Birds were especially important, and this importance is reflected in the many bird motifs in the Southeastern Ceremonial Complex." Hudson's fictional holy man at Coosa (see *Conversations*, 28–29) states that: "Creatures that are at home in more than one realm are special. Kingfisher flies, and so he is of the above. But he can also dive into the watery realm [and] completely immerse himself into it. . . . When I wish to know the hidden causes of things, how I would like to be Kingfisher, who enters the under world so easily."

34. Hudson, *Conversations*, 152. Hudson provides an extended treatment of the *posketa* on pp. 152–75.

35. Hudson (*Elements of Southeastern Indian Religion*, 20) suggests that the square ground "was very likely a microcosm of the world, so that in this act of refurbishing they symbolically made the earth anew, obliterating all traces of the previous year."

36. For a discussion of the use of emetics among Southeastern Indians, see Hudson, "Vomiting for Purity," 93–102.

37. Hudson, *Elements of Southeastern Indian Religion*, 20; Smith, *Coosa*, 64.

38. Hudson (*Elements of Southeastern Indian Religion*, 21, 25) summarizes the overall impact of the *posketa*: "It was as if the entire social fabric was dusted off, tidied up, and set in order . . . time stopped, and then started, and the world was made anew."

39. John E. Worth, "Spanish Exploration," *New Georgia Encyclopedia*, http://www.georgiaencyclopedia.org/nge/Article.jsp?id=h-1012&hl=y (accessed June 7, 2006); Hudson, "The Hernando de Soto Expedition," 74–103; and Hudson, *Knights of Spain*.

40. King, "Mississippian Period."

41. De Soto and his men traveled for months through what is today southwest, central, northeast, and northwest Georgia. Along the way they spent brief periods of time in several Indian chiefdoms, including not only Coosa, but also Ichisi, on the Ocmulgee River near modern Macon, and Ocute, southeast of modern Milledgeville. See Hudson, *Knights of Spain*.

42. See Worth, "Late Spanish Military Expeditions," 104–22.

43. Marvin T. Smith, *Coosa*, 37, 42–43; Marvin T. Smith, "Late Prehistoric/Early Historic Chiefdoms (ca. A.D. 1300–1850)," *New Georgia Encyclopedia*, http://www.georgiaencyclopedia.org/nge/Article.jsp?id=h-573&hl=y (accessed August 12, 2006).

44. Charles Hudson (*Knights of Spain*, 424) observes that "the general archaeological picture of the Southeastern chiefdoms between about 1550 and 1650 is the same everywhere. The populations declined sharply; some areas became very thinly populated, or even abandoned; the construction and maintenance of platform mounds ceased; and the level of ritual and artistic elaboration decreased."

45. See Marvin T. Smith, "Aboriginal Depopulation in the Postcontact Southeast," 257–75; and Marvin T. Smith, *Archaeology of Aboriginal Culture Change*.

46. Worth, "Before Creek and Cherokee."

47. Max E. White's vivid description (*Archaeology and History*, 94) is worth quoting at length: "The most devastating result of [De Soto's] expedition was what amounted to germ warfare, although it was unintentional. Members of the de Soto expedition apparently spread smallpox and other Old World diseases, and within a few years the southeastern tribes [*sic*] had been decimated by the tens of thousands. Isolated from the Old World for many thousands of years, they had no resistance to the diseases brought by the Europeans. They also had no treatments. Like Europeans at the time of the Black Death of the Middle Ages, they had no idea what was causing their sickness, how it spread, or how it could be treated. We can only imagine the anguish of the tribes [*sic*] as thousands sickened and died. With no form of writing, the people passed their collective knowledge from generation to generation by word of mouth. As death claimed old and young alike, with the elderly went much of the accumulated knowledge of the people. It is small wonder that in later years, local Indians sometimes expressed ignorance of the builders of the ancient temple mounds. The Indians encountered by the English in the eighteenth century were merely the survivors."

48. Marvin T. Smith, *Coosa*, 96–117.

49. Marvin T. Smith, "Aboriginal Depopulation," 272.

50. Milanich, "Franciscan Missions," 279–80; and John E. Worth, "Spanish Missions," *New Georgia Encyclopedia,* http://www.georgiaencyclopedia.org/nge/Article .jsp?id=h-572&hl=y (accessed May 11, 2006). See also Worth, *Struggle for the Georgia Coast*; and Worth, *The Timucuan Chiefdoms.*

51. Worth, "Spanish Missions"; and Worth, "Before Creek and Cherokee."

52. Thomas, *St. Catherines*, 17–44.

53. Cathy Hulbert, "Early Georgia Evangelists: Archaeologists Are Revising Their Ideas about Relations between Native Americans and Spanish Catholics at St. Catherines Island," *Atlanta Journal-Constitution*, January 21, 2006.

54. Milanich, "Franciscan Missions," 289.

55. Milanich, "The Legacy of Columbus," 38.

56. Milanich, *Laboring*, 148–49.

57. Worth, "Before Creek and Cherokee"; and Milanich, "Franciscan Missions," 280–81.

58. Arnade, *Siege of St. Augustine*, 1.

59. See Bowne, "The Rise and Fall of the Westo Indians"; Bowne, *The Westo Indians*; and Bowne, "'A Bold and Warlike People'."

60. Robbie Ethridge, "English Trade in Deerskins and Indian Slaves," *New Georgia Encyclopedia*, http://www.georgiaencyclopedia.org/nge/Article.jsp?id=h-585&hl=y (accessed May 21, 2006). See also Joel W. Martin, "Southeastern Indians and the English Trade," 304–24; and Gallay, *The Indian Slave Trade.*

61. See Ethridge, "Creating the Shatter Zone," 207–18.

62. Eric E. Bowne, "Westo Indians," *New Georgia Encyclopedia*, http://www .georgiaencyclopedia.org/nge/Article.jsp?id=h-575&hl=y (accessed May 9, 2006).

63. Worth, "Spanish Missions."

64. John E. Worth ("Prelude to Abandonment," 30) states that "by the late 1600s, the great majority of . . . surviving prehistoric societies had vanished, leaving most of interior Georgia a vast abandoned zone between the Spanish colonial frontier to the south and that of the English to the north."

65. Worth, "Before Creek and Cherokee." On the development of the Creeks, see also Knight, "The Formation of the Creeks," 373–92; and Schnell, "Beginnings of the Creeks," 24–29.

66. For the historical background of the Redstick revolt, see Saunt, *New Order of Things*, 249–72.

67. Joel W. Martin, *Sacred Revolt*, 121–22.

68. Ibid., 127–29.

69. Ibid., 1–2.

70. Charles Hudson, communication with the author, July 20, 2006.

71. Originally published as John Howard Payne, "The Green-Corn Dance," *Continental Monthly* 1 (1862): 19, and quoted in John R. Swanton, "The Green Corn Dance," *Chronicles of Oklahoma* 10 (1932): 176–77, http://digital.library.okstate.edu/chronicles/v010/v010p170.html (accessed May 10, 2006).

72. For further discussion of the Green Corn ceremony, see Ballard, *Yuchi Green Corn Ceremonial*; Hudson, *Southeastern Indians*, 365–75; Hudson, *Elements of Southeastern Indian Religion*, 19–21; and Hudson, *Conversations*, 152–75.

73. Antonio Waring (*Waring Papers*, 63) observed: "The Creek busk, certainly the most impressive ceremonial in the entire Southeast, was in all probability derived from the old rectangular townhouse ceremonial. In fact, evidence has been presented suggesting that the busk represents the clearest survival of mound ceremonial and that several elements of the busk refer to mound-building activity." Vernon James Knight Jr. ("Symbolism of Mississippian Mounds," 287) adds: "It seems justifiable, in light of the evidence for continuity, to claim that [there is] an unbroken southeastern ritual tradition. This tradition employs earth mounds, either figuratively or actually, as earth icons in communal world renewal ceremonialism. Such a ritual tradition evidently predates Mississippian culture, and it survives in the green corn ceremonialism of the displaced southeastern tribes of Oklahoma."

CHAPTER TWO. *Seeds Are Sown*

1. Cf. Bolton and Ross, *Debatable Land*. See Spalding, "Spain and the Coming of the English," 9–15.

2. A replica of the fort has been constructed and is maintained as Fort King George Historic Site in Darien. See http://gastateparks.org/info/ftkinggeorge/ (accessed May 13, 2006). See also Cook, *Fort King George*; and Kelso, *Excavations*.

3. Julie Anne Sweet, "Tomochichi (ca. 1644–1739)," *New Georgia Encyclopedia*, http://www.newgeorgiaencyclopedia.org/nge/Article.jsp?id=h-689&hl=y (accessed May 13, 2006). See also Charles C. Jones Jr., *Historical Sketch of Tomo-Chi-Chi*; and Todd, *Tomochichi*.

4. "James Edward Oglethorpe," http://ourgeorgiahistory.com/people/oglethorpe .html (accessed August 7, 2006).

5. Edwin L. Jackson, "James Edward Oglethorpe (1696–1785)," *New Georgia Encyclopedia*, http://www.georgiaencyclopedia.org/nge/Article.jsp?id=h-1058&hl=y (accessed August 7, 2006). See Ettinger, *James Edward Oglethorpe*; and Spalding and Jackson, *Oglethorpe in Perspective*.

6. Apparently, there was not another Indian group in the area. In a letter Oglethorpe wrote to the Georgia trustees in February 1733, he commented: "A little Indian nation the only one within fifty miles is not only at amity but desire to be subject to the Trustees." Phillips Collection of Egmont Manuscripts, Letters from Georgia, 14201, Hargrett Rare Book and Manuscript Library, University of Georgia Libraries.

7. Andrew K. Frank, "Mary Musgrove (ca. 1700–ca. 1763)," *New Georgia Encyclopedia*, http://www.newgeorgiaencyclopedia.org/nge/Article.jsp?id=h-688&hl=y (accessed May 13, 2006). See also Doris Fisher, *Mary Musgrove*; Baine, "Myths of Mary Musgrove," 428–35; Gillespie, "The Sexual Politics of Race and Gender," 187–201; Green, "Mary Musgrove," 29–47; and Morris, "Emerging Gender Roles," 1–24.

8. Davis, *Fledgling Province*, 193, 195.

9. Saye, *Georgia's Charter*, 49.

10. See Stern, "New Light," 169–99; and George Fenwick Jones, "Sephardim and Ashkenazim Jewish Settlers," 519–37. For overviews of the various religious groups in colonial Georgia, including Anglicans, Jews, Lutherans, Presbyterians, Congregationalists, Quakers, and Baptists, see Walker, "Georgia's Religion," 17–44; and Davis, *Fledgling Province*, 192–232.

11. See George Fenwick Jones, *Salzburger Saga*.

12. George Fenwick Jones, *Detailed Reports on the Salzburger Emigrants*, 1:60. For a discussion of the interactions of Jews and German Protestants in the New World, focusing on Savannah, see Snyder, "A Tree with Two Different Fruits," 855–82.

13. Though it is often assumed that Bolzius did not refer to Sheftall by name, Holly Snyder ("A Tree with Two Different Fruits," 870 n. 56) asserts that Bolzius "apparently named Sheftall in the ms. diary, and [the original editor] Urlsperger excised the reference in the published version." In any case, as George Fenwick Jones ("Sephardim and Ashkenazim Jewish Settlers," 521) notes, "it is generally agreed that the generous host was Benjamin Sheftall."

14. See Stern, "Sheftall Diaries," 243–77.

15. Schmier, "Sheftall Family," 690–91.

16. Bolzius explains the circumstances surrounding the move in George Fenwick Jones, *Secret Diary*. See also Charles C. Jones Jr., *Dead Towns of Georgia*, 10–44.

17. Harold E. Davis (*Fledgling Province*, 15) states that "the Salzburgers, through their industry and common sense, were to distinguish themselves as the community of settlers who came closest to fulfilling what the trustees desired of all immigrants. Devout and hard-working small farmers who earned their bread by the sweat of their brows, they opposed slavery and were content not to stupefy themselves with rum."

18. Loewald, Starika, and Taylor, "John Martin Bolzius Answers a Questionnaire," 251.

19. Codrina Cozma ("John Martin Bolzius and the Early Christian Opposition to Slavery," 466) notes that "it was Bolzius's strong conviction that by using slave labor for their sustenance, the Salzburgers might turn to idleness."

20. See Fries, *Moravians in Georgia*; and Jones and Peucker, "'We Have Come to Georgia with Pure Intentions,'" 84–120.

21. For an alternative view, see Aaron Spencer Fogleman, "Moravians," *New Georgia Encyclopedia*, http://www.newgeorgiaencyclopedia.org/nge/Article.jsp?id=h-1595&hl=y (accessed May 13, 2006); Fogleman asserts that "the ultimate cause for the dissolution of the pacifist Moravian colony was not the pressure to bear arms in the war against Spain, as some have suggested, but rather a crisis within the Moravian community." See also Fogleman, "Shadow Boxing in Georgia," 629–59.

22. See Parker, *Scottish Highlanders in Colonial Georgia*.

23. One of the reasons for their settling at this location was the presence of the mighty Altamaha River, which is formed by the confluence of the Ocmulgee and Oconee rivers. The Altamaha is the "third largest contributor of freshwater to the Atlantic Ocean on North America's eastern shore." See Christa S. Frangiamore and Whit Gibbons, "Altamaha River," *New Georgia Encyclopedia*, http://www.newgeorgiaencyclopedia .org/nge/Article.jsp?id=h-2834&hl=y (accessed May 13, 2006). For discussions of the importance of the river to Darien's history, see Sullivan, *Early Days on the Georgia Tidewater*; and Sullivan, *Darien and McIntosh County*.

24. Scott, *Cornerstones*, 34.

25. See Lanning, *The Diplomatic History of Georgia*. See also the "Georgians and the War of Jenkins' Ear" special section in *Georgia Historical Quarterly* 78, no. 3 (1994): 461–508, containing the following articles: Phinizy Spalding, "Oglethorpe, Georgia, and the Spanish Threat," 461–70; Harvey H. Jackson III, "Behind the Lines: Savannah during the War of Jenkins' Ear," 471–92; and J. T. Scott, "The Frederica Homefront in 1742," 493–508.

26. See Baine, "General James Oglethorpe," 197–229.

27. Conner, *Muskets, Knives, and Bloody Marshes*, 27–56; Julie Anne Sweet, "War of Jenkins' Ear," *New Georgia Encyclopedia*, http://www.georgiaencyclopedia.org/nge/Article .jsp?id=h-807 (accessed May 13, 2006).

28. On the malcontents and the controversy over slavery in Georgia, see Wood, "A Note on the Georgia Malcontents," 264–78; Wood, *Slavery in Colonial Georgia*, 24–87; and Wood, "James Edward Oglethorpe, Race, and Slavery: A Reassessment," 66–79. See also Reese, *The Clamorous Malcontents*.

29. Wood, "Oglethorpe, Race, and Slavery," 73.

30. Excerpts from this document are available in Scott, *Cornerstones*, 32–33. Thomas Stephens was the son of William Stephens, who served as the trustees' secretary in Savannah. Scott (p. 31) observes that William Stephens loyally supported the trustees' policies, and therefore that it was to his "chagrin" that his son "became a major voice for the malcontents."

31. Wood, *Slavery*, 32. Wood observes that "in 1739 the Trustees were under no real pressure to modify their labor policy; by 1743 they had all but conceded defeat in their attempt to exclude slavery from Georgia."

32. "The Petition of the Inhabitants of New Iverness" is available in Reese, *Clamorous Malcontents*, 249–50; and Scott, *Cornerstones*, 34–35.

33. See Wylly, *Seed That Was Sown*, 34.

34. See Wood, *Slavery*, 59–73; and Cozma, "John Martin Bolzius," 457–76.

35. See Thurmond, *Freedom*, 17–18.

36. Davis, *Fledgling Province*, 117.

37. "Inhabitants of Ebenezer to James Oglethorpe," Georgia Digital History Project, Georgia State University, http://msit.gsu.edu/dhr/gacolony/letters/ebenezer_1735.htm (accessed July 31, 2006). Elsewhere Bolzius suggested that Georgia summers were "not so very hot as idle and delicate people endeavor to persuade themselves and others" (quoted in Lane, *General Oglethorpe's Georgia*, 2:401).

38. Wood, "Oglethorpe, Race, and Slavery," 77.

39. Thurmond, *Freedom*, 32–33.

40. Cozma, "John Martin Bolzius," 475. Cozma notes that Bolzius nevertheless "remained adamant in his anti-slavery political and ethical objections."

41. Davis, *Fledgling Province*, 31–32.

42. On Sunbury, see Charles C. Jones Jr., *Dead Towns of Georgia*, 141–223. For Midway Church, see Stacy, *History of the Midway Congregational Church*; and Stacy, *History and Published Records of the Midway Congregational Church*.

43. The present Midway Congregational Church building dates to 1792 (an earlier building was destroyed during the Revolution).

44. Raboteau, *Slave Religion*, 46, 120, 125–26.

45. See Edward J. Cashin, "Royal Georgia, 1752–1776," *New Georgia Encyclopedia*, http://www.newgeorgiaencyclopedia.org/nge/Article.jsp?id=h-818&sug=y (accessed May 14, 2006). As Cashin notes elsewhere, the trusteeship ended one year early: "The failure of Parliament to vote a subsidy in 1751 caused the Trustees to enter into negotiations to turn the colony over to the government a year before the charter expired." See Edward J. Cashin, "Trustee Georgia, 1733–1752," *New Georgia Encyclopedia*, http://www.newgeorgiaencyclopedia.org/nge/Article.jsp?id=h-816 (accessed August 23, 2006).

46. Stan Deaton, "James Wright (1716–1785)," *New Georgia Encyclopedia*, http://www.newgeorgiaencyclopedia.org/nge/Article.jsp?id=h-669&hl=y (accessed May 14, 2006). See also Abbot, *Royal Governors of Georgia*.

47. Davis, *Fledgling Province*, 29.

48. Robert Scott Davis Jr., "Wrightsborough," *New Georgia Encyclopedia*, http://www.newgeorgiaencyclopedia.org/nge/Article.jsp?id=h-1096&hl=y (accessed June 10, 2006). See also Baker, *Story of Wrightsboro*; Dorothy M. Jones, *Wrightsborough*; and Davis, *Quaker Records*.

49. Candler, *Colonial Records of the State of Georgia*, 18:271–72.

50. For a discussion of the circumstances that brought Zubly to Georgia, see Roger A. Martin, "John J. Zubly Comes to America," 125–39.

51. Jim Schmidt, "John J. Zubly (1724–1781)," *New Georgia Encyclopedia*, http://www.newgeorgiaencyclopedia.org/nge/Article.jsp?id=h-662&sug=y (accessed May 13, 2006); Davis, *Fledgling Province*, 51.

52. See Nichols, "Religious Liberty," 1764, n. 432.

53. Davis, *Fledgling Province*, 183. Zubly's magnificent library would ultimately be thrown into the Savannah River. Before and during the Revolution, Zubly was a loyalist. He was banished from Savannah in July 1776, at which time a crowd of patriots entered his house and threw most of his books into the river. See Schmidt, "John J. Zubly." See also Miller, *"A Warm & Zealous Spirit"*; and Pauley, "Tragic Hero," 61–81.

54. [Zubly], "Letter of Rev. John J. Zubly," 215–16.

55. Davis, *Fledgling Province*, 204–5.

56. Ibid., 205.

57. Samuel Quincy to Mr. Newman, July 4, 1735. Phillips Collection of Egmont Manuscripts, Letters from Georgia, 14201, Hargrett Rare Book and Manuscript Library, University of Georgia.

58. Davis, *Fledgling Province*, 198.

59. [Zubly], "Letter of Rev. John J. Zubly," 219. Harold E. Davis (*Fledgling Province*, 197–98) observes that the overwhelming evidence is that colonial Georgians tended not to be deeply religious, and the atmosphere was such that "Georgians who showed themselves entirely uninterested in churches bore no stigma."

60. Thomas Jackson, *Journal of Charles Wesley*, 1:1.

61. Ibid., 1:2–4, 6, 8, 17, 36.

62. Ibid., 1:2, 4, 11, 16. Harold E. Davis (*Fledgling Province*, 194–95) explains that while "the official policy of the government was one of religious toleration for everybody except Roman Catholics . . . the government did not feel threatened by the very few Roman Catholics who actually lived in Georgia."

63. Harvey H. Jackson, "Parson and Squire," 57, 65.

64. Davis, *Fledgling Province*, 177–78.

65. Ibid., 193, 222.

66. Coleman, *Colonial Records of the State of Georgia*, 118.

67. Davis, *Fledgling Province*, 222–23.

68. See "John Wesley's American Parish," http://www.gcah.org/Heritage_Landmarks/Parish.htm (accessed August 12, 2006).

69. Curnock, *Journal of the Rev. John Wesley*, 3:434.

70. Frederick V. Mills, Sr., "John Wesley (1703–1791)," *New Georgia Encyclopedia*, http://www.newgeorgiaencyclopedia.org/nge/Article.jsp?id=h-1623&hl=y (accessed May 14, 2006).

71. Curnock, *Journal of John Wesley*, 1:400.

72. See Tyerman, *Life of the Rev. George Whitefield*; and Pollock, *George Whitefield*.

73. See Cashin, *Beloved Bethesda*.

74. Finke and Stark, *Churching of America*, 49.

75. Roger Finke and Rodney Stark (ibid., 54) state that "in 1776 the Congregationalists, Episcopalians, and Presbyterians seemed to be *the* colonial denominations. Of Americans active in a religious body, 55 percent belonged to one of the three." Edwin Scott Gaustad and Philip L. Barlow (*New Historical Atlas*, figure C.22) also refer to these denominations as the "Colonial 'Big Three.'"

76. Gardner, "Georgia Baptist Convention," 42.

77. Finke and Stark, *Churching of America*, 54.

CHAPTER THREE. *God Is Calling Ev'ry Nation*

1. See Asbury, *Methodist Saint*; and Rudolph, *Francis Asbury*.

2. For the foundational history of Methodism in Europe and the development of the Methodist Episcopal Church in America, see Bucke, *History of American Methodism*; Norwood, *Story of American Methodism*; Richey, *Early American Methodism*; and Hempton, *Methodism*.

3. Owen, *Sacred Flame*, 1–2, 4. A helpful digest of material from Asbury's journal relating to Georgia may be found in Lawrence, *Asbury's Georgia Visits*. A standard edition of the journal is Clark, Potts, and Payton, *Journal and Letters of Francis Asbury*.

4. Owen, *Sacred Flame*, 3–4, 11. See also Wayne Mixon, "Georgia," 291.

5. Finke and Stark, *Churching of America*, 23, 27, 35. Overall, Finke and Stark assert that, contrary to popular understanding, religious adherence has steadily grown in America from a low of approximately 17 percent of the population being churched (i.e., belonging to a congregation) on the eve of the Revolution, to approximately 37 percent at the start of the Civil War, 51 percent by 1906, and about 60 to 65 percent by the end of the twentieth century.

6. Owen, *Sacred Flame*, 7.

7. Walker, "Birth of Missions and Education," 59. Wilkes County was larger in the past than it is at present, having originally included Lincoln, Elbert, and parts of Hart, Madison, Oglethorpe, Taliaferro, Warren, and McDuffie counties; see http://wilkescounty.georgia.gov/03/home/0,2230,8356233,00.html;jsessionid =D0B85B5F3AF367BD8B23F282BB51FFBE (accessed August 2, 2006).

8. James C. Giesen, "Cotton," *New Georgia Encyclopedia*, http://www.newgeorgia encyclopedia.org/nge/Article.jsp?id=h-2087&hl=y (accessed August 13, 2006). James C. Bonner (*A History of Georgia Agriculture*, 52) notes that "to separate a pound of this cotton from the seed required a day's work."

9. Jeffrey Robert Young observes that "in 1790, just before the explosion in cotton production, some 29,264 slaves resided in the state. . . . By 1800 the slave population in Georgia had more than doubled, to 59,699; by 1810 the number of slaves had grown to 105,218." See Jeffrey Robert Young, "Slavery in Antebellum Georgia," *New Georgia Encyclopedia*, http://www.newgeorgiaencyclopedia.org/nge/Article.jsp?id=h-1019&hl=y (accessed June 18, 2006). As a result, Georgia led the world in cotton production by 1825. See Coleman, *Georgia History in Outline*, 39. On slavery in antebellum Georgia, see Reidy, *From Slavery to Agrarian Capitalism*; Julia Floyd Smith, *Slavery and Rice Culture*; Stewart, *"What Nature Suffers to Groe"*; and Young, *Domesticating Slavery*.

10. Evangelicals may be understood as those Protestants, such as Baptists, Methodists, and Presbyterians, who emphasize the conversion experience through faith in the atoning death of Jesus and regard the Bible as the ultimate religious authority. See Wells and Woodbridge, *The Evangelicals*.

11. The Baptist figure is based on May 2004 correspondence between the author and Robert G. Gardner. Regarding Methodists, Christopher H. Owen (*Sacred Flame*, 14) records that "by 1810 . . . 8,072 Methodists . . . lived in Georgia." As to Presbyterians, Ernest Trice Thompson (*Presbyterians*, 1:123) notes that "in 1810 there were still only five [Presbyterian] ministers in [Georgia], and the communicants reported were only 218."

12. Wesley M. Gewehr, *The Great Awakening in Virginia, 1740–1790* (Durham, N.C.: Duke University Press, 1930), 106, quoted in Ernest Trice Thompson, *Presbyterians*, 1:66. Gewehr observed: "Presbyterianism, 'with its intellectual demands of an elaborate creed' and its high standards of education for its ministry, was at best restricted in its appeal. It was never able to reach and to stir the common folk."

13. Gardner, "Baptists in Georgia," 10–13; and Davis, *Fledgling Province*, 32. See also Robert G. Gardner, "Baptists: Overview," *New Georgia Encyclopedia*, http://www .newgeorgiaencyclopedia.org/nge/Article.jsp?id=h-2923&hl=y (accessed June 20, 2006).

14. For a helpful compendium of materials relating to the growth of Georgia Baptists in the 1700s, see Gardner, "Primary Sources," 59–118.

15. See Mosteller, *History of the Kiokee Baptist Church*; and Harris and Mosteller, *Georgia's First Continuing Baptist Church*.

16. Gardner, "Baptists in Georgia," 13–15.

17. Ibid., 16.

18. See Hunt, "Daniel Marshall," 5–18.

19. The date of the creation of the Georgia Baptist Convention is not completely settled. It is possible that it was created in 1785 instead of 1784, but the earlier date is more generally accepted among scholars. See Gardner, "Georgia Baptist Convention," 42.

20. Robert G. Gardner, "Daniel Marshall (1706–1784)," *New Georgia Encyclopedia*, http://www.newgeorgiaencyclopedia.org/nge/Article.jsp?id=h-2853&hl=y (accessed May 20, 2006).

21. It is worth noting that though Daniel Marshall is most widely known for his association with "mighty men," his wife, Martha Stearns Marshall, became recognized as the model of the ideal minister's spouse. See Garmon, "Role of Women," 11.

22. Alfred Mann Pierce, *Lest Faith Forget*, 9.

23. Owen, *Sacred Flame*, 2; and Frederick V. Mills, Sr., "John Wesley (1703–1791)," *New Georgia Encyclopedia*, http://www.newgeorgiaencyclopedia.org/nge/Article .jsp?id=h-1623&hl=y (accessed May 14, 2006).

24. Owen, *Sacred Flame*, 4–7.

25. Lawrence, *Asbury's Georgia Visits*, 10–11, 24.

26. Data drawn from Owen, *Sacred Flame*, 190; and Gardner, "Baptists in Georgia," 12. The upper figure for Baptists (i.e., 5,315) is from 1801.

27. Wesley's views on slavery can be found in Wesley, *Thoughts upon Slavery*.

28. Owen, *Sacred Flame*, 7; and Gardner, "Baptists in Georgia," 17.

29. Owen, *Sacred Flame*, 4.

30. Gardner, "Baptists in Georgia," 16–17.

31. Owen, *Sacred Flame*, 24.

32. Lawrence, *Asbury's Georgia Visits*, 16, 20.

33. Boles, *Great Revival*, 81–82. For a historical overview of camp-meeting sites in Georgia, see Lawrence, *Feast of Tabernacles*.

34. Lumpkin, "Great Awakening," 310. See also Bumsted, *Great Awakening*.

35. See Pollock, *George Whitefield*.

36. Franklin, *Autobiography*, 177.

37. Frank Lambert ("'Pedlar in Divinity,'" 813) observes: "What was new about Whitefield was the skill as an entrepreneur, an impresario, that made him a full-fledged forerunner of evangelists like . . . Billy Graham."

38. Finke and Stark, *Churching of America*, 46–51, 88–89.

39. Lawrence, *Asbury's Georgia Visits*, 3.

40. Boles, *Irony of Southern Religion*, 18–19.

41. Ibid., 19–24. See also Boles, *Great Revival*.

42. Owen, *Sacred Flame*, 14.

43. Boles, *Great Revival*, 82.

44. See Moore, *Selling God*, 77.

45. Jesse Lee, letter to the editor in *Farmer's Gazette*, August 8, 1807, reprinted in Commons, *Documentary History*, 2:284–86.

46. Boles, *Irony of Southern Religion*, 28–29.

47. See Malinda Snow, "*The Sacred Harp*," *New Georgia Encyclopedia*, http://www .georgiaencyclopedia.org/nge/Article.jsp?id=h-549&hl=y (accessed February 1, 2007). See also Bealle, *Public Worship, Private Faith*; Ellington, "The Sacred Harp Tradition"; and Buell E. Cobb Jr., *Sacred Harp*. Also known as "shape-note" or "fasola" singing, Sacred Harp is a nondenominational, unaccompanied style of group singing. Using syllables (i.e., "do, re, mi, fa, sol, la, ti") to represent notes on a scale that originated in Europe before the nineteenth century, a notation system was developed in New England by 1801. In *The Sacred Harp*, White and King codified many aspects of the style, and their approach has been adopted and modified widely.

48. Bruce, *And They All Sang Hallelulah*, 95.

49. Owen, *Sacred Flame*, 22.

50. Raboteau, *Slave Religion*, 92. For discussions of how "revivalism . . . created the conditions for large-scale conversion of the slaves," see also pp. 132–33 and 148–49.

51. Art Rosenbaum, "McIntosh County Shouters," *New Georgia Encyclopedia*, http:// www.newgeorgiaencyclopedia.org/nge/Article.jsp?id=h-520&hl=y (accessed May 15, 2006). See also Rosenbaum, *Shout Because You're Free*.

52. Georgia author Corra Harris published an autobiographical novel in 1910 about a circuit rider and his family in north Georgia, which reflects much of the lifestyle that was present in the nineteenth century. See Corra Harris, *Circuit Rider's Wife*.

53. Owen, *Sacred Flame*, 14, 30.

54. Walker, "Birth of Missions," 83–84; and Walker, "Development of Organizations and Institutions," 119–21.

55. Baker, *Southern Baptist Convention and Its People*, 85.

56. Ibid., 105–13; and Walker, "Different Frontiers," 155.

57. Gardner, "Georgia Baptist Convention," 55; and Walker, "Development of Organizations and Institutions," 134. James Adams Lester (*History of the Georgia Baptist Convention*, 59) adds that in 1819 there were eight Baptist associations in Georgia, and only one (Piedmont) expressed any anti-mission sentiments.

58. Robert G. Gardner, "History of the Baptists in Georgia, 1733 to Present," http:// tarver.mercer.edu/archives/GaBaptists.php (accessed August 13, 2006).

59. John G. Crowley, "Primitive Baptists," http://www.georgiaencyclopedia.org/nge/ Article.jsp?id=h-1545&hl=y (accessed August 11, 2007). See Crowley, "Primitive Baptists of South Georgia"; and Crowley, *Primitive Baptists of the Wiregrass South*.

60. "The Georgia Baptist Convention, 1822–Present," http://www.gabaptist.org/ common/content.asp?PAGE=169 (accessed June 22, 2006).

61. See Burch, *Adiel Sherwood: Baptist Antebellum Pioneer*; and Burch, "Adiel Sherwood: Religious Pioneer," 22–47. See also Carswell, "Adiel Sherwood," 93–106; and Sanders, "Frontier to Forefront," 31–46.

62. Jarrett Burch, "Adiel Sherwood (1791–1879)," *New Georgia Encyclopedia*, http:// www.georgiaencyclopedia.org/nge/Article.jsp?id=h-2848&sug=y (accessed May 20, 2006).

63. "Generally the altar call is a time at the close of the sermon where, during some form of music, listeners are invited to come to the front in response to the message." Carey Hardy, "A Close Look at Invitations and Altar Calls," *Bible Bulletin Board*, http:// www.biblebb.com/files/MAC/SC03-1050CDNotes.htm (accessed August 12, 2006).

64. Burch, "Adiel Sherwood."

65. See Dowell, *A History of Mercer University*. See also Bryant, "From Penfield to Macon."

66. See Mondy, "Jesse Mercer," 349–59; Huddlestun, "Jesse Mercer's Influence," 41–66; Chute, *Piety above the Common Standard*; and William Brent Jones, "Jesse Mercer (1769–1841)," *New Georgia Encyclopedia*, http://www.georgiaencyclopedia.org/nge/Article .jsp?id=h-1611&hl=y (accessed May 20, 2006).

67. Mercer, *History of the Georgia Baptist Association*.

68. See Chase L. Peeples, "*Christian Index*," *New Georgia Encyclopedia*, http://www .georgiaencyclopedia.org/nge/Article.jsp?id=h-749&hl=y (accessed June 22, 2006). The paper remains the official publication of the GBC, and some regard it as the oldest religious newspaper in the United States still in publication. In the antebellum period, the editorial offices were housed in a succession of Georgia cities, including Washington and Macon. Since the Civil War, the paper has been published in Atlanta.

69. Gardner, "John Leadley Dagg," 246–63; and Gardner, "John Leadley Dagg of Georgia," 68–86.

70. Robert G. Gardner, "John Leadley Dagg (1794–1884)," *New Georgia Encyclopedia*, http://www.georgiaencyclopedia.org/nge/Article.jsp?id=h-787&hl=y (accessed May 20, 2006).

71. Lawrence, *Asbury's Georgia Visits*, 29.

72. Owen, *Sacred Flame*, 7, 27, 32.

73. See Wade, *Augustus Baldwin Longstreet*.

74. David Rachels, "Augustus Baldwin Longstreet (1790–1870)," *New Georgia Encyclopedia*, http://www.newgeorgiaencyclopedia.org/nge/Article.jsp?id=h-1235&hl=y (accessed August 11, 2007); and Owen, *Sacred Flame*, 33.

75. Christopher H. Owen (*Sacred Flame*, 8) points out that "as plantation agriculture became more profitable, it was increasingly difficult for Methodists to oppose the peculiar institution."

76. See Rachels, *Augustus Baldwin Longstreet's Georgia Scenes*. A contemporary literary scholar, Hugh Ruppersburg, has noted that "many regard Longstreet's collection of sketches and stories of frontier Georgia as the first true expression of indigenous American humor. . . . *Georgia Scenes* was the first in a rich succession of books and writers of southern humor, culminating at the end of the nineteenth century in the novels of Mark Twain, whose wry wit and rollicking characters owe a direct debt to Longstreet." See Hugh Ruppersburg, "Twelve Great Works of Georgia Fiction," *New Georgia Encyclopedia*, http://www.georgiaencyclopedia.org/nge/Feature.jsp?id=s-47&hl=y (accessed May 6, 2006).

77. See Bullock, *History of Emory University*.

78. Maddex, "Waddel, Moses," 819. Ernest Trice Thompson (*Presbyterians*, 1:251) observes that in the half-century following the Revolution, "the University of North Carolina and the University of Georgia, were for all practical purposes Presbyterian institutions." He also notes (1:263) that in 1829 "Georgia had thirty-two thousand Baptists, twenty-seven thousand Methodists, and three thousand Presbyterians," yet the religious affiliation of state university faculty members was "six Presbyterians, one Methodist, one Episcopalian, one Congregationalist, and a few others of no affiliation."

79. Owen, *Sacred Flame*, 42.

80. See Stacy, *History of the Presbyterian Church*, 108–57; and Paul Stephen Hudson, "Oglethorpe University," *New Georgia Encyclopedia*, http://www.georgiaencyclopedia.org/nge/Article.jsp?id=h-1450&hl=y (accessed May 17, 2006).

81. Thompson, *Presbyterians*, 1:123.

82. See Gabin, *Living Minstrelsy*; and Susan Copeland Henry, "Sidney Lanier (1842–1881)," *New Georgia Encyclopedia*, http://www.newgeorgiaencyclopedia.org/nge/Article.jsp?id=h-533&hl=y (accessed August 11, 2007).

83. See Erick D. Montgomery, "Woodrow Wilson in Georgia," *New Georgia Encyclopedia*, http://www.georgiaencyclopedia.org/nge/Article.jsp?id=h-2904&hl=y (accessed May 20, 2006). See also Osborn, *Woodrow Wilson*.

84. Jesse Griffin, "Christian Church (Disciples of Christ)," *New Georgia Encyclopedia*, http://www.georgiaencyclopedia.org/nge/Article.jsp?id=h-1549&hl=y (accessed May 17, 2006). See also Moseley, *Disciples of Christ*.

85. "First Christian Church (Disciples of Christ)," http://www.georgiahistory.com/first1.htm (accessed August 13, 2006).

86. "Emily Harvie Thomas Tubman, 1794–1885," http://www.georgiawomen.org (accessed May 20, 2006).

87. Moseley, *Disciples of Christ*, 137.

88. Tim Alan Garrison, "Cherokee Removal," *New Georgia Encyclopedia*, http://www.georgiaencyclopedia.org/nge/Article.jsp?id=h-2722&hl=y (accessed August 13, 2006).

89. Walker, "Birth of Missions and Education," 68.

90. See Schwarze, *History of the Moravian Missions*; McLoughlin, *Cherokees and Missionaries*; and Rowena McClinton, "Indian Missions," *New Georgia Encyclopedia*, http://www.georgiaencyclopedia.org/nge/Article.jsp?id=h-784&hl=y (accessed May 20, 2006).

91. N. Michelle Williamson, "Chief Vann House," *New Georgia Encyclopedia*, http://www.georgiaencyclopedia.org/nge/Article.jsp?id=h-2726&hl=y (accessed May 20, 2006); and McClinton, "Indian Missions."

92. McLoughlin, *Cherokees and Missionaries*, 336–37.

93. See Tim Alan Garrison, "*Worcester v. Georgia* (1832)," *New Georgia Encyclopedia*, http://www.georgiaencyclopedia.org/nge/Article.jsp?id=h-2720 (accessed August 13, 2006).

94. "*Worcester v. Georgia*, 1832," *Civics-Online*, http://www.civics-online.org/library/formatted/texts/worcester.html (accessed May 20, 2006). See Breyer, "Cherokee Indians and the Supreme Court"; Garrison, *Legal Ideology of Removal*; and Norgren, *Cherokee Cases*.

95. See Anderson, *Cherokee Removal*; and Perdue and Green, *Cherokee Removal*. Regarding the severity of the treatment of the displaced Cherokees, one Georgian who was a member of the federal detail and was later a Confederate colonel said: "I fought through the civil war and have seen men shot to pieces and slaughtered by thousands, but the Cherokee removal was the cruelest work I ever knew" (Thompson, *Presbyterians*, 1:203).

96. Haynes, *Noah's Curse*, 142, 144.

97. State Population Facts, http://www.npg.org/states/ga.htm (accessed August 20, 2006).

98. Gaustad and Barlow, *New Historical Atlas*, figure C.3.

CHAPTER FOUR. *The Crucible of Slavery*

1. Stephens and Lincoln were well acquainted. Stephens recollected after Lincoln's assassination: "I knew Mr. Lincoln well. We met in the House in December, 1847. We were together during the Thirtieth Congress. I was as intimate with him as with any other man of that Congress except perhaps one. That exception was my colleague, Mr. [Robert] Toombs. Mr. Lincoln was warm-hearted; he was generous; he was magnanimous; he was truly 'with malice toward none, with charity for all.'" See Avary, *Recollections of Alexander H. Stephens*, 61.

2. Basler, *Collected Works of Abraham Lincoln*, 4:160. Earlier in the year, on February 27, 1860, Lincoln had emphasized these points at Cooper Union in New York. Lincoln asserted that Southerners were demanding that the North "cease to call slavery *wrong*, and join them in calling it *right*." He added: "Their thinking it right, and our thinking it wrong, is the precise fact upon which depends the whole controversy." On the Cooper Union speech, see Holzer, *Lincoln at Cooper Union*; an authoritative text of the speech is found on pp. 249–84.

3. Stephens, *Constitutional View of the Late War*, 2: 269.

4. Stephens had opposed secession as a policy, but he also pledged to go along if Georgia chose that route: "I shall bow to the will of the people. Their cause is my cause, and their destiny is my destiny." See Schott, *Alexander H. Stephens*, 308.

5. Alexander H. Stephens, "Speech Delivered on the 21st March, 1861, in Savannah, Known as 'The Corner Stone Speech,' Reported in the Savannah Republican," in Cleveland, *Alexander H. Stephens*, 721. In reference to Stephens's assertion of the South's "corner-stone," Donald Grant (*Way It Was in the South*, 82) observes: "It was this racist bedrock, born of self-deception and assiduously cultivated since Georgia was founded, that obscured the relatively simple fact that slavery was an economic institution created to exploit the black worker. It was this racism that took Georgia out of the Union in 1861, that killed so many of its sons on the battlefields of the Civil War, impoverished its economy, and brought needless suffering to countless people, both black and white."

6. For a general overview of proslavery argumentation, see Tise, *Proslavery*. Tise (xvii) observes: "I found quite early in my research that the antebellum clergy provided essential social leadership in manners quite distinct from the patterns to which we are accustomed in the twentieth century. In the nineteenth century . . . one could find among the ranks of the ministry some of the most superbly educated, socially aware, and powerfully stationed (both symbolically and actually) leaders America could boast. As educators, writers, reformers, orators, and spiritual leaders, clergymen constituted the largest, most vocal, and most readily accessible national elite in American society. One measure of their significance is the fact that ministers wrote almost half of all defenses of slavery published in America."

7. On these matters, see especially Snay, *Gospel of Disunion*.

8. Chesebrough, *Clergy Dissent*. Mitchell Snay (*Gospel of Disunion*, 27) observes that antislavery sentiments "seemed limited to the upper South, especially North Carolina and Virginia."

9. Owen, *Sacred Flame*, 78. Owen (p. 33) notes: "Given the hostility of southern whites to criticisms of slavery, the muting of antislavery principles was a necessary condition to allow Methodism to expand, perhaps even to survive, in Georgia."

10. As Clarence L. Mohr ("Slaves and White Churches," 155) puts it: "If slavery had divine sanction, evangelizing blacks became a sacred duty."

11. See Raboteau, *Slave Religion*, 152–80.

12. For an overview of the interaction between white missionaries and slaves in the mid-eighteenth century, see Janet Duitsman Cornelius, *Slave Missions*.

13. Raboteau, *Slave Religion*, 154.

14. Charles Colcock Jones, *The Religious Instruction of the Negroes in the United States* (Savannah: Thomas Purse, 1842), v–xiii. Documenting the American South, University Library, The University of North Carolina at Chapel Hill, http://docsouth.unc.edu/church/jones/menu.html (accessed May 18, 2006).

15. Thompson, *Presbyterians*, 1:443–44.

16. Owen, *Sacred Flame*, 80.

17. Ayoub, "Islamic Tradition," 481.

18. Jones, *Religious Instruction*, 125.

19. Raboteau, *Slave Religion*, 46.

20. Austin, *African Muslims*, 99, 106.

21. See Coulter, *Thomas Spalding*.

22. Austin, *African Muslims*, 85–99.

23. Martin, "Sapelo Island's Arabic Document," 594–95, 598, 601. During the War of 1812, Bilali assured Spalding that he would defend his master's property on Sapelo Island, and Spalding gave him eighty muskets. Austin (*African Muslims*, 87) reports: "This appears to have been the only instance in which slaves were given guns in Georgia during the antebellum period. Bilali put his own faith on the line; he declared to Spalding that in the event of an attack, 'I will answer for every Negro of the true faith [i.e., Islam], but not for the *Christian dogs* you own'" (emphasis in original).

24. Jones, *Religious Instruction*, 129–30.

25. See Boles, *Irony of Southern Religion*, 47 ("biracial religion was a commonplace in the antebellum South and represented the normative worship experience for blacks"); and Boles, *Masters and Slaves*.

26. Waters, *On Jordan's Stormy Banks*, 45, 104, 149, 164.

27. Berlin et al., *Remembering Slavery*, 192. Cf. Ephesians 6:5–8: "Servants, be obedient to them that are your masters according to the flesh, with fear and trembling, in singleness of your heart, as unto Christ; Not with eyeservice, as menpleasers; but as the servants of Christ, doing the will of God from the heart; With good will doing service, as to the Lord, and not to men: Knowing that whatsoever good thing any man doeth, the same shall he receive of the Lord, whether he be bond or free."

28. Christopher H. Owen (*Sacred Flame*, 24) observes that "one should not exaggerate the degree of biracialism. . . . White Methodists . . . outnumbered black Wesleyans four to one in Georgia as a whole. . . . Whites kept a virtual monopoly on church offices, controlled the terms of worship, and dominated the denomination in leadership and outlook."

29. Mohr, "Slaves and White Churches," 156.

30. On such proceedings, see Wills, *Democratic Religion*.

31. Boles, *Irony of Southern Religion*, 60. Boles (p. 58) observes: "Church disciplinary procedures . . . were probably the most important way that slave members were accorded a degree of respect and equality."

32. Waters, *On Jordan's Stormy Banks*, 128, 149.

33. Raboteau, *Slave Religion*. See also Genovese, *Roll, Jordan, Roll*.

34. Waters, *On Jordan's Stormy Banks*, 164, 182, 191.

35. Ibid., 9–10.

36. Snay, *Gospel of Disunion*, 19, 30, 37.

37. Mitchell Snay (ibid., 12) asserts that for Southern clergy, "the Bible was the center of their defense of slavery." He discusses Southern claims concerning scriptural justification of slavery on pp. 54–59. See also Noll, "The Bible and Slavery," 43–73; and Haynes, *Noah's Curse*.

38. Joseph R. Wilson, *Mutual Relation of Masters and Slaves as Taught in the Bible: A Discourse Preached in the First Presbyterian Church, Augusta, Georgia, on Sabbath Morning,*

Jan. 6, 1861 (Augusta, Ga.: Steam Press of Chronicle & Sentinel, 1861). Documenting the American South, University Library, The University of North Carolina at Chapel Hill, http://docsouth.unc.edu/wilson/menu.html (accessed June 29, 2006).

39. Longstreet, *Letters on the Epistle of Paul to Philemon*, 9, 11.

40. Owen, *Sacred Flame*, 52, 67.

41. Henderson, "Patrick Hues Mell," 11–19; and Jarrett Burch, "Patrick Hues Mell (1814–1888)," *New Georgia Encyclopedia*, http://www.georgiaencyclopedia.org/nge/Article .jsp?id=h-2848&sug=y (accessed April 18, 2007).

42. [Mell], *Slavery*, 15, 37.

43. Ibid., 9, 15.

44. Dagg, *Elements of Moral Science*, 344. Cf. Haynes, *Noah's Curse*, 71.

45. [Mell], *Slavery*, 10, 15.

46. Stephens, "Speech Delivered on the 21st March, 1861," 722–23.

47. Cassels, "Conscience," 468.

48. Snay, *Gospel of Disunion*, 49.

49. See William Y. Thompson, *Robert Toombs*.

50. Morris Brown College, http://www.morrisbrown.edu/wwwroot/prototype/College %20Information/MBCCollegeInformationHistory.htm (accessed June 29, 2006).

51. Owen, *Sacred Flame*, 121, 166.

52. Berlin et al., *Remembering Slavery*, 21–22.

53. Raboteau, *Slave Religion*, 167.

54. Melanie Pavich-Lindsay, who has edited the extensive letters of one slave master, Anna Matilda Page King of St. Simons Island, summarizes that King lived closely with her slaves and could "work with them, nurse them, love them, even despise them." However, "she could never see them as deserving her fullest attention or sympathies." Pavich-Lindsay notes: "Rarely in [King's] letters does she talk about their lives independent of her own. Her racism, like that of many people of her time, was inherited, constant, and unquestioned. She never wavered in her belief that it was her right to own other human beings or in her understanding of the duties of that ownership." In short, King "never saw her enslaved workers as fully human." Pavich-Lindsay, *Anna*, xxvii.

55. Lane, *Neither More nor Less*, 157. An extract from Ball's autobiography is found on pp. 154–60. As an example of the cruelty Ball encountered, in one passage (pp. 157–58) he vividly portrays "cat-hauling," which he calls "the most excruciating punishment" of a slave that he ever observed. In this practice, a large cat would be placed on the back of a slave, near the shoulders, "and forcibly dragged by the tail down the back and along the bare thighs of the sufferer." Ball describes seeing such a cat-hauling: "The cat sunk his nails into the flesh and tore off pieces of the skin with his teeth. The man roared with the pain. . . . The overseer said he should have another touch of the cat, which was again drawn along his back, not as before from the head downwards, but from below the hips to the head." After this treatment, the slave's back was doused with salt water.

56. Catherine Clinton, "Fanny Kemble (1809–1893)," *New Georgia Encyclopedia*, http://www.georgiaencyclopedia.org/nge/Article.jsp?id=h-792&hl=y (accessed March 22, 2007); and "Fanny Kemble and Pierce Butler, 1806–1893," Africans in America, Public

Broadcasting System, WGBH Educational Foundation, http://www.pbs.org/wgbh/aia/ part4/4p1569.html (accessed August 13, 2006).

57. Kemble, *Journal.*

58. See Schneider and Schneider, *Eyewitness History*, 89.

59. Kemble, *Journal*, 10.

60. Ibid., 159–61, 240–41.

61. Holmes, "Duties of Christian Masters," 133, 135–36.

62. Wilson, *Mutual Relation of Masters and Slaves.*

63. See especially Snay, *Gospel of Disunion.*

64. Ibid., 128–29; and Goen, *Broken Churches*, 78–90.

65. Goen, *Broken Churches*, 90–98; and Snay, *Gospel of Disunion*, 134–38.

66. See Gardner, *Decade of Debate and Division*, 25–31, 65–73. Apparently, 138 of the registered Georgia delegates actually attended meetings.

67. Snay, *Gospel of Disunion*, 113.

68. Goen, *Broken Churches*, 101. Clay served in the U.S. Senate from 1831 until 1842, when he resigned. He was reelected to the Senate in 1849 and served until 1852. See Remini, *Henry Clay.*

69. Goen, *Broken Churches*, 99.

70. Cheek, *John C. Calhoun*, 695–97.

71. Daniel Webster, *Writings and Speeches*, 10:63, 92–93.

72. McCash, *Thomas R. R. Cobb*, 89. The article in which this statement appears was unsigned, but it has been ascribed to Cobb. See the discussion on p. 89 n. 65.

73. See Goen, *Broken Churches*, 68–78; and Snay, *Gospel of Disunion*, 115–26.

74. A. J. L. Waskey, "Presbyterian Church in the United States of America (PCUSA)," *New Georgia Encyclopedia*, http://www.georgiaencyclopedia.org/nge/Article.jsp?path=/ Religion/FaithsDenominations/Christianity/Presbyterian&id=h-1565 (accessed August 4, 2007).

75. See Faust, *Creation of Confederate Nationalism.*

76. Boles, *Irony of Southern Religion*, 80.

77. Snay, *Gospel of Disunion*, 151.

78. Porter, *Christian Duty in the Present Crisis*, 5–6.

79. Boles, *Irony of Southern Religion*, 83.

80. Palmer, *Thanksgiving Sermon*, 5–6, 9–10.

81. Snay, *Gospel of Disunion*, 179. Snay discusses Palmer's sermon at length on pp. 175–80.

82. Owen, *Sacred Flame*, 91.

83. Stowell, *Rebuilding Zion*, 33.

84. Owen, *Sacred Flame*, 98.

85. Pierce and Palmer, *Sermons*, 3–5.

86. Faust, "Christian Soldiers," 71. See also http://www.nps.gov/anti/ (accessed February 22, 2007).

87. See Boles, *Irony of Southern Religion*, 94.

88. Cf. Shattuck, *Shield and Hiding Place*, 40–41.

89. Stephen Elliott, *Extract from a Sermon Preached by Bishop Elliott, on the 18th September, Containing a Tribute to the Privates of the Confederate Army.* Documenting the American South, University Library, The University of North Carolina at Chapel Hill, http://docsouth.unc.edu/imls/elliotts1/elliott.html (accessed April 7, 2007); Stephen Elliott, *New Wine Not to Be Put into Old Bottles. A Sermon Preached in Christ Church, Savannah, on Friday, February 28th, 1862, being the Day of Humiliation, Fasting, and Prayer, Appointed by the President of the Confederate States* (Savannah: Steam Power Press of John M. Cooper, 1862). Documenting the American South, University Library, The University of North Carolina at Chapel Hill, http://docsouth.unc.edu/imls/elliott/menu .html (accessed April 7, 2007); Stephen Elliott, *Ezra's Dilemna [sic]. A Sermon Preached in Christ Church, Savannah, on Friday, August 21st, 1863, Being the Day of Humiliation, Fasting and Prayer, Appointed by the President of the Confederate States* (Savannah, Ga.: Power Press of George M. Nichols, 1863). Documenting the American South, University Library, The University of North Carolina at Chapel Hill, http://docsouth.unc.edu/imls/ elliottezra/menu.html (accessed April 7, 2007).

90. Stephen Elliott, *Vain Is the Help of Man. A Sermon Preached in Christ Church, Savannah, on Thursday, September 15, 1864, Being the Day of Fasting, Humiliation, and Prayer, Appointed by the Governor of the State of Georgia* (Macon, Ga.: Burke, Boykin, 1864). Documenting the American South, University Library, The University of North Carolina at Chapel Hill, http://docsouth.unc.edu/imls/elliotts/menu.html (accessed May 18, 2006).

91. Cf. Stowell, *Rebuilding Zion*, 8. See also Noll, *Civil War*.

92. Burr, *Secret Eye*, 276–77.

93. See especially Stowell, *Rebuilding Zion*, 33–48.

94. S. G. Hillyer, "To the Baptists of Georgia," *Christian Index*, November 9, 1865; and Henry H. Tucker, "All Things Work Together for Good to Them That Love God," *Christian Index*, January 13, 1866. Quoted in Stowell, *Rebuilding Zion*, 41.

95. Basler, *Collected Works of Abraham Lincoln*, 5:537.

96. Owen, *Sacred Flame*, 107.

CHAPTER FIVE. *A Racial Pas de Deux*

1. See Anne J. Bailey, *War and Ruin*; and Kennett, *Marching through Georgia*.

2. Anne J. Bailey, "Sherman's March to the Sea," *New Georgia Encyclopedia*, http:// www.newgeorgiaencyclopedia.org/nge/Article.jsp?id=h-641&sug=y (accessed May 6, 2006).

3. Carter, *Diary of Dolly Lunt Burge*, 161–62. Also available as Dolly Lunt Burge, *A Woman's Wartime Journal: An Account of the Passage over Georgia's Plantation of Sherman's Army on the March to the Sea, as Recorded in the Diary of Dolly Sumner Lunt (Mrs. Thomas Burge)* (New York: The Century Company, 1918), 29–30. Documenting the American South, University Library, The University of North Carolina at Chapel Hill, http:// docsouth.unc.edu/burge/menu.html (accessed May 6, 2006).

4. Johnson, *Black Savannah*, 173.

5. See Glatthaar, *March to the Sea*.

6. Berlin et al., *Free at Last*, 314.

7. For instance, Katherine Dvorak (*African-American Exodus*, 2) states that "the driving force in the segregation of the southern churches was the black Christians' surge toward self-separation acting on their own distinctive appropriation of Christianity. . . . Black initiative was decisive in the emergence of a pattern of racial separation in the southern churches." Conversely, Kenneth K. Bailey ("Post-Civil War Racial Separations," 463) asserts that "the eventual thrust toward explicit (and boastful) explicitly and discretely all-white, all-black denominationalism is considerably attributable largely to a white aversion to an ecclesiastical union with blacks."

8. Stowell, *Rebuilding Zion*, 80–81. Stowell (p. 80) points out that "the Presbyterian Synod of Georgia had few, if any, black members by 1870; that church had ceased reporting black membership statistics in 1866 because there were so few."

9. Boles, *Irony of Southern Religion*, 69–70.

10. See the chart of "White membership in southern denominations in Georgia, 1860–1877," in Stowell, *Rebuilding Zion*, 107.

11. Owen, *Sacred Flame*, 115.

12. See David S. Williams, "Lizzie Rutherford (1833–1873)," *New Georgia Encyclopedia*, http://www.newgeorgiaencyclopedia.org/nge/Article.jsp?id=h-2901&hl=y (accessed May 6, 2006).

13. Anna Caroline Benning, "Preface," in *A History of the Origins of Memorial Day* (Columbus: Thomas Gilbert, 1898), 6; quoted in Lloyd A. Hunter, "Immortal Confederacy," 190.

14. See David S. Williams, "Lost Cause Religion," *New Georgia Encyclopedia*, http://www.newgeorgiaencyclopedia.org/nge/Article.jsp?id=h-2723&hl=y (accessed May 6, 2006). Lloyd A. Hunter ("Immortal Confederacy," 186) observes that Lost Cause religion represents an "amalgam of Protestant evangelicalism and Southern romanticism."

15. Blight, *Race and Reunion*, 258.

16. Pollard, *Lost Cause*. It is noteworthy that on April 13, 1865, shortly before John Wilkes Booth shot Abraham Lincoln, he wrote in his diary that "our cause being almost lost, something decisive & great must be done" (Rhodehamel and Taper, *Right or Wrong*, 154).

17. Nolan, "Anatomy of the Myth," 13–14.

18. Pollard, *Lost Cause*, 751.

19. Charles Reagan Wilson (*Baptized in Blood*, 7) underscores that, among other groups, white religious figures in the South took up this message: "Fearing that crushing defeat might eradicate the identity forged in war, Southerners reasserted that identity with a vengeance. . . . The South's religious leaders and laymen defined this identity in terms of morality and religion: in short, Southerners were a virtuous people. Clergymen preached that Southerners were the chosen people, peculiarly blessed by God." Wilson goes on to note: "Unfortunately, the self-image of a chosen people leaves little room for self-criticism. This deficiency has led to the greatest evils of the religion-culture link in the South."

20. The following paragraphs are based on Hunter, "Immortal Confederacy," 185–218. Hunter's discussion of the distinction between civil religion and culture religion in n. 3 (pp. 209–11) is particularly valuable.

21. Ibid., 187–89.

22. For an overview of the assertions of the Lost Cause myth, see Nolan, "Anatomy of the Myth," 11–34.

23. There is no better capsule description of the Old South of the Lost Cause myth than the opening words of the film version of *Gone with the Wind*, with its elegiac reference to the now vanished pretty world of "Cavaliers and Cotton Fields," where gallantry "took its last bow." The term "Cavaliers" is not lightly used here. Alan T. Nolan ("Anatomy of the Myth," 16–17) discusses how one element of the Lost Cause myth held that "Northerners were . . . descended from the Anglo-Saxon tribes that had been conquered by the Norman cavaliers. The cavaliers were, of course, the ancestors of the Southerners according to this theory." Nolan points to the analysis found in Beringer et al. (*Why the South Lost*, 76): "Without its own distinctive past upon which to base its nationality, the Confederacy appropriated history and created a mythic past of exiled cavaliers and chivalrous knights."

24. One of the staunchest defenders of the glories of the Old South and the supposed benefits of slavery was the venerable Mildred Lewis Rutherford, historian-general of the United Daughters of the Confederacy, and long-time principal of the Lucy Cobb Institute for Girls in Athens. See Anne E. Marshall, "Mildred Lewis Rutherford (1851–1928)," *New Georgia Encyclopedia*, http://www.newgeorgiaencyclopedia.org/nge/Article.jsp?id=h-3178 &hl=y (accessed July 8, 2006). David W. Blight (*Race and Reunion*, 281) quotes Rutherford as asserting: "The Negroes under the institution of slavery were well-fed, well-clothed, and well-housed. How hard it was for us to make the North understand this!"

25. Several scholars identify this assertion as being, as David W. Blight (*Race and Reunion*, 259) puts it, "almost omnipresent in Lost Cause rhetoric." Lloyd A. Hunter ("Immortal Confederacy," 207) adds that "Confederates rejected the notion that they had gone to war for the purpose of maintaining or extending the institution of slavery. This refutation was a cardinal element in the myth of the culture religion, and about none were they so vociferous."

26. Blight, *Race and Reunion*, 257.

27. Evans, "Our Confederate Memorial Day," 228. Cf. Hunter, "Immortal Confederacy," 193.

28. Wilson, *Baptized in Blood*, 52. Cf. Hunter, "Immortal Confederacy," 196–99.

29. Hunter, "Immortal Confederacy," 200. See also Wert, "James Longstreet and the Lost Cause," 127–46.

30. Hunter, "Immortal Confederacy," 201. Hunter discusses the common pattern of Memorial Day activities on pp. 201–2.

31. Foster, *Ghosts of the Confederacy*, 273.

32. See Richard J. Lenz, "The Civil War in Georgia, an Illustrated Travelers Guide," *Sherpa Guides*, http://www.sherpaguides.com/georgia/civil_war/mid_ga/athens_area.html (accessed June 6, 2007).

33. Historic Oakland Foundation, http://www.oaklandcemetery.com/layout.html; and "Oakland Cemetery," *Roadside Georgia*, http://roadsidegeorgia.com/site/oakland.html (each accessed August 11, 2007).

34. "Savannah, Georgia Civil War Sites," *CivilWarAlbum.com*, http://www .civilwaralbum.com/misc6/savannah1.htm (accessed August 9, 2007).

35. See William Harris Bragg, "Charles C. Jones Jr. (1831–1893)," *New Georgia Encyclopedia*, http://www.newgeorgiaencyclopedia.org/nge/Article.jsp?id=h-678&hl=y (accessed July 6, 2006).

36. On this matter, see Nolan, "Anatomy of the Myth," 17, 22–24. As Nolan (p. 22) notes: "Historians concede the North's advantage in population and the capacity to make war but reject the inevitable loss tradition and its premise in regard to men and material wealth. Historians today generally believe that the South could have won the Civil War." Nolan (p. 23) also underscores the conclusion reached by Richard Beringer et al. (*Why the South Lost*, 16): "No Confederate army lost a major engagement because of a lack of arms, munitions or other essential supplies."

37. *Oration Pronounced by Col. Charles C. Jones, Jr. on the 31st October 1878, upon the Occasion of the Unveiling and Dedication of the Confederate Monument, Erected by the Ladies Memorial Association of Augusta, Georgia* (Augusta: 1878); quoted in Blight, *Race and Reunion*, 265.

38. Pollard, *Lost Cause*, 752.

39. Lang, "*Birth of a Nation*: History, Ideology, Narrative Form," 11.

40. Nolan, "Anatomy of the Myth," 12. For a penetrating exploration of the memory of the Civil War in the national consciousness and the implications for contemporary race relations, see Blight, *Race and Reunion*.

41. See David S. Williams, "J. William Jones (1836–1909)," *New Georgia Encyclopedia*, http://www.newgeorgiaencyclopedia.org/nge/Article.jsp?id=h-2898&hl=y (accessed May 6, 2006); and Wilson, *Baptized in Blood*, 119–38.

42. Wilson, *Baptized in Blood*, 127.

43. Hunter, "Immortal Confederacy," 204.

44. Wilson, *Baptized in Blood*, 120, 122, 124, 136.

45. J. William Jones, *Christ in the Camp; or Religion in Lee's Army* (Richmond: B. F. Johnson, 1888), reprinted as Jones, *Christ in the Camp*.

46. Wilson, *Baptized in Blood*, 123, 136.

47. Ellen G. Harris, "Incorporating 'Our Southern Zion': The Southern Baptist Convention 1880–1920," http://xroads.virginia.edu/~MA02/harris/sbc/hmb.html (accessed May 7, 2006).

48. "Appendix A: Forty-Seventh Annual Report of the Home Mission Board," in *Proceedings of the Southern Baptist Convention* (1892), x–xi.

49. "Appendix B: Forty-Sixth Annual Report of the Home Mission Board," in *Proceedings of the Southern Baptist Convention* (1891), xxxvi.

50. "Forty-Seventh Annual Report of the Home Mission Board," iv.

51. White and Heard are quoted in Harvey, *Redeeming the South*, 55–56, 63–64.

52. "Morehouse Legacy," *Morehouse College*, http://www.morehouse.edu/about/legacy .html (accessed August 9, 2007). See Edward A. Jones, *Candle in the Dark*.

53. For an overview of "five stages of accommodation" that white evangelicals experienced in the face of blacks withdrawing from formerly biracial churches, see Stowell, *Rebuilding Zion*, 85–88. Stowell (p. 85) remarks that "the larger pattern that emerges is one of whites' gradually relinquishing their control in response to black initiatives throughout the South, a process that was complete by the mid-1870s." In the end, as Stowell (p. 89) concludes, "white southern evangelicals firmly refused to treat as equals their black members, who increasingly determined to accept nothing less."

54. Quoted in Harvey, *Redeeming the South*, 36, 38.

55. Ibid., 46, 70–73.

56. Owen, *Sacred Flame*, 118, 120–21.

57. Ibid., 118–19, 130.

58. Ibid., 121.

59. Stephen Ward Angell, "Henry McNeal Turner (1834–1915)," *New Georgia Encyclopedia*, http://www.newgeorgiaencyclopedia.org/nge/Article.jsp?id=h-632&hl=y (accessed July 6, 2006).

60. Angell, *Bishop Henry McNeal Turner*, 249.

61. Owen, *Sacred Flame*, 123–24.

62. Angell, *Bishop Henry McNeal Turner*, 87.

63. See Perman, *Road to Redemption*.

64. *Atlanta Constitution*, January 13, 1872; reproduced at http://www.cviog.uga .edu/Projects/gainfo/tdgh-jan/jan12.htm (accessed June 7, 2007). Edmund L. Drago ("Black Legislators During Reconstruction," *New Georgia Encyclopedia*, http://www .newgeorgiaencyclopedia.org/nge/Article.jsp?id=h-635&hl=y [accessed May 6, 2006]) summarizes the impact of Redemption on black legislators: "Conservatives used terror, intimidation, and the Ku Klux Klan to 'redeem' the state [and] black legislators were killed, threatened, beaten, or jailed." See also Drago, *Black Politicians and Reconstruction*.

65. See C. H. Phillips, *The History of the Colored Methodist Episcopal Church in America: Comprising Its Organization, Subsequent Development and Present Status* (Jackson, Tenn.: C. M. E. Church Publishing House, 1925). Documenting the American South, University Library, The University of North Carolina at Chapel Hill, http://docsouth.unc .edu/church/phillips/menu.html (accessed May 6, 2006).

66. Owen, *Sacred Flame*, 125.

67. See Hitchcock, *Richard Malcolm Johnston*.

68. Lucius Henry Holsey, *Autobiography, Sermons, Addresses, and Essays of Bishop L. H. Holsey, D. D.* (Atlanta: Franklin Printing and Publishing Company, 1898), 16. Documenting the American South, University Library, The University of North Carolina at Chapel Hill, http://docsouth.unc.edu/holsey/menu.html (accessed May 6, 2006).

69. Stowell, *Rebuilding Zion*, 8–9.

70. Wheeler, *Uplifting the Race*, 38.

71. Eastman, *Ways of Religion*, 448.

72. Hill, *One Name but Several Faces*, 36.

73. Owen, *Sacred Flame*, 130. See also the chart showing "Cumulative black Methodist membership in Georgia, 1860–1877," in Stowell, *Rebuilding Zion*, 90.

74. See Duncan, *Freedom's Shore*.

75. Cf. Harvey, *Redeeming the South*, 46.

76. Owen, *Sacred Flame*, 127–28.

77. Harvey, *Redeeming the South*, 72.

78. This observation was repeated in various forms by King. One striking use came during a question and answer period following a speech on December 18, 1963, at Western Michigan University, when King stated: "We must face the fact that . . . the church is still the most segregated major institution in America. At 11:00 on Sunday morning when we stand and sing . . . we stand at the most segregated hour in this nation. This is tragic. Nobody of honesty can overlook this." Western Michigan University Archives and Regional History Collections, http://www.wmich.edu/~ulib/archives/mlk/q-a.html (accessed May 6, 2006).

CHAPTER SIX. *In the Shadow of Jim Crow*

1. Garrett, *Atlanta and Environs*, 2:666–67.

2. Lang, *Birth of a Nation*, 183.

3. Ibid., 114.

4. Robert Lang (ibid., 12) writes that "the protection of white women is precisely what gets narrativized in the film. . . . It is, in fact, the film's core." Lang also notes that Thomas Dixon, the author of the novel upon which the film is based, *The Clansman*, stated in an interview that his purpose in having *The Birth of a Nation* produced was "to create a feeling of abhorrence in white people, especially white women against colored men." Dixon stated further that "the Ku Klux Klan was formed to protect the white women from Negro men, to restore order and to reclaim political control for the white people of the South. . . . The Ku Klux Klan was not only engaged in restoring law and order, but was of a religious nature."

5. "The Birth of a Nation," *AfricanAmericans.com*, http://www.africanamericans .com/BirthofANation.htm (accessed June 5, 2007).

6. Garrett, *Atlanta and Environs*, 2:667–68.

7. Tolnay and Beck, *Festival of Violence*, 273.

8. E. M. Beck and Stewart E. Tolnay, "Lynching," *New Georgia Encyclopedia*, http:// www.newgeorgiaencyclopedia.org/nge/Article.jsp?id=h-2717&hl=y (accessed June 5, 2007).

9. While lynching is sometimes equated with hanging, the term can refer to a variety of violent acts, including shooting and burning. Lynching can be defined as mob action to execute someone without due process of law.

10. On December 7, 1915, the day *The Birth of a Nation* premiered in Atlanta, the *Atlanta Journal* carried on the same page an ad for the film and another for "The World's Greatest Secret Social, Patriotic, Fraternal, Beneficiary Order," the Knights of the Ku Klux Klan. The ad mentioned that the organization had received a charter from the State of Georgia the previous day. See Lutholtz, *Grand Dragon*, 23–24. It is reported that several thousand Klan members and sympathizers marched through Atlanta's streets in support of the showing of *The Birth of a Nation*.

11. Owen, *Sacred Flame*, 190; and May 2004 correspondence between the author and Robert G. Gardner.

12. Robert G. Gardner records 1,206,457 Baptists out of a total state population of 3,444,578 in 1950. See Gardner, "History of the Baptists in Georgia, 1733 to Present," *Jack Tarver Library*, http://tarver.mercer.edu/archives/GaBaptists.php (accessed August 13, 2006). By 1950, Baptists had some 2,736 churches in Georgia, while Methodists had 1,566. See Gaustad and Barlow, *New Historical Atlas*, 402.

13. Owen, *Sacred Flame*, 150–53. The following paragraphs are largely based on Owen's discussion in pp. 150–87.

14. Frederick V. Mills Sr., "George Foster Pierce (1811–1884)," *New Georgia Encyclopedia*, http://www.georgiaencyclopedia.org/nge/Article.jsp?id=h-1615&sug=y (accessed August 13, 2006).

15. Owen, *Sacred Flame*, 23, 134.

16. Ibid., 136.

17. See Mann, *Atticus Greene Haygood*; and Frederick V. Mills Sr., "Atticus G. Haygood (1839–1896)," *New Georgia Encyclopedia*, http://www.newgeorgiaencyclopedia .org/nge/Article.jsp?id=h-1605&hl=y (accessed August 13, 2006).

18. Owen, *Sacred Flame*, 149.

19. Atticus G. Haygood, *Our Brother in Black: His Freedom and His Future* (New York: Phillips and Hunt, 1881), 122. Documenting the American South, University Library, The University of North Carolina at Chapel Hill, http://docsouth.unc.edu/ church/haygood/menu.html (accessed May 6, 2006).

20. Owen, *Sacred Flame*, 149–50. See John E. Fisher, *John F. Slater Fund*.

21. Kathryn W. Kemp, "Warren Akin Candler (1857–1941)," *New Georgia Encyclopedia*, http://www.newgeorgiaencyclopedia.org/nge/Article.jsp?id=h-754&hl=y (accessed May 6, 2006). See also Bauman, *Warren Akin Candler*.

22. See John E. Talmadge, *Rebecca Latimer Felton*; and David B. Parker, "Rebecca Latimer Felton (1835–1930), *New Georgia Encyclopedia*, http://www .newgeorgiaencyclopedia.org/nge/Article.jsp?id=h-904&hl=y (accessed May 21, 2006).

23. Owen, *Sacred Flame*, 160.

24. John E. Talmadge, *Rebecca Latimer Felton*, 118.

25. David B. Parker, "Sam Jones (1847–1906)," *New Georgia Encyclopedia*, http://www .newgeorgiaencyclopedia.org/nge/Article.jsp?id=h-1606&hl=y (accessed May 6, 2006). See also Minnix, *Laughter in the Amen Corner*. Chad Gregory ("Sam Jones," 242) notes that Jones "vindicated his use of blunt language" by claiming that he suited his speech to his audience: "Speaking in a service for men only, Jones joked, 'I cannot reach some of you without it.'"

26. See Parker, "'Quit Your Meanness.'"

27. Wayne Mixon, "Georgia," 298.

28. Owen, *Sacred Flame*, 180–85.

29. Ibid., 172.

30. R. V. Pierard, "American Holiness Movement," http://mb-soft.com/believe/text/ holiness.htm (accessed May 7, 2006).

31. Owen, *Sacred Flame*, 162–63, 172–73. See also Turley, *Wheel within a Wheel*.

32. Owen, *Sacred Flame*, 151–52. Owen (p. 186) later writes that "divisions of race, class, gender, geography, and theology infiltrated and weakened Georgia Wesleyanism. . . .

By 1900 several links in the chain of belief that bound Georgia Methodists together had snapped."

33. Gaustad and Barlow, *New Historical Atlas*, figure C.17.

34. Wayne Mixon, "Georgia," 299.

35. Leroy Fitts (*History of Black Baptists*, 244) observes that "alcohol . . . was deemed a moral wrong [by black Baptists] and total abstinence was a moral position of the Baptist church."

36. Flynt, "Impact of Social Factors," 23.

37. Finke and Stark, *Churching of America*, 176.

38. Bureau of the Census, Religious Bodies, 1906: [Excerpts Relating to African American Religious Bodies]: Electronic Edition. Documenting the American South, University Library, The University of North Carolina at Chapel Hill, http://docsouth.unc .edu/church/census/census.html (accessed May 22, 2006); Wayne Mixon, "Georgia," 299; and Owen, *Sacred Flame*, 190.

39. Harvey, *Redeeming the South*, 73.

40. Shurden, "Southern Baptist Synthesis," 6–7.

41. Boles, *Irony of Southern Religion*, 65.

42. John E. Talmadge, *Rebecca Latimer Felton*, 114.

43. Litwack, "Hellhounds," 9; and Dray, *At the Hands of Persons Unknown*, 4–5.

44. Litwack, "Hellhounds," 9; and Dray, *At the Hands of Persons Unknown*, 12–14.

45. Wells-Barnett was a well-known opponent of lynching and racial violence at the time. Later, she would become a cofounder of the National Association for the Advancement of Colored People (NAACP). An online text of her pamphlet is available at http://memory.loc.gov/, and an image of the cover page may be found at http://cas1 .elis.rug.ac.be/avrug/illdia/lynch.htm (each accessed February 17, 2007). E. M. Beck and Stewart E. Tolnay note that 1899 was the peak year for lynchings in Georgia in the 1880s and 1890s, with twenty-seven victims in all. See "Lynching," *New Georgia Encyclopedia*, http://www.georgiaencyclopedia.org/nge/Article.jsp?id=h-2717 (accessed February 17, 2007).

46. Sledd, "The Negro: Another View," 65–68.

47. Terry L. Matthews, "Voice of a Prophet: Andrew Sledd Revisited," *Journal of Southern Religion* 6 (2003), jsr.as.wvu.edu/2003/Matthews.pdf (accessed May 7, 2006). See also Reed, "Emory College and the Sledd Affair of 1902."

48. Sledd, "The Negro: Another View," 66.

49. Wheeler, *Uplifting the Race*, 37–38.

50. Ibid., 38, 44, 46.

51. Ibid., 38–39.

52. Hill, *One Name but Several Faces*, 38. Hill adds: "Neither northern liberal Social Gospel nor southern revivalistic evangelicalism, the black church theology crafted in the late nineteenth century was sui generis. A century later we enjoy a vantage from which to view its integrity and forcefulness."

53. A speech Smith delivered on January 10, 1906, in Columbus is representative of his rhetoric. He began by declaring: "I urge the adoption of an amendment to the

Constitution of Georgia, which will eliminate by law all possible danger from the use of ignorant, purchasable negro votes." Until that time, he indicated, the threat of racial violence would have to do: "It is only the mental and physical domination of the white man that protects. THE WHITE MEN WOULD RATHER DIE THAN BE RULED BY IGNORANT, PURCHASABLE NEGROES, AND THIS FACT HAS KEPT THEM IN CONTROL." Smith ended by asserting: "THIS IS A CONTEST BY THE PEOPLE OF GEORGIA. IT RISES FAR ABOVE A PERSONAL RACE. WE ARE DETERMINED TO PRESERVE WHITE SUPREMACY AND TO PROTECT IT WITH EVERY ADDITIONAL LEGAL MEANS FOR THE WELFARE OF THOSE OF TODAY, AND FOR OUR CHILDREN." Hoke Smith, "Speech of Hoke Smith at Columbus, Georgia, January 10, 1906, in His Debate with Clark Howell," MS 2334, box no. 15:15, Hargrett Rare Book and Manuscript Library, University of Georgia Libraries, 12, 15.

54. Gregory Mixon and Clifford Kuhn, "Atlanta Race Riot of 1906," *New Georgia Encyclopedia*, http://www.newgeorgiaencyclopedia.org/nge/Article.jsp?id=h-3033&hl=y (accessed August 11, 2007). See Bauerlein, *Negrophobia*; Godshalk, *Veiled Visions*; and Gregory Mixon, *Atlanta Riot*.

55. Litwack, "Hellhounds," 9.

56. Oney, *And the Dead Shall Rise*, 566–67.

57. Donald G. Mathews, "The Southern Rite of Human Sacrifice," *Journal of Religion* 3 (2000), http://jsr.as.wvu.edu/mathews.htm (accessed May 7, 2006). It should be noted that segregation was conceived by some, such as New South advocate Henry Grady, as having an important economic role as well, by promising to achieve and maintain a racial stability that would enable an industrial economy to flourish in the South. See Cobb, *Brown Decision*, 27–28.

58. Williamson, *Crucible of Race*, 308.

59. Litwack, "Hellhounds," 9–10.

60. Mathews, "Southern Rite of Human Sacrifice."

61. The words to "Just As I Am" were written by Charlotte Elliott in 1835. The influence of this hymn can be sensed by noting that Billy Graham chose it as the title to his autobiography. See Graham, *Just As I Am*.

62. Lillian Smith, *Killers of the Dream*, 101.

63. Newman, *Getting Right with God*, 7.

64. See Dinnerstein, *Leo Frank Case*; and Oney, *And the Dead Shall Rise*.

65. Leonard Dinnerstein, "The Leo Frank Case," *New Georgia Encyclopedia*, http://www.newgeorgiaencyclopedia.org/nge/Article.jsp?id=h-906&hl=y (accessed July 8, 2006).

66. Oney, *And the Dead Shall Rise*, 503.

67. Dinnerstein, *Leo Frank Case*.

68. A copy of the pardon statement may be found in Scott, *Cornerstones of Georgia History*, 162–63.

69. Oney, *And the Dead Shall Rise*, 560–66. Oney (p. 566) provides a vivid quote from the August 17, 1915, edition of the *Atlanta Journal* concerning the clamor to view the scene that day: "They swarmed the road from both directions. They seemed to rise up out of the ground, so fast they came. The automobiles came careening. . . . Horse-drawn vehicles came at a gallop. Pedestrians came running. The vehicles stopped in the road at

the grove and soon packed the road and overflowed into the fields. As the vehicles would stop, their occupants would jump out and run to the grove, bending forward, panting, wild-eyed. Women came. Children came. Even babes in arms."

70. Dinnerstein, *Leo Frank Case*, 146.

71. Carol Pierannunzi, "Thomas E. Watson (1856–1922)," *New Georgia Encyclopedia*, http://www.newgeorgiaencyclopedia.org/nge/Article.jsp?id=h-906&hl=y (accessed August 11, 2007). Following the Leo Frank case, Watson was elected to the U.S. Senate in 1920.

72. Leonard Dinnerstein (*Leo Frank Case*, 119) observes that "the attacks upon Frank . . . thrust Watson, who had suffered years of setbacks, to the apex of his popularity in Georgia. During his crusade against the "jewpervert" [his] sales more than tripled and profits soared."

73. Watson, "Celebrated Case," 234–35.

74. Oney, *And the Dead Shall Rise*, 558.

75. A commemorative plaque, erected by the Jewish Community of Cobb County, now marks the area where Frank was hanged; the plaque reads: "Leo Frank (1884–1915). Wrongly accused, Falsely convicted, Wantonly murdered."

76. See Theoharis and Cox, *The Boss*, 45. Leonard Dinnerstein ("Leo Frank Case") observes that, on a broader basis, the lynching "struck fear in Jewish southerners, causing them to monitor their behavior in the region closely for the next fifty years."

77. Greene, *Temple Bombing*, 74–75.

78. Dinnerstein, *Leo Frank Case*, 150.

79. It is possible that the burning cross derived from the Thomas Dixon play, *The Clansman*, which Dixon brought to Atlanta's Grand Theater in October 1905. Owing to the visual medium afforded by the play, Dixon included spectacles that were unique for the time, including having live horses on stage. He was also able to underscore a number of religious themes by means of visual elements, such as the presentation of crosses by Klan members, as well as prominent crosses on their uniforms. In reference to the death of a central white female character in the play, the Grand Dragon of the Klan held aloft a cross and announced: "In olden times, the Fiery Cross . . . called every clansman from the [Scottish] hills. . . . Here on this spot made holy ground by the sacrifice of a daughter of the South, I raise the symbol of an unconquered race of men." See Millin, "Defending the Sacred Hearth," 28–31.

80. Bauerlein, *Negrophobia*, 288.

81. Lutholtz, *Grand Dragon*, 24.

82. On the formation and nature of the second Ku Klux Klan, see Chalmers, *Hooded Americanism*; and MacLean, *Behind the Mask*. Regarding Atlanta's prominence within the Klan, see Kenneth T. Jackson, *Ku Klux Klan in the City*, 29–44; and Chalmers, *Hooded Americanism*, 70–77. Jackson (p. 29) remarks that "a recurrent theme in the history of the Ku Klux Klan has been its continuing relationship with the city of Atlanta. . . . Atlantans have exercised a disproportionate influence in Klan affairs." Similarly, Chalmers (p. 70) observes: "One of the major themes in the history of the Ku Klux Klan in the twentieth century has been its long-lived relationship with the state of Georgia. The Klan was

reborn there . . . and consecrated on the top of Stone Mountain, which for almost fifty years has been sacred soil for the Invisible Empire. . . . Klan leadership has traditionally been strongly Georgian. . . . Atlanta was the capital of the order. . . . For fifty years, Imperial Wizards have come to Atlanta to take up their reigns. . . . The Klan has dwelt in Georgia for half a century. . . . And through the years, Georgia has been its tabernacle."

83. Ellis, "The Commission on Interracial Cooperation," 7–13; and Ann Ellis Pullen, "Commission on Interracial Cooperation," *New Georgia Encyclopedia*, http://www .newgeorgiaencyclopedia.org/nge/Article.jsp?id=h-2919&hl=y (accessed July 16, 2006). Alexander was born in Missouri, but came to Atlanta in 1917.

84. Sosna, *In Search of the Silent South*, 23.

85. See Pilkington, "Trials of Brotherhood."

86. Ellis, "Commission on Interracial Cooperation," 23–25.

87. Ibid., 25–29, 83, 104–5.

88. Boles, *Irony of Southern Religion*, 101.

89. Newman, *Getting Right with God*, 7.

90. Ann Wells Ellis ("Commission on Interracial Cooperation," 104) observes that "the ASWPL women in no way attacked Southern mores, seeking not to end the practice of segregation itself, but merely to end what they saw as a barbaric and unchristian practice [i.e., lynching]. . . . Southern attitudes concerning the inferiority of the Negro were not changed by the activities of the CIC and the ASWPL."

91. Thomas P. Bailey, *Race Orthodoxy in the South*, 92–93.

92. History of the Unitarian Universalist Congregation of Atlanta, http://www.uuca .org/About/History/Financial.asp (accessed May 1, 2006).

93. Lillian Smith, *Killers of the Dream*, 28–29.

94. Lester, *History of the Georgia Baptist Convention*, 539.

95. Randall L. Patton notes: "Like many of Georgia's rural county leaders, Rivers was active in both the state legislature and the Ku Klux Klan." See "E. D. Rivers," *New Georgia Encyclopedia*, http://www.georgiaencyclopedia.org/nge/Article.jsp?id=h-1390 (accessed June 7, 2007).

96. Larry Worthy, "Gone with the Wind Premiere," *About North Georgia*, http:// ngeorgia.com/feature/gwtwpremiere.html (accessed April 29, 2006).

CHAPTER SEVEN. *Things Are Stirring*

1. Martin Luther King Jr., "An Autobiography of Religious Development," Box 106, Folder 22, Martin Luther King Papers, 1954–1968, Boston University. Available at Martin Luther King Jr. Papers Project, Stanford University, http://www.stanford.edu/group/King/ publications/papers/vol1/501122-An_Autobiography_of_Religious_Development.htm (accessed May 2, 2006). There is some confusion as to when and how the name change from Michael L. King Jr. to Martin Luther King Jr. occurred. For a discussion of the issues and the evidence, see Branch, *Parting the Waters*, 46–47.

2. Reg Murphy, "Carter's Inaugural Speech: Like 1966," *Atlanta Constitution*, January 13, 1971.

3. For an overview of the civil rights struggle in Georgia, see Stephen G. N. Tuck, "Civil Rights Movement," *New Georgia Encyclopedia*, http://www.georgiaencyclopedia .org/nge/Article.jsp?id=h-2716 (accessed July 29, 2006). See also Tuck, *Beyond Atlanta*. The three phases identified here reflect chapter titles in *Beyond Atlanta*.

4. J. Pius Barbour, "Borders Re-elected President of Georgia Baptist Missionary and Educational Convention," *National Baptist Voice* 32 (1948), 3; quoted in Manis, *Southern Civil Religions*, 35–36.

5. Charles Elmore, "Ralph Mark Gilbert Civil Rights Museum," *New Georgia Encyclopedia*, http://www.georgiaencyclopedia.org/nge/Article.jsp?id=h-2734&hl=y (accessed May 2, 2006).

6. Tuck, *Beyond Atlanta*, 45.

7. Elmore, "Ralph Mark Gilbert."

8. Tuck, *Beyond Atlanta*, 48.

9. Smith, *Killers of the Dream*, 94.

10. Bruce Clayton, "Lillian Smith, 1897–1966," *New Georgia Encyclopedia*, http://www .georgiaencyclopedia.org/nge/Article.jsp?id=h-463&hl=y (accessed May 2, 2006). See also Loveland, *Lillian Smith*.

11. Margaret Rose Gladney, "Introduction to the 1994 Edition," in Smith, *Killers of the Dream*.

12. Ralph McGill, "Miss Smith and Freud," *Atlanta Constitution*, November 24, 1949; quoted in Loveland, *Lillian Smith*, 104.

13. Clayton, "Lillian Smith."

14. See Lee, *Cotton Patch*; Chancey, "Race, Religion, and Agricultural Reform," 246–65; Chancey, "Race, Religion, and Reform"; K'Meyer, *Interracialism and Christian Community*; Coble, *Cotton Patch for the Kingdom*; and O'Connor, "The Politics of Industrialization," 527.

15. Jordan, *No Such Thing*, 121. On the creation of Koinonia, see Chancey, "'A Demonstration Plot for the Kingdom of God,'" 321–53.

16. Andrew S. Chancey, "Clarence Jordan (1912–1969)," *New Georgia Encyclopedia*, http://www.georgiaencyclopedia.org/nge/Article.jsp?id=h-1607&hl=yy (accessed August 11, 2007).

17. Tracy Elaine K'Meyer (*Interracialism and Christian Community*, 34) points out that "the last straw was his practice of dining with African Americans. For many southerners eating together was a sign of social equality, and thus dining with African Americans was one thing they just could not abide."

18. Jordan, *No Such Thing*, 129.

19. Chancey, "Clarence Jordan."

20. Jordan, *No Such Thing*, 122.

21. Lee, *Cotton Patch*, 46.

22. Scott E. Buchanan, "Herman Talmadge (1913–2002)," *New Georgia Encyclopedia*, http://www.georgiaencyclopedia.org/nge/Article.jsp?id=h-590&hl=y (accessed August 11, 2007).

23. *New York Times*, August 15, 1948; quoted in Tuck, *Beyond Atlanta*, 76.

24. Tuck, *Beyond Atlanta*, 74–79.

25. Ibid., 77.

26. Herman E. Talmadge, *You and Segregation*, 1.

27. Ibid., 1, 42, 44–45, 78.

28. Newman, *Getting Right with God*, 48, 54.

29. Ibid., 53.

30. Basler, *Collected Works of Abraham Lincoln*, 8:333.

31. Newman, *Getting Right with God*, 57–58.

32. Manis, *Southern Civil Religions*, 97–98.

33. Newman, *Getting Right with God*, 175–76.

34. Mark Newman (ibid., 176) concludes that state and regional religious groups, together with lay people and most clergy, "were generally no more willing to desegregate . . . than Southern Baptists, whatever the statements of their leading southern or national bodies."

35. Dorgan, "Response of the Main-line," 23–25. Dorgan (p. 25) observes that "there were abundant parallels in the South to McNeill's experience. Most white ministers who made any statement, or took any action, in support of integration quickly found that the clerical cloth did not protect them from the abuse typically given violators of segregationist principles." See also Newman, *Getting Right with God*, 180.

36. Edith Holbrook Riehm, "Dorothy Rogers Tilly (1883–1970)," *New Georgia Encyclopedia*, http://www.newgeorgiaencyclopedia.org/nge/Article.jsp?id=h-1619&sug=y (accessed July 16, 2006).

37. Riehm, "Dorothy Tilly and the Fellowship of the Concerned," 26.

38. Riehm, "Dorothy Rogers Tilly."

39. Manis, "'City Mothers,'" 136.

40. Riehm, "Dorothy Tilly and the Fellowship of the Concerned," 24.

41. Manis, "'City Mothers,'" 142.

42. "About the Temple," *The Temple*, http://www.the-temple.org/do/genericContent View?sectionTypeId=6 (accessed August 1, 2007).

43. See Sibley, *Dear Store*.

44. On the differences between the established German-Jewish elite and the eastern European Jews who arrived in Atlanta in the late nineteenth and early twentieth centuries, see Mark K. Bauman, "Jewish Community of Atlanta," http://www.georgiaencyclopedia .org/nge/Article.jsp?id=h-2731 (accessed August 1, 2007). The play, "The Last Night of Ballyhoo," by Alfred Uhry (also the author of "Driving Miss Daisy"), explores the intergroup dynamics in 1939-era Atlanta between the German Jews and "the other kind," that is, the eastern European Jews. See Uhry, *Last Night of Ballyhoo*.

45. Greene, *Temple Bombing*, 6–7.

46. Ibid., 6.

47. Ibid., 190, 232–33.

48. Ibid., 237–39.

49. Ralph McGill, "A Church, a School," *Atlanta Constitution*, October 13, 1958.

50. Greene, *Temple Bombing*, 246, 260.

51. Jordan, *No Such Thing*, 132.

52. K'Meyer, *Interracialism and Christian Community*, 84; and Lee, *Cotton Patch*, 105–6, 108, 110, 112. There are a few stirring stories of individuals standing up to the prevailing anti-Koinonia sentiments in Sumter County. At one point, some of the congregants of Calvary Episcopal Church in Americus were proposing to exclude the members of the Koinonia commune, in line with other churches in the area. One courageous congregant, Quenelle Harrold Sheffield, a scion of the family that had established the church in 1858, spoke against the proposal. Her grandson, Atlantan Sheffield Hale, interviewed her about the event in the 1990s and recounts: "Grandmother related, 'I got up and made my valedictory response. . . . I told them that this church was not our church, but that it was God's church, and I could not imagine how we could keep anyone from attending God's church and that if that was the case, it was certainly not the church [I] grew up in and that furthermore, it was a terribly unchristian thing to do.'" After she spoke, another woman, a schoolteacher, stood up and said: "I agree and I'm going home." The meeting broke up shortly after, with the result that the members of the Koinonia commune were not banned from Calvary Church. Sheffield Hale, unpublished memorandum, August 22, 1997.

53. Jordan, *No Such Thing*, 134–35.

54. K'Meyer, *Interracialism and Christian Community*, 86–87; and Lee, *Cotton Patch*, 123–24.

55. Lee, *Cotton Patch*,118.

56. Ibid., 118–20, 131–32.

57. Egerton, *Speak Now against the Day*, 127.

58. Jordan, *No Such Thing*, 118, 138–39.

59. On the interconnection between Koinonia and the development of Habitat for Humanity, see Fuller and Scott, *Love in the Mortar Joints*; and Edward A. Hatfield, "Habitat for Humanity International," *New Georgia Encyclopedia*, http://www .georgiaencyclopedia.org/nge/Article.jsp?id=h-2511 (accessed August 11, 2007).

60. Tuck, *Beyond Atlanta*, 178.

61. Jordan, *No Such Thing*, 122–23.

62. John A. Kirk, "Martin Luther King Jr. (1929–1968)," *New Georgia Encyclopedia*, http://www.newgeorgiaencyclopedia.org/nge/Article.jsp?id=h-1009 (accessed May 2, 2006). Standard studies of King's civil rights career include Taylor Branch's *Parting the Waters, Pillar of Fire*, and *At Canaan's Edge*; and Garrow, *Bearing the Cross*.

63. Garrow, *Bearing the Cross*, 85.

64. See Abernathy, *And the Walls Came Tumbling Down*.

65. Garrow, *Bearing the Cross*, 91. It is worth noting that Ralph David Abernathy assumed leadership of the new group, eventually known as the Southern Christian Leadership Conference, in 1968 after King was assassinated, a position he would hold until 1977. Following these two Baptist ministers, Joseph E. Lowery, a Methodist minister, then served as president of the Southern Christian Leadership Conference from 1977 to 1997, a length of time that earned him a popular designation as "dean of the civil rights movement."

66. Ibid., 90, 97. David J. Garrow (p. 97) notes that one of his advisors tried to dissuade King from adding the word "Christian" out of concern that it might put off nonreligious supporters, but King was resolute.

67. Pomerantz, *Where Peachtree Meets Sweet Auburn*, 252.

68. Garrow, *Bearing the Cross*, 57, 625.

69. Kirk, "Martin Luther King Jr."

70. Andrew Young, correspondence with the author, February 4, 2004.

71. See Christopher Allen Huff, "Sibley Commission," *New Georgia Encyclopedia*, http://www.newgeorgiaencyclopedia.org/nge/Article.jsp?id=h-2617&hl=y (accessed August 7, 2007).

72. Tuck, *Beyond Atlanta*, 102.

73. Kathryn Nasstrom, "Frances Pauley (1905–2003)," *New Georgia Encyclopedia*, http://www.newgeorgiaencyclopedia.org/nge/Article.jsp?id=h-745&hl=y (accessed May 2, 2006). See also Nasstrom, *Everybody's Grandmother*.

74. Manis, "'City Mothers,'" 116, 126.

75. Knotts, *Fellowship of Love*, 18.

76. Hempton, *Methodism*, 42.

77. Huff, "Sibley Commission." See Pratt, *We Shall Not Be Moved*.

78. Lee W. Formwalt, "Albany Movement," *New Georgia Encyclopedia*, http://www.georgiaencyclopedia.org/nge/Article.jsp?id=h-1057&hl=y (accessed June 7, 2007).

79. Branch, *Parting the Waters*, 557.

80. Martin Luther King Jr., "Letter from Birmingham City Jail," in Washington, *Testament of Hope*, 290.

81. On the lessons of Albany, and the success of the Birmingham campaign, see Branch, *Parting the Waters*, 673–802; and Garrow, *Bearing the Cross*, 225–64.

82. King, "Letter from Birmingham City Jail," 289–90.

83. On these events, see especially Branch, *Parting the Waters*.

84. Garrow, *Bearing the Cross*, 283.

85. Taylor Branch (*Parting the Waters*, 882) suggests that, when King wandered off his text, "there was no alternative but to preach."

86. Martin Luther King Jr., "I Have a Dream," in Washington, *Testament of Hope*, 219.

87. Ibid., 220.

88. Tuck, *Beyond Atlanta*, 127, 132. Tuck (p. 133) observes that Law achieved "celebrity status in Savannah," and he quotes a March 1961 *Pittsburgh Courier* story that stated: "In Savannah circles Mr. Law's word is the law."

89. Ibid., 139, 142.

90. Aldon Morris, *Origins of the Civil Rights Movement: Black Communities Organizing for Change* (New York: Collier Macmillan, 1984), 4, quoted in Tuck, *Beyond Atlanta*, 247.

91. Tuck, *Beyond Atlanta*, 247.

92. Garrow, *Bearing the Cross*, 56–57.

93. Ibid., 57–58; and King's draft of his 1956 sermon, "Our God is Able," displayed at the Atlanta History Center in the temporary exhibit, "I Have A Dream: The Morehouse College Martin Luther King Jr. Collection," January-May 2007.

94. Garrow, *Bearing the Cross*, 622.

95. Smith and Zepp, "Martin Luther King's Vision," 361.

96. Martin Luther King Jr., *"Where Do We Go from Here: Chaos or Community?,"* in Washington, *A Testament of Hope*, 632.

97. King, *Where Do We Go from Here*. David J. Garrow ("Where Martin Luther King, Jr., Was Going," 736) remarks that this book "remains far and away the best starting point in all of King's published writings for the reader who wants to reflect upon where King had come from and where he potentially was going."

CHAPTER EIGHT. *Culture and Worship Wars*

1. *Doe v. Bolton*, 410 U.S. 179 (1973), http://caselaw.lp.findlaw.com/scripts/getcase .pl?court=US&vol=410&invol=179 (accessed September 1, 2006); Frost-Knappman and Cullen-Dupont, *Women's Rights on Trial*, 182–83; and *Our Georgia History*, http:// ourgeorgiahistory.com/chronpop/2285 (accessed July 19, 2006).

2. Hunter, *Culture Wars*, xi.

3. *Internet Brigade*, http://www.buchanan.org/pa-92-0817-rnc.html (accessed April 18, 2006).

4. "Judge: Evolution Stickers Unconstitutional," *CNN.com*, January 13, 2005, http:// www.cnn.com/2005/LAW/01/13/evolution.textbooks.ruling/ (accessed April 18, 2006).

5. Kristen Wyatt, "Jimmy Carter Breaks Lifelong Ties to Southern Baptists," *CNN .com*, October 20, 2000, http://edition.cnn.com/2000/ALLPOLITICS/stories/10/20/ carter.baptists.ap/ (accessed May 7, 2006).

6. "Baptist Faith and Message," Southern Baptist Convention, http://www.sbc.net/ bfm/bfm2000.asp (accessed April 18, 2006).

7. Wyatt, "Jimmy Carter."

8. Ammerman, *Baptist Battles*; Barnhart, *Southern Baptist Holy War*; and Shurden, *Struggle for the Soul of the SBC*.

9. Morgan, *New Crusades*, x. David T. Morgan provides a convenient summary of the Baptist struggles: "The 'conservative resurgence' (as the fundamentalists called it) and the 'takeover' of the Southern Baptist Convention (as the moderates called it) was in fact both a crusade for truth, at least in the minds of the fundamentalist crusaders, *and* a bid for power through the use of secular political means. The moderates denied the former, and the fundamentalists seldom admitted the latter." Thus, as Morgan concludes: "Moderates called what happened a 'takeover,' while fundamentalists called it a 'take back.'"

10. Daniel Vestal, "The History of the Cooperative Baptist Fellowship," in Shurden and Shepley, *Going for the Jugular*, 259.

11. Ibid., 259–61.

12. Cooperative Baptist Fellowship, http://www.thefellowship.info/Inside%20CBF/ Who%20we%20are.icm (accessed May 7, 2006).

13. Morgan, *New Crusades*, 177–78.

14. "Statement on Sexuality," Southern Baptist Convention, http://www.sbc.net/ aboutus/pssexuality.asp (accessed April 18, 2006).

15. "Resolution On Disney Company Policy," Southern Baptist Convention, http://www.sbc.net/resolutions/amResolution.asp?ID=435 (accessed April 18, 2006).

16. "On the Disney Boycott," Southern Baptist Convention, http://www.sbcannual meeting.net/sbc05/resolutions/sbcresolution.asp?ID=5 (accessed April 18, 2006).

17. Candace Chellew, "Kicked Out of the House: Two Georgia Baptist Churches Find Hope in Expulsion," *Whosoever: An Online Magazine for Gay, Lesbian, Bisexual, and Transgender Christians,* http://www.whosoever.org/v4i4/baptists.html (accessed July 31, 2007).

18. Blier, "A 'Catholic' Catholic Church," 74.

19. Alice M. Smith, "Conference Disagrees with Emory President about Same-Sex Union Ceremonies on Campus," United Methodist News Service, June 17, 1997, http://www.umaffirm.org (accessed May 7, 2006).

20. Laderman, *Religions of Atlanta,* 8.

21. The Pluralism Project, Harvard University, http://www.pluralism.org (accessed November 25, 2003).

22. Barry A. Kosmin, Egon Mayer, and Ariela Keysar, *American Religious Identification Survey 2001,* The Graduate Center of the City University of New York, http://www.gc.cuny.edu/faculty/research_briefs/aris/key_findings.htm (accessed May 7, 2006).

23. Colleen O'Connor, "Georgia Parish Welcomes Muslim Neighbors," Every Voice Network, http://www.everyvoice.net/modules.php?op=modload&name=News&file=index &catid=&topic=12&allstories=1 (accessed May 7, 2006).

24. Ibid.

25. "Interview: James Merritt," *Religion and Ethics Newsweekly,* episode no. 534, April 26, 2002, http://www.pbs.org/wnet/religionandethics/week534/jmerritt.html (accessed April 18, 2006).

26. "Free Resources on Cults and Sects," North American Mission Board, http://www.namb.net/site/c.9qKILUOzEpH/b.232957/k.50D8/Free_Resources_on_Cults__Sects.htm (accessed May 7, 2006).

27. Erin McClam, "In Georgia, a Fight over Religion and Land," Belief.net, http://www.beliefnet.com/story/101/story_10146.html (accessed May 7, 2006).

28. Steve Prothero, "To Live and Die in Gwinnett County," *Religion and Ethics Newsweekly,* April 26, 2002, http://www.pbs.org/wnet/religionandethics/week534/webexclusive.html (accessed May 7, 2006).

29. "Exploring Religious America," *Religion and Ethics Newsweekly,* April 26, 2002, http://www.pbs.org/wnet/religionandethics/week534/cover.html (accessed May 7, 2006).

30. Ibid.

31. McClam, "In Georgia."

32. Prothero, "To Live and Die."

33. Citing appeals to the Founding Fathers and "what America is really all about" in the abortion debate, James Davison Hunter (*Culture Wars,* 50) observes that "the contemporary culture war is ultimately a struggle over national identity—over the meaning of America, who we have been in the past, who we are now, and perhaps most important, who we, as a nation, will aspire to be in the new millennium."

34. Tom W. Smith and Seokho Kim, "The Vanishing Protestant Majority," National Opinion Research Center at the University of Chicago, www.norc.uchicago.edu/issues/ PROTSGO8.pdf (accessed May 7, 2006). See also "America's Protestant Majority Is Fading NORC Research Shows," http://www-news.uchicago.edu/releases/04/040720 .protestant.shtml (accessed July 19, 2006).

35. Kosmin et al., *American Religious Identification Survey 2001*.

36. Data compiled from Gaustad and Barlow, *New Historical Atlas*, figures C.17 and C.18; and Kosmin et al., *American Religious Identification Survey 2001*. Gerald R. Webster ("Geographical Patterns of Religious Denomination Affiliation in Georgia," 25, 47) notes that "Southern Baptists are representing a declining share of the state's population, most particularly in Georgia's urban areas," while "Catholics are rapidly increasing in the state's urban areas."

37. Brendan J. Buttimer, "Catholicism," *New Georgia Encyclopedia*, http://www .newgeorgiaencyclopedia.org/nge/Article.jsp?id=h-2922&hl=y (accessed May 6, 2006).

38. Diocese of Savannah, http://diosav.org/about (accessed May 7, 2006).

39. Buttimer, "Catholicism"; Blier, "A 'Catholic' Catholic Church," 71; Archdiocese of Atlanta, http://www.archatl.com/ (accessed June 3, 2007); and "Archdiocese of Atlanta," http://www.catholic-hierarchy.org/diocese/datla.html (accessed July 31, 2007).

40. See Buttimer, "Catholicism."

41. Dewey Weiss Kramer, "History," The Monastery of the Holy Spirit, http://www .trappist.net/newweb/hist3.html (accessed May 7, 2006).

42. Paula G. Shakelton, "Conyers Apparitions of the Virgin Mary," *New Georgia Encyclopedia*, http://www.newgeorgiaencyclopedia.org/nge/Article.jsp?id=h-750&hl=y (accessed May 7, 2006); and Balaban, "The Marian Apparition Site," 215–26.

43. Blier, "A 'Catholic' Catholic Church," 81.

44. "Hispanics by the Numbers in Georgia," Small Business Development Center, University of Georgia, www.sbdc.uga.edu/pdfs/hispanicfactsheet.pdf (accessed May 7, 2006). See also Leon F. Bouvier and John L. Martin, "Shaping Georgia: The Effects of Immigration, 1970–2020," Center for Immigration Studies, http://www.cis.org/articles/ 1995/georgia.html (accessed May 7, 2006).

45. "Latinos are Leaving the Roman Catholic Church, but Taking Beliefs with Them," *ChristianityToday.com*, http://www.christianitytoday.com/ct/2001/119/12.0.html (accessed April 23, 2006).

46. "Archbishop Marino: Hispanic Presence Is Gift and Challenge," *The Georgia Bulletin*, January 4, 1990, http://www.georgiabulletin.org/local/1990/01/04/a/ (accessed April 18, 2006).

47. Kosmin et al., *American Religious Identification Survey 2001*.

48. See Blumhofer, "Pentecostalism," 584; and Mills, "Glossalalia." Watson E. Mills (p. 305) notes that "glossolalia was relatively infrequent in its appearance until its phenomenal rise in connection with Pentecostalism in America."

49. See Synan, *The Holiness-Pentecostal Tradition*.

50. Synan, "Franklin Springs, Georgia"; and Synan, "King, Joseph Hillery."

51. Vinson Synan, "Memphis 1994: Miracle and Mandate," Pentecostal/Charismatic Churches of North America, http://pccna.org/About_Us/history.cfm (accessed April 23, 2006).

52. "Racial Reconciliation Manifesto," Pentecostal/Charismatic Churches of North America, http://www.pctii.org/manifesto.html (accessed May 7, 2006).

53. "Resolution on Racial Reconciliation on the 150th Anniversary of the Southern Baptist Convention," Southern Baptist Convention, http://www.sbc.net/resolutions/amResolution.asp?ID=899 (accessed April 23, 2006).

54. John Blake, "An Unfulfilled Promise? After a 1995 Apology for Racism, Southern Baptists Say They're Making Progress toward Including Blacks in Decision-Making, but Some Complain It's Not Fast Enough," *Atlanta Journal-Constitution*, June 14, 2003.

55. Stroupe and Fleming, *While We Run This Race*, 15.

56. Stroupe, *Where Once We Feared Enemies*, 7.

57. Oakhurst Presbyterian Church, http://home.earthlink.net/~oakpres/oak_who .html (accessed April 23, 2006).

58. See New Birth, http://www.newbirth.org/home.asp (accessed August 11, 2007).

59. See Scott Thumma, "Exploring the Megachurch Phenomena: Their Characteristics and Cultural Context," Hartford Institute for Religion Research, http://hirr.hartsem.edu/bookshelf/thumma_article2.html (accessed April 23, 2006). See also Thumma, "The Kingdom, the Power, and the Glory."

60. John Blake, "Big on Worship: Large Congregations Rely on Conservative Values, Strong Pastors, Study Finds," *Atlanta Journal-Constitution*, February 15, 2006. See "Megachurches Today 2005," Hartford Institute for Religion Research, available at http://hirr.hartsem.edu; and "Megachurches More Numerous Than Researchers Thought, Study Shows," ABPnews.com, http://www.abpnews.com/318.article (accessed April 23, 2006).

61. Chaves, *Congregations in America*, 18–19.

62. "Database of Megachurches in the U.S.," Hartford Institute for Religion Research, http://hirr.hartsem.edu/org/faith_megachurches_database.html (accessed April 23, 2006); and "Top 10 U.S. States with Highest Proportion of Megachurch Members, 2001," http://www.adherents.com/largecom/com_mega.html (accessed February 17, 2007).

63. Blake, "Big on worship."

64. "Metro Atlanta Megachurches, World Changers Church International," *Atlanta Journal-Constitution*, April 19, 2003.

65. Thumma, "Exploring the Megachurch Phenomena."

66. "Megachurches Today 2000," http://hirr.hartsem.edu/org/faith_megachurches_ FACTsummary.html#location (accessed February 17, 2007).

67. Mike Dorning, "Obama Addresses California Megachurch on Friday," *Chicago Tribune*, December 1, 2006, http://master.redorbit.com/news/politics/750676/obama _addresses_california_megachurch_on_friday/index.html# (accessed June 6, 2007).

68. Todd E. Johnson, "Disconnected Rituals," 54. See Lathrop, "New Pentecost or Joseph's Britches?"

69. See Finke and Stark, *Churching of America*, 46; and Moore, *Selling God*, 41–49.

70. Ostwalt, *Secular Steeples*, 30, 57.

71. Finke and Stark, *Churching of America*, 51; and Ostwalt, *Secular Steeples*, 57.

72. "Jesus, CEO," *The Economist*, December 20, 2005, http://www.teachingamerican history.org/library/index.asp?documentprint=1443 (accessed February 4, 2007).

73. Bill Leonard, quoted in Ostwalt, *Secular Steeples*, 30.

74. Julian Borger, "Bush Poll Campaign Courts Religious Right," *Guardian*, July 3, 2004, http://www.guardian.co.uk/international/story/0,,1252932,00.html (accessed February 4, 2007).

75. Cf. Ostwalt, *Secular Steeples*, 59–60.

76. C. Kirk Hadaway, "FACTS on Growth: A new look at the dynamics of growth and decline in American congregations based on the Faith Communities Today 2005 national survey of congregations," available at http://fact.hartsem.edu/products/index.html (accessed February 4, 2007).

77. Ostwalt, *Secular Steeples*, 66–67.

78. "Megachurches Today 2000."

79. Mark R. Bell, "Continued Captivity: Religion in Bartow County Georgia," *Journal of Southern Religion* 2 (1999), http://jsr.fsu.edu/mbell2.htm (accessed May 7, 2006). Though published in 1999, the majority of Bell's field work was performed in 1996.

80. Ibid.

81. Hill, *Southern Churches in Crisis*, 73, 76–77.

82. Bell, "Continued Captivity."

83. Hill, *Southern Churches in Crisis Revisited*, xxxviii.

84. Bell, "Continued Captivity."

85. Georgia Statistics System, University of Georgia, http://www.georgiastats.uga.edu (accessed June 6, 2007).

86. "Georgia," Encarta, http://encarta.msn.com/text_761571609__1/Georgia_(state) .html (accessed August 11, 2007); and Economic Research Service, U.S. Department of Agriculture, http://www.ers.usda.gov/StateFacts/GA.HTM (accessed April 24, 2006). For an important analysis of urban and rural population patterns in Georgia, see Douglas C. Bachtel, "The Four Georgias," Georgia Facts and Figures, University of Georgia, http:// www.fcs.uga.edu/hace/gafacts/ (accessed May 7, 2006).

87. Les Christie, "100 Fastest Growing Counties," CNNMoney.com, April 14, 2005, http://money.cnn.com/2006/03/15/real_estate/fastest_growing_US_counties/ (accessed April 23, 2006).

88. Georgia Statistics System, University of Georgia, http://www.georgiastats.uga.edu/ (accessed August 11, 2007).

89. Eiesland, *Particular Place*, 1, 82, 207.

90. Leon Bouvier and Sharon McCloe Stein, "Georgia's Dilemma: The Unintended Consequences of Population Growth," Negative Population Growth, http://www.npg .org/ga_poll/georgia.html (accessed April 23, 2006).

91. Reid Ewing, Rolf Pendall, and Don Chen, "Measuring Sprawl and Its Impact," Smart Growth America, http://www.smartgrowthamerica.org/sprawlindex/sprawlindex .html (accessed April 23, 2006).

92. Haya El Nasser and Paul Overberg, "A Comprehensive Look at Sprawl in America," *USAToday.com*, February 22, 2001, http://www.usatoday.com/news/sprawl/main.htm (accessed May 7, 2006).

93. Brian Feagans, "Atlanta Growth Tops in Nation," *Atlanta Journal-Constitution*, April 5, 2007.

94. "Texas Becomes Nation's Newest 'Majority-Minority' State, Census Bureau Announces," U.S. Census Bureau, http://www.census.gov/Press-Release/www/releases/archives/population/005514.html (accessed July 19, 2006). It is worth noting that the U.S. Census Bureau announced in May 2007 that the United States had reached the symbolic milestone of a minority population of 100 million (http://www.census.gov/Press-Release/www/releases/archives/population/010048.html [accessed May 22, 2007]). Bureau Director Louis Kincannon stated: "About one in three U.S. residents is a minority. . . . To put this into perspective, there are more minorities in this country today than there were people in the United States in 1910. In fact, the minority population in the U.S. is larger than the total population of all but 11 countries."

95. Janice Morrill, "Ethnic Celebrations," *New Georgia Encyclopedia*, http://www.newgeorgiaencyclopedia.org/nge/Article.jsp?id=h-774&sug=y (accessed August 14, 2007).

96. "Interview: Gary Laderman," *Religion and Ethics Newsletter*, episode no. 534, April 26, 2002, http://www.pbs.org/wnet/religionandethics/week534/gladerman.html (accessed October 29, 2004).

97. Du Bois, *Souls of Black Folk*, 3.

Epilogue

1. Stephen Elliott, "Our Cause in Harmony with the Purposes of God in Christ Jesus. A Sermon Preached in Christ Church, Savannah, on Thursday, September 18th, 1862." Documenting the American South, University Library, The University of North Carolina at Chapel Hill, http://docsouth.unc.edu/imls/elliott5/menu.html (accessed May 6, 2006).

2. Ibid.

3. Owen, *Sacred Flame*, 127.

4. For an overview of the cemetery and its history, see Taliaferro, *Historic Oakland Cemetery*.

5. Du Bois, *Souls of Black Folk*, 84. It is worth noting that Du Bois remarks shortly before this observation that "a little past Atlanta . . . not far from where Sam Hose was crucified, you may stand on a spot which is to-day the center of the Negro problem."

6. Tuck, *Beyond Atlanta*, 1.

7. Nobel presentation speeches may be accessed at the Nobel Prize web site; Martin Luther King Jr., http://nobelprize.org/nobel_prizes/peace/laureates/1964/king-acceptance.html; and Jimmy Carter, http://nobelprize.org/nobel_prizes/peace/laureates/2002/carter-lecture.html (each accessed May 7, 2006).

8. Washington, *Testament of Hope*, 617.

9. Julia L. Coleman was inducted into the Georgia Women of Achievement in 2001. See "Julia L. Coleman," *Georgia Women of Achievement*, http://www.georgiawomen.org/_honorees/colemanj/index.htm (accessed June 6, 2007).

Bibliography

Abbot, W. W. *The Royal Governors of Georgia, 1754–1775.* Chapel Hill: University of North Carolina Press, 1959.

Abernathy, Ralph David. *And the Walls Came Tumbling Down: An Autobiography.* New York: Harper and Row, 1989.

Ammerman, Nancy Tatom. *Baptist Battles: Social Change and Religious Conflict in the Southern Baptist Convention.* New Brunswick, N.J.: Rutgers University Press, 1990.

Anderson, William L., ed. *Cherokee Removal: Before and After.* Athens: University of Georgia Press, 1991.

Angell, Stephen Ward. *Bishop Henry McNeal Turner and African-American Religion in the South.* Knoxville: University of Tennessee Press, 1992.

Arnade, Charles W. *The Siege of St. Augustine in 1702.* Gainesville: University of Florida Press, 1959.

Asbury, Herbert. *A Methodist Saint: The Life of Bishop Asbury.* New York: Alfred A. Knopf, 1927.

Austin, Allan D. *African Muslims in Antebellum America: Transatlantic Stories and Spiritual Struggles.* New York: Routledge, 1997.

Avary, Myrta Lockett, ed. *Recollections of Alexander H. Stephens: His Diary Kept When a Prisoner at Fort Warren, Boston Harbour, 1865; Giving Incidents and Reflections of his Prison Life and Some Letters and Reminiscences.* 1910. Reprint, Baton Rouge: Louisiana State University Press, 1998.

Ayoub, Mahmoud M. "The Islamic Tradition." In *World Religions: Western Traditions,* edited by Willard G. Oxtoby, 352–491. New York: Oxford University Press, 1996.

Bailey, Anne J. *War and Ruin: William T. Sherman and the Savannah Campaign.* Wilmington, Del.: Scholarly Resources, 2003.

Bailey, Cornelia, with Christena Bledsoe. *God, Dr. Buzzard, and the Bolito Man: A Saltwater Geechee Talks about Life on Sapelo Island.* New York: Doubleday, 2000.

Bailey, Kenneth K. "The Post–Civil War Racial Separations in Southern Protestantism: Another Look." *Church History* 46, no. 4 (1977): 453–73.

Bailey, Thomas P. *Race Orthodoxy in the South, and Other Aspects of the Negro Question.* New York: Neale Publishing Co., 1914.

Baine, Rodney E. "General James Oglethorpe and the Expedition against St. Augustine." *Georgia Historical Quarterly* 84, no. 2 (2000): 197–229.

———. "Myths of Mary Musgrove." *Georgia Historical Quarterly* 76, no. 2 (1992): 428–35.

Baker, Pearl. *The Story of Wrightsboro, 1768–1964.* Thomson, Ga.: Warrenton Clipper, 1965.

Baker, Robert A. *The Southern Baptist Convention and Its People, 1607–1972*. Nashville: Broadman Press, 1974.

Balaban, Victor. "The Marian Apparition Site at Conyers, Georgia." In Laderman, *Religions of Atlanta*, 215–26.

Ballard, W. L. *The Yuchi Green Corn Ceremonial: Form and Meaning*. Los Angeles: University of California Press, 1978.

Barnes, Roy E. "Foreword." In Thurmond, *Freedom*, v–vi.

Barnhart, Joe Edward. *The Southern Baptist Holy War*. Austin: Texas Monthly Press, 1986.

Basler, Roy P. ed. *The Collected Works of Abraham Lincoln*. 8 vols. New Brunswick, N.J.: Rutgers University Press, 1953.

Bauerlein, Mark. *Negrophobia: A Race Riot in Atlanta, 1906*. San Francisco: Encounter Books, 2001.

Bauman, Mark K. *Warren Akin Candler: The Conservative as Idealist*. Metuchen, N.J.: Scarecrow Press, 1981.

Bealle, John. *Public Worship, Private Faith: Sacred Harp and American Folksong*. Athens: University of Georgia Press, 1997.

Beringer, Richard E., Herman Hattaway, Archer Jones, and William N. Still. *Why the South Lost the Civil War*. Athens: University of Georgia Press, 1986.

Berlin, Ira, Barbara J. Fields, Steven F. Miller, Joseph P. Reidy, and Leslie S. Rowland, eds. *Free at Last: A Documentary History of Slavery, Freedom, and the Civil War*. New York: New Press, 1993.

Berlin, Ira, Marc Favreau, and Steven F. Miller, eds. *Remembering Slavery: African Americans Talk about Their Personal Experiences of Slavery and Freedom*. New York: New Press, 1998.

Blier, Helen. "A 'Catholic' Catholic Church: The Roman Catholic Community of Atlanta." In Laderman, *Religions of Atlanta*, 67–86.

Blight, David W. *Race and Reunion: The Civil War in American Memory*. Cambridge: Harvard University Press, 2001.

Blumhofer, Edith. "Pentecostalism." In Hill, *Encyclopedia of Religion in the South*, 584–87.

Boles, John B. *The Great Revival: Beginnings of the Bible Belt*. 1972. Reprint, Lexington: University Press of Kentucky, 1996.

———. *The Irony of Southern Religion*. New York: Peter Lang, 1994.

———, ed. *Masters and Slaves in the House of the Lord: Race and Religion in the American South, 1740–1870*. Lexington: University Press of Kentucky, 1988.

Bolton, Herbert E., and Mary Ross. *The Debatable Land: A Sketch of the Anglo-Spanish Contest for the Georgia Country*. Berkeley: University of California Press, 1925.

Bonner, James C. *A History of Georgia Agriculture, 1732–1860*. Athens: University of Georgia Press, 1964.

Bowne, Eric E. "'A Bold and Warlike People': The Basis of Westo Power." In Pluckhahn and Ethridge, *Light on the Path*, 123–32.

———. "The Rise and Fall of the Westo Indians: An Evaluation of the Documentary Evidence." *Early Georgia* 28 (2000): 56–78.

———. *The Westo Indians: Slave Traders of the Colonial South*. Tuscaloosa: University of Alabama Press, 2005.

Branch, Taylor. *At Canaan's Edge: America in the King Years, 1965–68.* New York: Simon and Schuster, 2006.

———. *Parting the Waters: America in the King Years, 1954–1963.* New York: Simon and Schuster, 1988.

———. *Pillar of Fire: America in the King Years, 1963–65.* New York: Simon and Schuster, 1998.

Breyer, Stephen. "The Cherokee Indians and the Supreme Court." *Georgia Historical Quarterly* 87, nos. 3–4 (2003): 408–26.

Bruce, Dickson D., Jr. *And They All Sang Hallelujah: Plain-Folk Camp-Meeting Religion, 1800–1845.* Knoxville: University of Tennessee Press, 1974.

Brundage, W. Fitzhugh. *Lynching in the New South: Georgia and Virginia, 1880–1930.* Urbana: University of Illinois Press, 1993.

Bryant, James C. "From Penfield to Macon: Mercer University's Problematic Move." *Georgia Historical Quarterly* 89, no. 4 (2005): 462–84.

Bucke, Emory S., general ed. *The History of American Methodism.* 3 vols. Nashville: Abingdon Press, 1964.

Bullock, Henry Morton. *A History of Emory University.* Nashville: Parthenon Press, 1936.

Bumsted, J. M., ed. *The Great Awakening: The Beginnings of Evangelical Pietism in America.* Waltham, Mass.: Blaisdell, 1970.

Burch, Jarrett. *Adiel Sherwood: Baptist Antebellum Pioneer in Georgia.* Macon, Ga.: Mercer University Press, 2003.

———. "Adiel Sherwood: Religious Pioneer of Nineteenth-Century Georgia." *Georgia Historical Quarterly* 87 (2003): 22–47.

Burr, Virginia Ingraham, ed. *The Secret Eye: The Journal of Ella Gertrude Clanton Thomas, 1848–1889.* Chapel Hill: University of North Carolina Press, 1990.

Candler, Allen D., ed. *The Colonial Records of the State of Georgia.* 26 vols. Atlanta: State of Georgia, 1904–1916.

Carneiro, Robert L. "What Happened at the Flashpoint? Conjectures on Chiefdom Formation at the Very Moment of Conception." In Redmond, *Chiefdoms and Chieftaincy,* 18–42.

Carswell, W. J. "Adiel Sherwood." *Viewpoints* 2 (1969): 93–106.

Carter, Christine Jacobson, ed. *The Diary of Dolly Lunt Burge, 1848–1879.* Athens: University of Georgia Press, 1997.

Cashin, Edward. *Beloved Bethesda: A History of George Whitefield's Home for Boys, 1740–2000.* Macon, Ga.: Mercer University Press, 2001.

Cassels, Samuel J. "Conscience—Its Nature, Office and Authority." *Southern Presbyterian Review* 6 (1853): 467–68.

Chalmers, David M. *Hooded Americanism: The History of the Ku Klux Klan.* Durham: Duke University Press, 1987.

Chancey, Andrew S. "'A Demonstration Plot for the Kingdom of God': The Establishment and Early Years of Koinonia Farm." *Georgia Historical Quarterly* 75, no. 2 (1991): 321–53.

———. "Race, Religion, and Agricultural Reform: The Communal Vision of Koinonia Farm." In *Georgia in Black and White: Explorations in the Race Relations of a Southern*

State, 1865–1950, edited by John C. Inscoe, 246–65. Athens: University of Georgia Press, 1994.

———. "Race, Religion, and Reform: Koinonia's Challenge to Southern Society, 1942–1992." Ph.D. diss., University of Florida, 1998.

Chaves, Mark. *Congregations in America*. Cambridge: Harvard University Press, 2004.

Cheek, H. Lee, Jr., ed. *John C. Calhoun: Selected Writings and Speeches*. Washington, D.C.: Regnery Publishing, 2003.

Chesebrough, David B. *Clergy Dissent in the Old South, 1830–1865*. Carbondale: Southern Illinois University Press, 1996.

Chute, Anthony L. *A Piety above the Common Standard: Jesse Mercer and Evangelistic Calvinism*. Macon, Ga.: Mercer University Press, 2004.

Clark, Elmer E., J. Manning Potts, and Jacob S. Payton, eds. *The Journal and Letters of Francis Asbury*. 3 vols. Nashville: Abingdon Press, 1958.

Cleveland, Henry, ed. *Alexander H. Stephens, in Public and Private: With Letters and Speeches, before, during, and since the War*. Philadelphia: National Publishing Company, 1866.

Cobb, Buell E., Jr. *The Sacred Harp: A Tradition and Its Music*. Athens: University of Georgia Press, 1978.

Cobb, James C. *The Brown Decision, Jim Crow, and Southern Identity*. Athens: University of Georgia Press, 2005.

Coble, Ann Louise. *Cotton Patch for the Kingdom: Clarence Jordan's Demonstration Plot at Koinonia Farm*. Scottdale, Pa.: Herald Press, 2002.

Coleman, Kenneth, ed., *The Colonial Records of the State of Georgia: Trustees' Letter Book, 1745–1752*. Athens: University of Georgia Press, 1986.

———. *Georgia History in Outline*. Athens: University of Georgia Press, 1978.

———. *A History of Georgia*. 2nd ed. Athens: University of Georgia Press, 1991.

Commons, John R., general ed. *A Documentary History of American Industrial Society*. 2 vols. 1909. Reprint, New York: Russell and Russell, 1958.

Conner, Judson J. *Muskets, Knives, and Bloody Marshes: The Fight for Colonial Georgia*. St. Simons Island: Saltmarsh Press, 2001.

Cook, Jeannine. *Fort King George: Step One to Statehood*. Darien, Ga.: Darien News, 1990.

Cornelius, Elias. "On the Geology, Mineralogy, Scenery, and Curiosities of Parts of Virginia, Tennessee, and the Alabama and Mississippi Territories, &c. with Miscellaneous Remarks, in a Letter to the Editor." *American Journal of Science* 1 (1818): 214–26, 317–31.

Cornelius, Janet Duitsman. *Slave Missions and the Black Church in the Antebellum South*. Columbia: University of South Carolina Press, 1999.

Coulter, E. Merton. *Thomas Spalding of Sapelo*. Baton Rouge: Louisiana State University Press, 1940.

Cozma, Codrina. "John Martin Bolzius and the Early Christian Opposition to Slavery in Georgia." *Georgia Historical Quarterly* 88, no. 4 (2004): 457–76.

Crowley, John G. "The Primitive Baptists of South Georgia and Florida." Ph.D. diss., Florida State University, 1996.

————. *Primitive Baptists of the Wiregrass South: 1815 to the Present.* Gainesville: University Press of Florida, 1998.

Curnock, Nehemiah, ed. *The Journal of the Rev. John Wesley.* 3 vols. 1912. Reprint, London: Epworth Press, 1938.

Dagg, J. L. *The Elements of Moral Science.* New York: Sheldon, 1860.

Davis, Harold E. *The Fledgling Province: Social and Cultural Life in Colonial Georgia, 1733–1776.* Chapel Hill: University of North Carolina Press, 1976.

Davis, Robert Scott. *Quaker Records in Georgia: Wrightsborough 1772–1793, Friendsborough 1776–1777.* Augusta, Ga.: Augusta Genealogical Society, 1986.

Davis, William C. *The Cause Lost: Myths and Realities of the Confederacy.* Lawrence, Kans.: University Press of Kansas, 1996.

DePratter, Chester B. "The Archaic in Georgia." *Early Georgia* 3 (1975): 1–16.

Dinnerstein, Leonard. *The Leo Frank Case.* 1966. Reprint, Athens: University of Georgia Press, 1987.

Dorgan, Howard. "Response of the Main-line Southern White Protestant Pulpit to *Brown v. Board of Education,* 1954–1965." In *A New Diversity in Contemporary Southern Rhetoric,* edited by Calvin M. Logue and Howard Dorgan, 15–51. Baton Rouge: Louisiana State University Press, 1987.

Dowell, Spright. *A History of Mercer University, 1833–1953.* Macon, Ga.: Mercer University Press, 1958.

Drago, Edmund L. *Black Politicians and Reconstruction in Georgia: A Splendid Failure.* Athens: University of Georgia Press, 1992.

Dray, Philip. *At the Hands of Persons Unknown: The Lynching of Black America.* New York: Random House, 2002.

Du Bois, W. E. B. *Dusk of Dawn: An Essay toward an Autobiography of a Race Concept.* New York, 1940.

————. *The Souls of Black Folk.* 1903. Reprint, New York: Vintage Books, 1990.

Duncan, Russell. *Freedom's Shore: Tunis Campbell and the Georgia Freedmen.* Athens: University of Georgia Press, 1986.

Dvorak, Katherine. *An African-American Exodus: The Segregation of the Southern Churches.* Brooklyn, N.Y.: Carlson Publishing, 1991.

Eastman, Roger, ed. *The Ways of Religion: An Introduction to the Major Traditions,* 3rd ed. New York: Oxford University Press, 1999.

Egerton, John. *Speak Now against the Day: The Generation before the Civil Rights Movement in the South.* Chapel Hill: University of North Carolina Press, 1994.

Eiesland, Nancy L. *A Particular Place: Urban Restructuring and Religious Ecology in a Southern Exurb.* New Brunswick, N.J.: Rutgers University Press, 2000.

Ellington, Charles Linwood. "The Sacred Harp Tradition of the South: Its Origin and Evolution." Ph.D. diss., Florida State University, 1969.

Ellis, Ann Wells. "The Commission on Interracial Cooperation, 1919–1944: Its Activities and Results." Ph.D. diss., Georgia State University, 1976.

Eskew, Glenn T. "Black Elitism and the Failure of Paternalism in Postbellum Georgia: The Case of Bishop Lucius Henry Holsey." *Journal of Southern History* 58 (1992): 637–66.

Ethridge, Robbie. "Creating the Shatter Zone: Indian Slave Traders and the Collapse of the Southeastern Chiefdoms." In Pluckhahn and Ethridge, *Light on the Path*, 207–18.

Ettinger, Amos Aschbach. *James Edward Oglethorpe: Imperial Idealist*. Oxford: Clarendon Press, 1936.

Evans, Clement A. "Our Confederate Memorial Day." *Confederate Veteran* 4 (1896): 222–28.

Faust, Drew Gilpin. "Christian Soldiers: The Meaning of Revivalism in the Confederate Army." *Journal of Southern History* 53, no. 1 (1987): 63–90.

———. *The Creation of Confederate Nationalism: Ideology and Identity in the Civil War South*. Baton Rouge, La.: Louisiana State University Press, 1988.

Finke, Roger, and Rodney Stark. *The Churching of America, 1776–1990: Winners and Losers in Our Religious Economy*. New Brunswick, N.J.: Rutgers University Press, 2000.

Fisher, Doris. "Mary Musgrove: Creek Englishwoman." Ph.D. diss., Emory University, 1990.

Fisher, John E. *The John F. Slater Fund: A Nineteenth Century Affirmative Action for Negro Education*. Lanham, Md.: University Press of America, 1986.

Fitts, Leroy. *A History of Black Baptists*. Nashville: Broadman Press, 1985.

Flynt, J. Wayne. "The Impact of Social Factors on Southern Baptist Expansion, 1800–1914." *Baptist History and Heritage* 17 (1982): 20–31.

Fogleman, Aaron Spencer. "Shadow Boxing in Georgia: The Beginnings of the Moravian-Lutheran Conflict in British North America." *Georgia Historical Quarterly* 83, no. 4 (1999): 629–59.

Foster, Gaines M. *Ghosts of the Confederacy: Defeat, the Lost Cause, and the Emergence of the New South, 1865 to 1913*. New York: Oxford University Press, 1987.

Franklin, Benjamin. *The Autobiography of Benjamin Franklin*. 1868. Reprint, Garden City, N.Y.: Garden City Publishing Company, 1916.

Fries, Adelaide L. *The Moravians in Georgia, 1735–1740*. 1905. Reprint, Baltimore: Genealogical Publishing Company, 1967.

Frost-Knappman, Elizabeth, and Kathryn Cullen-Dupont. *Women's Rights on Trial: 101 Historic Trials from Anne Hutchinson to the Virginia Military Institute Cadets*. Detroit: Gale, 1997.

Fuller, Millard, and Diane Scott. *Love in the Mortar Joints: The Story of Habitat for Humanity*. Chicago: Association Press, 1980.

Fundaburk, Emma Lila, and Mary Douglass Foreman, eds. *Sun Circles and Human Hands: The Southeastern Indians—Art and Industry*. 1957. Reprint, Tuscaloosa: University of Alabama Press, 2001.

Gabin, Jane S. *A Living Minstrelsy: The Poetry and Music of Sidney Lanier*. Macon, Ga.: Mercer University Press, 1985.

Gallagher, Gary W., and Alan T. Nolan, eds. *The Myth of the Lost Cause and Civil War History*. Bloomington: Indiana University Press, 2000.

Gallay, Alan. *The Indian Slave Trade: The Rise of the English Empire in the American South, 1670–1717*. New Haven, Conn.: Yale University Press, 2002.

Galloway, Patricia, ed. *The Southeastern Ceremonial Complex: Artifacts and Analysis*. Lincoln: University of Nebraska Press, 1989.

Gardner, Robert G. "Baptists in Georgia, 1733–1801." In Gardner, Walker, Huddlestun, and Harris, *A History of the Georgia Baptist Convention*, 9–39.

———. *A Decade of Debate and Division: Georgia Baptists and the Formation of the Southern Baptist Convention*. Macon, Ga.: Mercer University Press, 1995.

———. *A Decade of Freedom and Faithfulness: The Cooperative Baptist Fellowship of Georgia, 1992–2002*. Macon, Ga.: Cooperative Baptist Fellowship of Georgia, 2002.

———. "The Georgia Baptist Convention, 1784–1801." In Gardner, Walker, Huddlestun, and Harris, *A History of the Georgia Baptist Convention*, 41–57.

———. "John Leadley Dagg." *Review and Expositor* 54 (1957): 246–63.

———. "John Leadley Dagg of Georgia." *Viewpoints* 1 (1968): 68–86.

———. "Primary Sources in the Study of Eighteenth-Century Georgia Baptist History." *Viewpoints* 7 (1980): 59–118.

Gardner, Robert G., Charles O. Walker, J. R. Huddlestun, and Waldo P. Harris III. *A History of the Georgia Baptist Association, 1784–1984*. Atlanta: Georgia Baptist Historical Society, 1996.

Garmon, Connie D. "The Role of Women in Georgia Baptist Life, 1733–1840." *Viewpoints* 12 (1990): 11.

Garrett, Franklin M. *Atlanta and Environs: A Chronicle of Its People and Events*. 2 vols. Athens: University of Georgia Press, 1954. Facsimile reprint, University of Georgia Press, 1969.

Garrison, Tim Alan. *The Legal Ideology of Removal: The Southern Judiciary and the Sovereignty of Native American Nations*. Athens: University of Georgia Press, 2002.

Garrow, David J., ed. *Atlanta, Georgia, 1960–1961*. Brooklyn, N.Y.: Carlson, 1989.

———. *Bearing the Cross: Martin Luther King, Jr., and the Southern Christian Leadership Conference*. New York: William Morrow, 1986.

———. "Where Martin Luther King, Jr., Was Going: *Where Do We Go from Here* and the Traumas of the Post-Selma Movement." *Georgia Historical Quarterly* 75, no. 4 (1991): 719–36.

Gaustad, Edwin Scott, and Philip L. Barlow. *New Historical Atlas of Religion in America*. New York: Oxford University Press, 2001.

Genovese, Eugene D. *Roll, Jordan, Roll: The World the Slaves Made*. New York: Pantheon Books, 1974.

Gillespie, Michele. "The Sexual Politics of Race and Gender: Mary Musgrove and the Georgia Trustees." In *The Devil's Lane: Sex and Race in the Early South*, edited by Catherine Clinton and Michele Gillespie, 187–201. New York: Oxford University Press, 1997.

Glatthaar, Joseph T. *The March to the Sea and Beyond: Sherman's Troops in the Savannah and Carolinas Campaign*. New York: New York University Press, 1985.

Godshalk, David Fort. *Veiled Visions: The 1906 Atlanta Race Riot and the Reshaping of American Race Relations*. Chapel Hill: University of North Carolina Press, 2005.

Goen, C. C. *Broken Churches, Broken Nation: Denominational Schisms and the Coming of the Civil War*. Macon, Ga.: Mercer University Press, 1985.

Goldstein, Doris H. "Inside/Outside: The Jewish Community of Atlanta." In Laderman, *Religions of Atlanta*, 87–102.

Graham, Billy. *Just As I Am: The Autobiography of Billy Graham*. New York: Harper-Collins, 1997.

Grant, Donald. *The Way It Was in the South: The Black Experience in Georgia*. Athens: University of Georgia Press, 1993.

Grantham, Bill. *Creation Myths and Legends of the Creek Indians*. Gainesville: University Press of Florida, 2002.

Green, Michael D. "Mary Musgrove: Creating a New World." In *Sifters: Native American Women's Lives*, edited by Theda Purdue, 29–47. New York: Oxford University Press, 2001.

Greene, Melissa Fay. *The Temple Bombing*. New York: Fawcett Columbine, 1996.

Gregory, Chad. "Sam Jones: Masculine Prophet of God." *Georgia Historical Quarterly* 86, no. 2 (2002): 231–52.

Gresham, Thomas H. "Historic Patterns of Rock Piling and the Rock Pile Problem." *Early Georgia* 18 (1990): 1–40.

Harris, Corra. *A Circuit Rider's Wife*. 1910. Reprint, Athens: University of Georgia Press, 1998.

Harris, Waldo P., III, and James D. Mosteller. *Georgia's First Continuing Baptist Church*. Appling, Ga.: Kiokee Baptist Church, 1997.

Harvey, Paul. *Redeeming the South: Religious Cultures and Racial Identities among Southern Baptists, 1865–1925*. Chapel Hill: University of North Carolina Press, 1997.

Haynes, Stephen R. *Noah's Curse: The Biblical Justification of American Slavery*. Oxford: Oxford University Press, 2002.

Hempton, David. *Methodism: Empire of the Spirit*. New Haven, Conn.: Yale University Press, 2005.

Henderson, Steven R. "Patrick Hues Mell: The Life, Character, and Influence of a Baptist King." *Viewpoints* 19 (2004): 11–19.

Hill, Samuel S., ed. *Encyclopedia of Religion in the South*. Macon, Ga.: Mercer University Press, 1997.

———. *One Name but Several Faces: Variety in Popular Christian Denominations in Southern History*. Athens: University of Georgia Press, 1996.

———. *Southern Churches in Crisis*. New York: Holt, Rinehart and Winston, 1966.

———. *Southern Churches in Crisis Revisited*. Tuscaloosa: University of Alabama Press, 1999.

Hitchcock, Bert. *Richard Malcolm Johnston*. Boston: Twayne, 1978.

Holmes, A. T. "The Duties of Christian Masters." In H. N. McTyeire, C. F. Sturgis, and A. T. Holmes, *Duties of Masters to Servants: Three Premium Essays*, 129–51. Charleston, S.C.: Southern Baptist Publication Society, 1851.

Holzer, Harold. *Lincoln at Cooper Union: The Speech That Made Abraham Lincoln President*. New York: Simon and Schuster, 2005.

Horton, James Oliver. "Confronting Slavery and Revealing the 'Lost Cause.'" *Cultural Resource Management* 21 (1998): 14–20.

Howard, James H. *The Southeastern Ceremonial Complex and Its Interpretation*. Columbia: Missouri Archaeological Society, 1968.

Huddlestun, J. R. "Jesse Mercer's Influence on the Georgia Baptist Convention."
Viewpoints 3 (1972): 41–66.

Hudson, Charles M. *Conversations With the High Priest of Coosa*. Chapel Hill: University
of North Carolina Press, 2003.

———. *Elements of Southeastern Indian Religion*. Leiden: E. J. Brill, 1984.

———. "The Hernando de Soto Expedition, 1539–1543." In Hudson and Tesser, *The
Forgotten Centuries*, 74–103.

———. *Knights of Spain, Warriors of the Sun: Hernando de Soto and the South's Ancient
Chiefdoms*. Athens: University of Georgia Press, 1997.

———. "Meaning in Mississippian Art." In *Of Sky and Earth: Art of the Southeastern
Indians*, edited by Roy S. Dickens, Jr., 18–21. Knoxville: University of Tennessee Press,
1982.

———. *The Southeastern Indians*. Knoxville: University of Tennessee Press, 1978.

———. "Uktena: A Cherokee Anomalous Monster." *Journal of Cherokee Studies* 3 (1978):
62–73.

———. "Vomiting for Purity: Ritual Emesis in the Aboriginal Southeastern United
States." In *Symbols and Society: Essays on Belief Systems in Action*, edited by C. Hill,
93–102. Athens: University of Georgia Press, 1975.

Hudson, Charles M., and Carmen Chaves Tesser, eds. *The Forgotten Centuries: Indians
and Europeans in the American South, 1521–1704*. Athens: University of Georgia Press,
1994.

Hunt, Gregory L. "Daniel Marshall: Energetic Evangelist for the Separate Baptist Cause."
Baptist History and Heritage 21 (April 1986): 5–18.

Hunter, James Davison. *Culture Wars: The Struggle to Define America*. New York: Basic
Books, 1991.

Hunter, Lloyd A. "The Immortal Confederacy: Another Look at Lost Cause Religion." In
Gallagher and Nolan, *The Myth of the Lost Cause*, 185–218.

Jackson, Harvey H. "Parson and Squire: James Oglethorpe and the Role of the Anglican
Church in Georgia, 1733–1736." In Spalding and Jackson, *Oglethorpe in Perspective*,
44–65.

Jackson, Harvey H., and Phinizy Spalding, eds. *Forty Years of Diversity: Essays on Colonial
Georgia*. Athens: University of Georgia Press, 1984.

Jackson, Kenneth T. *The Ku Klux Klan in the City, 1915–1930*. New York: Oxford
University Press, 1967.

Jackson, Thomas, ed. *The Journal of Charles Wesley*. 2 vols. 1849. Reprint, Grand Rapids:
Baker Book House, 1980.

Johnson, Todd E. "Disconnected Rituals." In *The Conviction of Things Unseen: Worship
and Ministry in the 21st Century*, edited by Todd E. Johnson, 53–66. Grand Rapids,
Mich.: Brazos Press, 2002.

Johnson, Whittington B. *Black Savannah, 1788–1864*. Fayetteville: University of Arkansas
Press, 1996.

Jones, Charles C., Jr. *The Dead Towns of Georgia*. 1878. Reprint, Spartanburg: Reprint
Company, 1974.

———. *Historical Sketch of Tomo-Chi-Chi, Mico of the Yamacraws.* Albany, N.Y.: J. Munsell, 1868.

Jones, Dorothy M. *Wrightsborough 1768, Wrightsboro 1799, McDuffie County, Georgia 1870.* Thomson, Ga.: Wrightsborough Quaker Community Foundation, 1982.

Jones, Edward A. *A Candle in the Dark: A History of Morehouse College.* Valley Forge, Pa.: Judson Press, 1967.

Jones, George Fenwick, ed. *Detailed Reports on the Salzburger Emigrants Who Settled in America . . . Edited by Samuel Urlsperger.* 17 vols. Athens: University of Georgia Press, 1993.

———. *The Salzburger Saga: Religious Exiles and Other Germans along the Savannah.* Athens: University of Georgia Press, 1984.

———, ed. *The Secret Diary of Pastor Johann Martin Boltzius.* [Savannah, Ga.]: Georgia Salzburger Society, 1975.

———. "Sephardim and Ashkenazim Jewish Settlers in Colonial Georgia." *Georgia Historical Quarterly* 85, no. 4 (2001): 519–37.

Jones, George Fenwick, and Paul Martin Peucker, eds. and trans. "'We Have Come to Georgia with Pure Intentions': Moravian Bishop August Gottlieb Spangenberg's Letters from Savannah, 1735." *Georgia Historical Quarterly* 82, no. 1 (1998): 84–120.

Jones, J. William. *Christ in the Camp: The True Story of the Great Revival during the War between the States* 1888. Reprint, Harrisonburg, Va.: Sprinkle Publications, 1999.

Jordan, Hamilton. *No Such Thing as a Bad Day: A Memoir.* Atlanta: Longstreet Press, 2000.

Kelso, William M. *Excavations at the Fort King George Historical Site: Darien, Georgia, the 1967 Survey.* Atlanta: Georgia Historical Commission, 1968.

Kemble, Frances Anne. *Journal of a Residence on a Georgia Plantation in 1838–1839.* 1863. Reprint, Athens: University of Georgia, 1984.

Kennett, Lee B. *Marching through Georgia: The Story of Soldiers and Civilians during Sherman's Campaign.* New York: HarperCollins, 1995.

King, Adam. *Etowah: The Political History of a Chiefdom Capital.* Tuscaloosa: University of Alabama Press, 2003.

King, Martin Luther, Jr. *Where Do We Go from Here: Chaos or Community?* New York: Harper & Row, 1967.

K'Meyer, Tracy Elaine. *Interracialism and Christian Community in the Postwar South: The Story of Koinonia Farm.* Charlottesville: University Press of Virginia, 1997.

Knight, Vernon James, Jr. "The Formation of the Creeks." In Hudson and Tesser, *The Forgotten Centuries*, 373–92.

———. "The Institutional Organization of Mississippian Religion." *American Antiquity* 51 (1986): 675–87.

———. "Symbolism of Mississippian Mounds." In *Powhatan's Mantle: Indians in the Colonial Southeast*, edited by Peter H. Wood, Gregory A. Waslkov, and M. Thomas Hatley, 279–91. Lincoln: University of Nebraska Press, 1989.

Knight, Vernon James, Jr., James A. Brown, and George E. Lankford. "On the Subject Matter of Southeastern Ceremonial Complex Art." *Southeastern Archaeology* 20 (2001): 129–41.

Knotts, Alice G. *Fellowship of Love: Methodist Women Changing American Racial Attitudes, 1920–1968.* Nashville: Kingswood Books, 1996.

Laderman, Gary, ed. *Religions of Atlanta: Religious Diversity in the Centennial Olympic City.* Atlanta: Scholars Press, 1996.

Lambert, Frank. "'Pedlar in Divinity': George Whitefield and the Great Awakening, 1737–1745." *Journal of American History* 77 (1990): 812–37.

Lane, Mills, ed., *General Oglethorpe's Georgia: Colonial Letters: 1733–1743.* 2 vols. Savannah, Ga.: Beehive Press, 1975.

———. *Neither More nor Less than Men: Slavery in Georgia.* Savannah, Ga.: Beehive Press, 1993.

Lang, Robert, ed., *The Birth of a Nation: D. W. Griffith, Director.* New Brunswick, N.J.: Rutgers University Press, 1994.

———. "*The Birth of a Nation*: History, Ideology, Narrative Form." In Lang, *The Birth of a Nation*, 3–24.

Lanning, John Tate. *The Diplomatic History of Georgia: A Study of the Epoch of Jenkins' Ear.* Chapel Hill: University of North Carolina Press, 1936.

Larson, Lewis H., Jr. "The Etowah Site." In Galloway, *The Southeastern Ceremonial Complex*, 133–41.

Lathrop, Gordon. "New Pentecost or Joseph's Britches? Reflections on the History and Meaning of the Worship Ordo in the Megachurches." *Worship* 72, no. 6 (1998): 521–38.

Lawrence, Harold, ed. *Asbury's Georgia Visits.* Tignall, Ga.: Boyd Publishing Company, 1988.

———. *A Feast of Tabernacles: Georgia Campgrounds and Campmeetings.* Tignall, Ga.: Boyd Publishing, 1990.

Lee, Dallas. *The Cotton Patch Evidence: The Story of Clarence Jordan and the Koinonia Farm Experiment (1942–1970).* New York: Harper and Row, 1971.

Leff, Leonard J. "*Gone with the Wind* and Hollywood's Racial Politics." *Atlantic Monthly* 284 (1999): 106–14.

Lester, James Adams. *A History of the Georgia Baptist Convention, 1822–1972.* N.p.: Executive Committee, Baptist Convention of the State of Georgia, 1972.

Lewis, David Levering. *W. E. B. Du Bois: Biography of a Race, 1868–1919.* New York: Henry Holt, 1993.

Litwack, Leon F. "Hellhounds." In James Allen, Hilton Als, Congressman John Lewis, and Leon F. Litwack, *Without Sanctuary: Lynching Photography in America*, 8–37. New York: Twin Palms Publishers, 2000.

Loewald, Klaus G., Beverly Starika, and Paul S. Taylor, trans. and eds. "John Martin Bolzius Answers a Questionnaire on Carolina and Georgia." Part II. *William and Mary Quarterly* 15 (1958): 228–52.

Longstreet, Augustus Baldwin. *Letters on the Epistle of Paul to Philemon: Or, the Connection of Apostolical Christianity with Slavery.* Charleston, S.C.: B. Jenkins, 1845.

Loveland, Anne C. *Lillian Smith: A Southerner Confronting the South.* Baton Rouge: Louisiana State University Press, 1986.

Lumpkin, William L. "Great Awakening." In Hill, *Encyclopedia of Religion in the South*, 309–10.

Lutholtz, M. William. *Grand Dragon: D. C. Stephenson and the Ku Klux Klan in Indiana.* West Lafayette, Ind.: Purdue University Press, 1991.

MacLean, Nancy. *Behind the Mask of Chivalry: The Making of the Second Ku Klux Klan.* New York: Oxford University Press, 1994.

Maddex, Jack P., Jr. "Waddel, Moses." In Hill, *Encyclopedia of Religion in the South,* 819.

Manis, Andrew M. "'City Mothers': Dorothy Tilly, Georgia Methodist Women, and Black Civil Rights." In *Before Brown: Civil Rights and White Backlash in the Modern South,* edited by Glenn Feldman, 116–43. Tuscaloosa: University of Alabama Press, 2004.

———. *Southern Civil Religions in Conflict: Civil Rights and the Culture Wars.* Macon, Ga.: Mercer University Press, 2002.

Mann, Harold W. *Atticus Greene Haygood: Methodist Bishop, Editor, and Educator.* Athens: University of Georgia Press, 1965.

Martin, B. G. "Sapelo Island's Arabic Document: The 'Bilali Diary' in Context." *Georgia Historical Quarterly* 77, no. 3 (1994): 589–601.

Martin, Joel W. *Sacred Revolt: The Muskogees' Struggle for a New World.* Boston: Beacon Press, 1991.

———. "Southeastern Indians and the English Trade in Skins and Slaves." In Hudson and Tesser, *The Forgotten Centuries,* 304–24.

Martin, Roger A. "John J. Zubly Comes to America." *Georgia Historical Quarterly* 61 (1977): 125–39.

McCash, William B. *Thomas R. R. Cobb: The Making of a Southern Nationalist.* Macon, Ga.: Mercer University Press, 1983.

McFeely, William S. *Sapelo's People: A Long Walk into Freedom.* New York: Norton, 1994.

McLoughlin, William G. *Cherokees and Missionaries: 1789–1839.* Norman: University of Oklahoma Press, 1995.

[Mell, Patrick Hues.] *Slavery. A Treatise, showing that Slavery is neither a moral, political, nor social evil.* Penfield: Benjamin Brantley, 1844.

Mercer, Jesse. *A History of the Georgia Baptist Association Compiled at the Request of that Body.* Washington, Ga.: [s.n.], 1838.

Milanich, Jerald T. "Franciscan Missions and Native Peoples." In Hudson and Tesser, *The Forgotten Centuries,* 276–303.

———. *Laboring in the Fields of the Lord: Spanish Missions and Southeastern Indians.* Washington: Smithsonian Institution Press, 1999.

———. "The Legacy of Columbus." *Archaeology* 45, no. 2 (1992): 38–42.

Miller, Randall M., ed. *"A Warm & Zealous Spirit": John J. Zubly and the American Revolution, Selection of His Writings.* Macon, Ga.: Mercer University Press, 1982.

Millin, Eric T. "Defending the Sacred Hearth: Religion, Politics, and Racial Violence in Georgia, 1904–1906." M.A. thesis, University of Georgia, 2002.

Mills, Watson E. "Glossolalia." In Hill, *Encyclopedia of Religion in the South,* 305–6.

Minnix, Kathleen. *Laughter in the Amen Corner: The Life of Evangelist Sam Jones.* Athens: University of Georgia Press, 1993.

Mitchell, Margaret. *Gone with the Wind.* 1936. Reprint, New York: Macmillan, 1979.

Mixon, Gregory. *The Atlanta Riot: Race, Class, and Violence in a New South City.* Gainesville: University Press of Florida, 2005.

Mixon, Wayne. "Georgia." In Hill, *Encyclopedia of Religion in the South,* 289–304.

Mohr, Clarence L. "Slaves and White Churches in Confederate Georgia." In Boles, *Masters and Slaves,* 153–72.

Mondy, Robert W. "Jesse Mercer and the Baptist College Movement." *Georgia Historical Quarterly* 40 (1956): 349–59.

Mooney, James. *Myths of the Cherokee.* 1900. Reprint, New York: Dover Publications, 1995.

Moore, R. Laurence. *Selling God: American Religion in the Marketplace of Culture.* New York: Oxford University Press, 1994.

Morgan, David T. *The New Crusades, the New Holy Land: Conflict in the Southern Baptist Convention, 1969–1991.* Tuscaloosa: University of Alabama Press, 1996.

Morris, Michael. "Emerging Gender Roles for Southeastern Indian Women: The Mary Musgrove Story Reconsidered." *Georgia Historical Quarterly* 89, no.1 (2005): 1–24.

Moseley, J. Edward. *Disciples of Christ in Georgia.* St. Louis: Bethany Press, 1954.

Mosteller, James D. *A History of the Kiokee Baptist Church in Georgia.* Ann Arbor, Mich.: Edwards Brothers, Inc., 1952.

Murray, Gail S., ed. *Throwing Off the Cloak of Privilege: White Southern Women Activists in the Civil Rights Era.* Gainesville: University Press of Florida, 2004.

Nasstrom, Kathryn L. *Everybody's Grandmother and Nobody's Fool: Frances Freeborn Pauley and the Struggle for Social Justice.* Ithaca, N.Y.: Cornell University Press, 2000.

Newman, Mark. "The Georgia Baptist Convention and Desegregation, 1945–1980." *Georgia Historical Quarterly* 83, no.4 (1999): 683–711.

———. *Getting Right with God: Southern Baptists and Desegregation, 1945–1995.* Tuscaloosa: University of Alabama Press, 2001.

Nichols, Joel A. "Religious Liberty in the Thirteenth Colony: Church-State Relations in Colonial and Early National Georgia." *New York University Law Review* 80 (2005): 1693–1772.

Nolan, Alan T. "The Anatomy of the Myth." In Gallagher and Nolan, *The Myth of the Lost Cause,* 11–34.

Noll, Mark. "The Bible and Slavery." In *Religion and the American Civil War,* edited by Randall M. Miller, Harry S. Stout, and Charles Reagan Wilson, 43–73. New York: Oxford University Press, 1998.

———. *The Civil War as a Theological Crisis.* Chapel Hill: University of North Carolina Press, 2006.

Norgren, Jill. *The Cherokee Cases: Two Landmark Federal Decisions in the Fight for Sovereignty.* Norman: University of Oklahoma Press, 2004.

Norwood, Frederick A. *The Story of American Methodism: A History of the United Methodists and Their Relations.* Nashville: Abingdon Press, 1974.

O'Connor, Charles S. "The Politics of Industrialization in Sumter County, Georgia: Koinonia Farm in the 1950s." *Georgia Historical Quarterly* 89, no. 4 (2005): 505–27.

Oney, Steve. *And the Dead Shall Rise: The Murder of Mary Phagan and the Lynching of Leo Frank.* New York: Pantheon Books, 2003.

Osborn, George C. *Woodrow Wilson: The Early Years.* Baton Rouge: Louisiana State University Press, 1968.

Ostwalt, Conrad. *Secular Steeples: Popular Culture and the Religious Imagination.* Harrisburg, Pa.: Trinity Press International, 2003.

Owen, Christopher H. *The Sacred Flame of Love: Methodism and Society in Nineteenth-Century Georgia.* Athens: University of Georgia Press, 1998.

Palmer, B. M. *Thanksgiving Sermon, Delivered in the First Presbyterian Church, New Orleans, on Thursday, Nov. 29, 1860.* Milledgeville: Boughton, Nisbet & Barnes, 1860.

Parker, Anthony W. *Scottish Highlanders in Colonial Georgia: The Recruitment, Emigration, and Settlement at Darien, 1735–1748.* Athens: University of Georgia Press, 1997.

Parker, David B. "'Quit Your Meanness': Sam Jones's Theology for the New South." *Georgia Historical Quarterly* 77, no. 4 (1993): 711–27.

Pauley, William E. "Tragic Hero: Loyalist John J. Zubly." *Journal of Presbyterian History* 54 (1976): 61–81.

Pavich-Lindsay, Melanie, ed. *Anna: The Letters of a St. Simons Island Mistress, 1817–1859.* Athens: University of Georgia Press, 2002.

Perdue, Theda, and Michael D. Green, eds. *The Cherokee Removal: A Brief History with Documents.* Boston: St. Martin's Press, 1995.

Perman, Michael. *The Road to Redemption: Southern Politics, 1869–1879.* Chapel Hill: University of North Carolina Press, 1984.

Pierce, Alfred Mann. *Lest Faith Forget: The Story of Methodism in Georgia.* Atlanta: Georgia Methodist Information, 1951.

Pierce, George Foster, and Benjamin Morgan Palmer. *Sermons of Bishop Pierce and Rev. B. M. Palmer, D.D. Delivered before the General Assembly at Milledgeville, Ga., on Fast Day, March 27, 1863.* Milledgeville, Ga.: Boughton, Nisbet and Barnes, 1863.

Pilkington, Charles Kirk. "The Trials of Brotherhood: The Founding of the Commission on Interracial Cooperation." *Georgia Historical Quarterly* 69, no. 1 (1985): 55–80.

Pluckhahn, Thomas J. *Kolomoki: Settlement, Ceremony, and Status in the Deep South, A.D. 350 to 750.* Tuscaloosa: University of Alabama Press, 2003.

Pluckhahn, Thomas J., and Robbie Ethridge, eds. *Light on the Path: The Anthropology and History of the Southeastern Indians.* Tuscaloosa: University of Alabama Press, 2006.

Pollard, Edward A. *The Lost Cause: A New Southern History of the War of the Confederates.* New York: E. B. Treat, 1867.

Pollock, John. *George Whitefield and the Great Awakening.* Garden City, N.Y.: Doubleday, 1972.

Pomerantz, Gary M. *Where Peachtree Meets Sweet Auburn: The Saga of Two Families and the Making of Atlanta.* New York: Scribner, 1996.

Porter, R. K. *Christian Duty in the Present Crisis: The Substance of a Sermon Delivered in the Presbyterian Church in Waynesboro, Georgia . . . December 9, 1860.* Savannah, Ga.: J. M. Cooper and Company, 1860.

Power, Susan C. *Early Art of the Southeastern Indians: Feathered Serpents and Winged Beings.* Athens: University of Georgia Press, 2004.

Pratt, Robert A. *We Shall Not Be Moved: The Desegregation of the University of Georgia.* Athens: University of Georgia Press, 2002.

Proceedings of the Southern Baptist Convention. Atlanta: Franklin Publishing House, 1891.

Proceedings of the Southern Baptist Convention. Atlanta: Franklin Publishing House, 1892.

Raboteau, Albert J. *Canaan Land: A Religious History of African Americans.* New York: Oxford University Press, 1999.

———. *Slave Religion: The "Invisible Institution" in the Antebellum South.* New York: Oxford University Press, 1978.

Rachels, David, ed. *Augustus Baldwin Longstreet's Georgia Scenes Completed: A Scholarly Text.* Athens: University of Georgia Press, 1998.

Redmond, Elsa M., ed. *Chiefdoms and Chieftaincy in the Americas.* Gainesville: University Press of Florida, 1988.

Reed, Ralph E., Jr. "Emory College and the Sledd Affair of 1902: A Case Study in Southern Honor and Racial Attitudes." *Georgia Historical Quarterly* 72, no. 3 (1988): 463–92.

Reese, Trevor R., ed. *The Clamorous Malcontents: Criticisms and Defenses of the Colony of Georgia, 1741–1743.* Savannah, Ga.: The Beehive Press, 1973.

Reidy, Joseph P. *From Slavery to Agrarian Capitalism in the Cotton Plantation South: Central Georgia, 1800–1880.* Chapel Hill: University of North Carolina Press, 1992.

Remini, Robert V. *Henry Clay: Statesman for the Union.* New York: W. W. Norton, 1991.

Rhodehamel, John H., and Louise Taper, eds. *"Right or wrong, God judge me": The Writings of John Wilkes Booth.* Urbana: University of Illinois Press, 1997.

Richey, Russell E. *Early American Methodism.* Bloomington: Indiana University Press, 1991.

Riehm, Edith Holbrook. "Dorothy Tilly and the Fellowship of the Concerned." In Murray, *Throwing Off the Cloak of Privilege,* 23–48.

Rosenbaum, Art. *Shout Because You're Free: The African American Ring Shout Tradition in Coastal Georgia,* with photographs by Margo Newmark Rosenbaum. Athens: University of Georgia Press, 1998.

Rudolph, L. C. *Francis Asbury.* Nashville: Abingdon Press, 1966.

Sanders, Daniel P. "Frontier to Forefront: Adiel Sherwood and the Shaping of Georgia Baptists, 1818–1841." *Viewpoints* 12 (1990): 31–46.

Saunt, Claudio. *A New Order of Things: Property, Power, and the Transformation of the Creek Indians, 1733–1816.* New York: Cambridge University Press, 1999.

Saye, Albert B., ed. *Georgia's Charter of 1732.* Athens: University of Georgia Press, 1942.

Schmier, Louis. "Sheftall Family." In Hill, *Encyclopedia of Religion in the South,* 691.

Schnecken, John. *The Good Life.* Cincinnati, Ohio: Babka Publishing, 1998.

Schneider, Dorothy, and Carl J. Schneider. *An Eyewitness History of Slavery in America: From Colonial Times to the Civil War.* New York: Checkmark Books, 2001.

Schnell, Frank T. "The Beginnings of the Creeks: Where Did They First 'Sit Down'?" *Early Georgia* 17 (1989): 24–29.

Schott, Thomas E. *Alexander H. Stephens of Georgia: A Biography.* Baton Rouge: Louisiana State University Press, 1988

Schwarze, Edmund. *History of the Moravian Missions among Southern Indian Tribes.* Bethlehem, Pa.: Times Publishing, 1923.

Scott, Thomas A., ed. *Cornerstones of Georgia History: Documents That Formed the State.* Athens: University of Georgia Press, 1995.

Shattuck, Gardiner H., Jr. *A Shield and Hiding Place: The Religious Life of the Civil War Armies*. Macon, Ga.: Mercer University Press, 1987.

Sherman, William T. *Memoirs of Gen. W. T. Sherman, Written by Himself*. 2 vols. New York: Charles L. Webster & Co., 1892.

Shurden, Walter B. "The Southern Baptist Synthesis: Is It Breaking?" *Baptist History and Heritage* 16 (April 1981): 2–19.

Shurden, Walter B., ed. *The Struggle for the Soul of the SBC: Moderate Responses to the Fundamentalist Movement*. Macon, Ga.: Mercer University Press, 1993.

Shurden, Walter, and Randy Shepley, eds. *Going for the Jugular: A Documentary History of the SBC Holy War*. Macon, Ga.: Mercer University Press, 1996.

Sibley, Celestine. *Dear Store: An Affectionate Portrait of Rich's*. Atlanta: Peachtree Publishers, 1990.

Sledd, Andrew. "The Negro: Another View." *Atlantic Monthly* 90 (1902): 65–73.

Smith, Julia Floyd. *Slavery and Rice Culture in Low Country Georgia, 1750–1860*. Knoxville: University of Tennessee Press, 1985.

Smith, Kenneth L., and Ira G. Zepp, Jr. "Martin Luther King's Vision of the Beloved Community." *Christian Century* 91 (1974): 361–63.

Smith, Lillian. *Killers of the Dream*. Reissue with an introduction by Margaret Rose Gladney. 1949. Reprint, New York: W. W. Norton, 1994.

———. *Strange Fruit*. 1944. Reprint, New York: Harvest, 1992.

Smith, Marvin T. "Aboriginal Depopulation in the Postcontact Southeast." In Hudson and Tesser, *The Forgotten Centuries*, 257–75.

———. *Archaeology of Aboriginal Culture Change in the Interior Southeast: Depopulation during the Early Historic Period*. Gainesville: University of Florida Press, 1987.

———. *Coosa: The Rise and Fall of a Southeastern Mississippian Chiefdom*. Gainesville: University Press of Florida, 2000.

Smith, Philip E. *Aboriginal Stone Constructions in the Southern Piedmont*. Athens: University of Georgia Laboratory of Archaeology, 1962.

Snay, Mitchell. *Gospel of Disunion: Religion and Separatism in the Antebellum South*. Chapel Hill: University of North Carolina Press, 1993.

Snyder, Holly. "A Tree with Two Different Fruits: The Jewish Encounter with German Pietists in the Eighteenth-Century Atlantic World." *William and Mary Quarterly* 58 (2001): 855–82.

Sosna, Morton. *In Search of the Silent South: Southern Liberals and the Race Issue*. New York: Columbia University Press, 1977.

Spalding, Phinizy. "Spain and the Coming of the English." In Coleman, *A History of Georgia*, 9–15.

Spalding, Phinizy, and Harvey H. Jackson, Jr., eds. *Oglethorpe in Perspective: Georgia's Founder after Two Hundred Years*. Tuscaloosa: University of Alabama Press, 1989.

Stacy, James. *History and Published Records of the Midway Congregational Church, Liberty County, Georgia*. 1903. Reprint, Spartanburg, S.C.: Reprint Company Publishers, 1979.

———. *History of the Midway Congregational Church, Liberty County, Georgia*. Newnan, Ga.: S.W. Murray, 1903.

————. *A History of the Presbyterian Church in Georgia.* Elberton, Ga.: Press of the Star, 1912.

Stephens, Alexander H. *A Constitutional View of the Late War between the States; Its Causes, Character, Conduct and Results.* 2 vols. 1870. Reprint, New York: Kraus Reprint Company, 1970.

Stern, Malcolm H. "New Light on the Jewish Settlement of Savannah." *American Jewish Historical Society Quarterly* 52 (1962–1963): 169–99.

————. "The Sheftall Diaries: Vital Records of Savannah Jewry (1733–1808)." *American Jewish Historical Quarterly* 54 (1965): 243–77.

Stewart, Mart A. *"What Nature Suffers to Groe": Life, Labor, and Landscape on the Georgia Coast, 1680–1920.* Athens: University of Georgia Press, 1996.

Stowell, Daniel. *Rebuilding Zion: The Religious Reconstruction of the South, 1863–1877.* New York: Oxford University Press, 1998.

Stroupe, Nibs. *Where Once We Feared Enemies: Inclusive Membership, Prophetic Vision, and the American Church.* Edited by Chris Boesel. Lima, Ohio: css Publishing, 2005.

Stroupe, Nibs, and Inez Fleming. *While We Run This Race: Confronting the Power of Racism in a Southern Church.* Maryknoll, N.Y.: Orbis Books, 1995.

Stroupe, Nibs, and Caroline Leach. *O Lord, Hold Our Hands: How a Church Thrives in a Multicultural World, the Story of Oakhurst Presbyterian Church.* Louisville, Ky.: Westminster John Knox Press, 2003.

Sullivan, Buddy. *Darien and McIntosh County.* Charleston, S.C.: Arcadia, 2000.

————. *Early Days on the Georgia Tidewater: The Story of McIntosh County and Sapelo.* 5th ed. Darien, Ga.: McIntosh County Board of Commissioners, 1997.

Synan, Vinson. "Franklin Springs, Georgia." In Hill, *Encyclopedia of Religion in the South*, 268.

————. *The Holiness-Pentecostal Tradition: Charismatic Movements in the Twentieth Century.* Grand Rapids: William B. Eerdmans, 1997.

————. "King, Joseph Hillery." In Hill, *Encyclopedia of Religion in the South*, 393.

Taliaferro, Tevi. *Historic Oakland Cemetery.* Charleston, S.C.: Arcadia Publishing, 2001.

Talmadge, Herman E. *You and Segregation.* Birmingham, Ala.: Vulcan Press, 1955.

Talmadge, John E. *Rebecca Latimer Felton: Nine Stormy Decades.* Athens: University of Georgia Press, 1960.

Theoharis, Athan G., and John Stuart Cox. *The Boss: J. Edgar Hoover and the Great American Inquisition.* Philadephia: Temple University Press, 1988.

Thomas, David Hurst. *St. Catherines: An Island in Time.* Atlanta: Georgia Endowment for the Humanities, 1988.

Thompson, Ernest Trice. *Presbyterians in the South.* 3 vols. Richmond, Va.: John Knox Press, 1963–1973.

Thompson, William Y. *Robert Toombs of Georgia.* Baton Rouge: Louisiana State University Press, 1966.

Thumma, Scott. "The Kingdom, the Power, and the Glory: Megachurches in Modern American Society." Ph.D. diss., Emory University, 1996.

Thurmond, Michael. *Freedom: Georgia's Antislavery Heritage, 1733–1865.* Atlanta: Longstreet Press, 2002.

Tise, Larry E. *Proslavery: A History of the Defense of Slavery in America, 1701–1840*. Athens: University of Georgia Press, 1987.

Todd, Helen. *Tomochichi: Indian Friend of the Georgia Colony*. Atlanta: Cherokee Publishing, 1977.

Tolnay, Stewart E., and E. M. Beck. *A Festival of Violence: An Analysis of Southern Lynchings, 1882–1930*. Urbana: University of Illinois Press, 1995.

Tuck, Stephen G. N. *Beyond Atlanta: The Struggle for Racial Equality in Georgia, 1940–1980*. Athens: University of Georgia Press, 2001.

Turley, Briane K. *A Wheel within a Wheel: Southern Methodism and the Georgia Holiness Association*. Macon, Ga.: Mercer University Press, 1999.

Twining, Mary A., and Keith E. Baird, eds. *Sea Island Roots: African Presence in the Carolinas and Georgia*. Trenton, N.J.: Africa World Press, 1991.

Tyerman, Luke. *The Life of the Rev. George Whitefield*. 2 vols. London: Hodder and Stoughton, 1876–77.

Uhry, Alfred. *The Last Night of Ballyhoo*. New York: Theatre Communications Group, 1997.

Wade, John Donald. *Augustus Baldwin Longstreet: A Study of the Development of Culture in the South*. New York: Macmillan, 1924.

Walker, Charles O. "Birth of Missions and Education, 1800–1820." In Gardner, Walker, Huddlestun, and Harris, *A History of the Georgia Baptist Convention*, 59–98.

———. "Development of Organizations and Institutions, 1821–1840." In Gardner, Walker, Huddlestun, and Harris, *A History of the Georgia Baptist Convention*, 99–141.

———. "Different Frontiers, 1841–1850." In Gardner, Walker, Huddlestun, and Harris, *A History of the Georgia Baptist Convention*, 143–76.

———. "Georgia's Religion in the Colonial Era, 1733–1790." *Viewpoints* 5 (1976): 17–44.

Waring, Antonio. *The Waring Papers: The Collected Works of Antonio J. Waring, Jr.* Edited by Stephen Williams. Cambridge, Mass.: Peabody Museum, 1968.

Waring, Antonio, and Preston Holder. "A Prehistoric Ceremonial Complex in the Southeastern United States." *American Anthropologist* 7 (1945): 1–34.

Washington, James M., ed. *Testament of Hope: The Essential Writings and Speeches of Martin Luther King, Jr.* New York: HarperCollins 1986.

Waters, Andrew, ed. *On Jordan's Stormy Banks: Personal Accounts of Slavery in Georgia*. Winston-Salem, N.C.: John F. Blair, 2000.

Watson, Tom. "The Celebrated Case of the State of Georgia vs. Leo Frank." *Watson's Magazine* 21, no. 4 (1915): 182–235.

Webster, Daniel. *The Writings and Speeches of Daniel Webster*. 18 vols. Boston: Little, Brown, and Company, 1903.

Webster, Gerald R. "Geographical Patterns of Religious Denomination Affiliation in Georgia, 1970–1990: Population Change and Growing Urban Diversity." *Southeastern Geographer* 40, no. 1 (2000): 25–51.

Wells, David F., and John D. Woodbridge, eds. *The Evangelicals: What They Believe, Who They Are, Where They Are Changing*. Nashville: Abingdon Press, 1975.

Wert, Jeffry D. "James Longstreet and the Lost Cause." In Gallagher and Nolan, *The Myth of the Lost Cause*, 127–46.